ARTHURIAN LITERATURE AND SOCIETY

Arthurian Literature and Society

Stephen Knight

St. Martin's Press   New York

For Elizabeth Bronwen

Contents

List of Illustrations

Acknowledgements

In a book which ranges so widely, a writer must depend heavily on the advice and assistance of friends and colleagues. I would like to acknowledge with my grateful thanks the generous and expert help given me by Helen Fulton, Alex Jones, Annette Krausmann, Pamela Law, Bernard Martin, Simon Petch, Nick Shimin, Richard Tardif, John O. Ward and Michael Wilding. Without the help of A. G. Veysey and Tecwyn Roberts I could not have found the illustration of Maen Huail, Plate 1, and without the efficient, friendly guidance of T. M. Farmiloe, Julia Steward, Susan Dickinson and Margaret Leach at Macmillan this book would hardly exist. I am grateful to the University of Sydney for research funds and study leave, and also to many librarians for their help, at the British Library, the London Library, the Courtauld Institute, and particularly at the University of Sydney's Fisher Library. I owe special gratitude to Jan O'Reilly, who has helped to produce the book with her usual skill and tolerance. And just as Malory does of Queen Guinevere, I 'make here a lytyll mencion' of Margaret Knight, who has contributed so much to this book in so many ways.

Stephen Knight

The author and publishers wish to acknowledge the following for permission to reproduce illustrations:

The British Library for Plates 2, 9, 10, 11, 12, 13, 14, 15, 16, 18
Tecwyn Roberts of Ruthin for Plate 1
The University of Wales Press for Plate 3
Phaidon Press for Plates 4, 5 and 6
The Courtauld Institute of Art for Plate 7
Nationalmuseet, Copenhagen for Plate 8

Lady Lever Art Gallery, Port Sunlight, for Plate 17, Burne-
   Jones's *The Beguiling of Merlin*
Museo de Arte de Ponce, Puerto Rico, for Plate 19
City of Manchester Art Galleries for Plate 20
Chatto and Windus for Plates 21–7
Weidenfeld and Nicolson for Plate 28

Introduction

The legend of King Arthur is great in a number of ways. It is very old, first occurring, it seems, nearly fifteen hundred years ago. Great age has not brought frailty: the legend is still vigorous and Arthurian material appears regularly in print and in the newly dominant narrative forms of cinema and television. The dissemination of literature about Arthur and his knights has also been prodigious. Originally recorded in Welsh and Latin, the medieval legend spread quickly to French, German and English and was subtly developed in those languages. Italian and Spanish also had a rich late medieval and Renaissance literature about Arthur, little-known in the English-speaking world. Furthermore, within one language, such as English, the cultural range of Arthurian material is very great. Readers and writers tend to think of literature as the dominant form, but fairy-tales from the past and cartoons and comics, their modern equivalents, have introduced many children to the world of Arthur, and those adults who rarely read also know him well both through the media of popular culture and the elusive processes of folk-lore and myth, often supported by place-name associations.

The amazing wealth and variety of Arthurian material makes it the more surprising and disappointing that studies of the legend have been so restricted in method. There is really only one approach, a more or less scholarly version of a dubiously 'historical' treatment. The pattern is a general survey of the literary material: it may be scholarly and specialised like R. S. Loomis's essay collection *Arthurian Literature in the Middle Ages* or general like R. W. Barber's *King Arthur in Legend and History*, the best of the handbooks. It may be lighter in tone and popular in intention like Joseph Clancy's *Pendragon*, aimed at children, or Helen Miller's *The Realms of Arthur*, which has a geographical emphasis. These are the best and liveliest of a whole set of Arthurian histories.

The problem with such books is that they are not so much

historical as idealist: they treat the Arthurian legend and its literature as if it exists in a world of its own, not in the periods and the societies that produced and consumed the material. Such literary idealism has long seemed a charming and comfortable haven from the brawling world of history and society, but it is an attitude to literature and culture in general which is steadily becoming less tenable. Both the academy and the cosy literary life have been penetrated by social reality in recent years, whether the cause has been the radical dissent of the immediate past or the economic distress of the painful present.

This failure to historicise fully the legend of Arthur is particularly glaring because the central 'greatness' of the whole legend is that it has always dealt with the issue of greatness itself. Arthur has always been a figure of authority and the many versions of the legend have consistently realised the contemporary ways of becoming, and the contemporary problems of remaining, great. The Arthurian legend, especially in its most sophisticated literary versions, is about power in the real world: the texts are potent ideological documents through which both the fears and the hopes of the dominant class are realised.

That is the major reason why the legend has survived so long; not only because it trails clouds of antique mystery and emotive tragedy; not only because there are mythic traces in king, queen, knights and their enemies; not only because the conflict of king and his greatest baron is an age-old conflict whether it is for the crown or the queen – or implicitly for both together. All these features have force in the survival of the legend, but essentially it is still potent because the central idea of a very powerful and glorious régime which ends in chaos is for those with power to sponsor literature a compelling story, compelling both as a model of glory to be relished as the product of power, and as a stern message from the past about the instability of such a position. There is a dynamic political tension inherent in the essential Arthurian story that has enabled its potent recreation in a remarkable range of versions and periods.

In consequence a proper history of the Arthurian legend will investigate its historical function. It will ask what these texts were written for, what role they fulfilled in their period. It will be a history not of the legend itself, but of its integration in history.

Because Arthurian texts deal with authority in a way that is much more historical and credible than has often been realised – a

point which will be brought out more fully in each chapter – they
are particularly rich material for a study of the role of culture in
different periods; they reveal under close study just what the
ruling forces in each period were worried about and how their
cultural support-system was able partly to deflect and partly to
console those worries. A history of Arthurian literature which is
socially and historically responsible can take its place as a part of
the striking – and increasingly available – history of the part
literary culture has played in the defence of power within the
state. That ideological process is continuing today, of course, in
various ways in various states. The last chapter deals with
modern material to show different attitudes embodied in
Arthurian forms, and the contemporary appropriateness of this
type of historical study of Arthurian authorities is itself shown by
the fact that several of the texts are themselves deeply critical of
the modern forms of authority, of the uses and abuses of power.
The study of Arthurian literature is not, should not be, a trip
round an appealingly antique museum, but can be and should be
an investigation of part of the historical process that is still in action.

Obviously there is far too much material for one book to study in
any socio-historical depth, even if the rich and largely unstudied
Arthurian popular culture is set aside and the literary material is
made the focus, as it is here. Accordingly, this book restricts its
discussion to texts that seem of major importance and relevance to
the English-speaking world – the language of the book has
conditioned its range. So, for example, there is here no considera-
tion of the German medieval works, among which the *Parzival* of
Wolfram von Eschenbach and the *Tristan* of Gottfried von
Strassburg can make a convincing claim to be of all the Arthurian
texts two of the most subtle, most artistically powerful and indeed
most interesting in a socio-historical context. Similarly the riches
of the Spanish and Italian Round Table romances and epics have
been passed over. But for the same reason the French poetry of
Chrétien de Troyes has been included because it has had such a
deep impact on all Arthurian literature.
   A simple lack of space has restricted the treatment of texts in
English. The medieval verse romances range from frank naïvety
to the subtle power found in *Sir Gawain and the Green Knight*. This

was omitted with reluctance, but although its social context is currently being studied it seemed that a text surviving in one manuscript and with such a restricted audience and influence could not find a place in a book emphasising the social and historical force of the legend. Spenser's *Faerie Queene* suffered the same disability, though it is also only partly Arthurian, see Chapter 5, section I. Intrinsic rarity also caused two intriguing English alliterative romances to be set aside, the uniquely early Layamon's *Brut* and the alliterative *Morte Arthure*, a surprisingly late heroic poem. Among more modern material for which another volume would provide room, some of which is briefly mentioned in the text, are the under-examined *Tristram of Lyonesse* by Swinburne, the little-known Arthurian texts of the seventeenth and eighteenth centuries, poems by William Morris and Edwin Arlington Robinson and many Arthurian novels ranging from serious (or sometimes just ponderous) to light and popular.

Equally interesting, especially in the context of a social and historical interest, would be the non-literary Arthurian material – place-names and their associations, fairy-tales, comics, film and television versions. The range here is stupendous, stretching in one character, for example from the grotesque giant wooer of the ballad 'Kempy Kay' to the Sir Kay of the British television series *Sir Lancelot*, which displayed his Battle of Britain values in his military bearing and his perfect 'Flying Officer Kite' moustache. All these exceptions and omissions have been necessary to enable this book to chart in sufficient depth and detail the function of the major Arthurian texts, ranging through the whole history of the legend from the earliest period in the British Dark Ages to the present day.

The first three chapters deal with Arthurian material written in Welsh, Latin and French. For all his modern associations with the English-speaking world, Arthur was a latecomer to that language, largely because the languages of medieval England were class-divided, the serious clergy using Latin and the aristocracy French. In discussing these early texts I have used well-known translations; those in Chapters 1 and 2 are excellent, but I have at times had to comment on Comfort's translation of Chrétien de Troyes in Chapter 3. Other translations, mostly small pieces of Welsh or French material, are my own. Later chapters quote from texts which are both authoritative and widely available.

Stephen Knight

1 'Chief of the princes of this island': the early British Arthurian legend

I

Pen teyrnedd yr ynys hon, 'Chief of the princes of this island': that is Arthur's title in the earliest substantial story in his legend, *Culhwch ac Olwen* ('Culhwch and Olwen'). For over a thousand years artists have recreated the legend of King Arthur and new versions keep appearing. 'Chief of the princes' has proved a fair description.

The original language of that title is Welsh. Arthur is not only the major royal figure of British legend: he is truly British. That adjective properly describes the Celts who inhabited Britain before and during the Roman period and then, in the fifth century AD after the Romans withdrew, faced the Germanic invaders usually called the Anglo-Saxons. These British Celts lost control of modern England, but they survived in the west and to some extent the north of England; their language and culture still exist in modern Wales.

That conflict between the British and the Germanic invaders is often thought to have produced the Arthurian legend itself. Many modern commentators accept that a man called Arthur lived around the year 500 AD. They believe he was a leader of a British defence, which was successful for a while – perhaps for a generation. In the end the Celts were defeated, but they apparently carried with them in their newly restricted territory the memory of Arthur as a great hero. His name was magnified by details borrowed from the rich Celtic resources of fabulous narrative, hero-tale and pagan religion. The developed legend was so popular and so powerful that Arthur's glory was transmit-

1

ted to other cultures when they came into contact with British tradition. They in turn passed on the legend as a fable, even by now a myth, of glorious authority.

So goes the legend of the legend. Scholars have become fascinated by it and have pored over the slender threads of evidence; a recent book has gathered, reviewed and extended their work (Alcock, 1971). There is probably truth in the notion of a historical Arthur – but no more than that can be said. No single detail about him can be unequivocally verified, unless some remarkable archaeological discovery is made. The quest for the 'real' Arthur fascinates modern people because it is itself a modern version of the legend, which should take its place beside the others as one more reworking of the Arthurian story. Accordingly the historical Arthur industry will be discussed with other modern versions of the legend in the last chapter of this book.

The present chapter will examine the early references to Arthur in Latin and Welsh, not to assess their truth or falsehood but to discover what social functions are fulfilled by them and the texts in which they appear. Two things will emerge. First there is a remarkable amount of ideological material in the texts, easily visible once you look for it. And second, this early material is very various in its functions: there were many versions of Arthur before he was known outside the British Isles.

Not all of those Arthurs were heroes. In order to stress the crucial part played by a social formation in sponsoring a particular version of the legend, this examination of Arthurian texts will begin with stories that show him as a villain.

Several lives of British saints were written in Latin about the year 1100, but they plainly preserve earlier British traditions about Arthur (Tatlock, 1950, pp. 184–9). He cuts a poor figure as the typical *rex tyrannus*, a king who tyrannises the church. However, the saintly heroes of the stories defeat and humiliate their secular oppressor. In the life of St Cadog Arthur is lustful and deceitful and the saint frustrates him in various ways; in another story he tries to steal St Padarn's coat, but is buried in the earth up to his neck until he begs the saint's pardon and promises to amend his ways; from St Carantoc Arthur does manage to steal an altar because he wants it for his drinking table, but the holy furniture keeps tipping the sinful vessels to the ground, and again Arthur must submit.

These saints' lives were not particularly well-known or influential. They are classic examples of texts with a limited and specific function, serving the interests and asserting the values of a particular social milieu, the Celtic church. They realise the threat of the secular military power but assert that saints can invoke a greater power to defend their position and possessions – a material interest comes clearly through the religious concern.

Other stories, less precisely preserved, recount Arthur's conflicts with his fellow Celts. One tells how Arthur became jealous of the sexual success of Huail, son of Caw, and finally tricked and beheaded him (T. Jones, 1968). The stone where Huail allegedly died still stands in Ruthin High Street (Plate 1). The same story is mentioned in Caradoc's 'Life of St Gildas' because Gildas, whose account of the 'Arthurian' period will be discussed shortly, is also one of Caw's twenty-four sons. Another version of the story, favourable to Arthur, is mentioned in *Culhwch ac Olwen* (to be discussed at length later in this chapter). There probably also existed a narrative unsympathetic to Arthur and favouring the dynasty of Caw (Chadwick, 1953, p. 127), which included the Huail story, showing Arthur as a cruel and whimsical tyrant. Caw may well have been a Pict, and so may have had both racial and territorial hostility to the historic Arthur, whom some scholars think was a northern hero, though others dispute that view. Bromwich (1975–6) surveys the evidence and advocates the northern case; it is opposed by Alcock (1971, pp. 81–5).

Another hero of the north who confronts Arthur without himself being a villain is Owein of Rheged. Undoubtedly a historic figure, he and his father Urien were both patrons of Taliesin, the earliest known poet in Welsh. As Yvain and Uwayne, Owein is well-known in later medieval Arthurian literature, but he is not mentioned in any early British texts as a member of Arthur's warband (though his sister Morfudd is one of the Arthurian ladies in *Culhwch ac Olwen*). A strange ritualised hostility between Owein and Arthur is central to *Breudwyt Ronabwy* which is medieval in date but still retains knowledge of early British tradition, apparently including a tribally based dislike of Arthur ('The Dream of Ronabwy', Richards, (ed.) 1948).

A different negative attitude to Arthur is found in an important sixth-century work by Gildas, the British monk who is said to have been brother to Huail son of Caw. Where the stories of

Huail, Owein and the British saints made Arthur a villain, Gildas ignores him completely. He produced his *De Excidio Britanniae* in the mid-sixth century; the title means 'About the Destruction of Britain', and the book explains the Germanic invasions as the product of British sin and sloth (Gildas, 1978). Much of it is a moral harangue, but Gildas calls it a 'tearful history', and it does include some brief, enigmatic narrative about the British defence. It mentions Ambrosius Aurelianus as the British leader and specifies the siege of 'Mons Badonicus' as a great native success. Mount Baddon is the most accurate version of this Latin name and the double 'd' should be pronounced in the Welsh way, like 'th' in 'fathom'. Later references will connect Mount Baddon firmly with Arthur, but Gildas does not mention him at all.

This is a difficult problem for those who believe in a historical Arthur. Gildas lived through the period, wrote about Baddon and British leaders and must have known of Arthur if he existed. So perhaps he did not exist. But the absence in the text does not prove that either, because Gildas's viewpoint demands that any successful military leader must be omitted unless, like Ambrosius, he can be represented as fully Roman and fully Christian. Those are Gildas's primary loyalties and as a member of the Christian church those are the basic elements of his social and cultural context (Hanning, 1966, ch. 2). The selective perception with which Gildas constructed his version of the contemporary world has no place for a warrior hero whose values do not match those of the text, and who worked only against the Germanic invaders, not against the threat of religious backsliding, Gildas's true enemy. If Arthur did exist, Gildas's silence about him is the first of many ideological treatments of his legend.

II

Two other sources from the early British church do use the name of Arthur in what has been taken as a historical context. The manuscript collection known as *The British Historical Miscellany* contains texts usually called the *Annales Cambriae* ('The Cambrian – i.e. Welsh – Annals') and Nennius's *Historia Brittonum* ('History of the Britons', see Alcock, 1971, for texts and translations of both). Although these were brought together in a twelfth-century manuscript, they were originally apart and should still be treated separately, because their handling of Arthur is somewhat different.

'The Cambrian Annals' are a collection of historical jottings. The fact that these annals are simple, brief remarks has made them attractive and credible to modern historians. At most they are a date, a name or two, a place, an event: as they stand simply on the page, they seem the very stuff of history (see Plate 2). But even among such apparently objective fragments ideology can lurk. The details recorded in the 'Cambrian Annals' have a specifically British slant (Chadwick, 1964; Alcock, 1971, pp. 45–55; Hughes, 1980, chs 5 and 6). The text must have been copied by monks, and a dual interest in British tradition and Christianity is evident – a less narrowly Christian and more nationalistic attitude than that taken by Gildas. The first entry about Arthur shows this plainly:

Bellum badonis in quo Arthur portavit crucem domini nostri Jesu Christi tribus diebus et tribus noctibus in humeros suos et brittones victores fuerunt.

[The battle of Baddon, in which Arthur carried the cross of our lord Jesus Christ for three days and three nights on his shoulders and the British were the victors.]

The year works out as 518 AD, reasonably close to Gildas's rather enigmatic date for Baddon. There is no doubt that such a battle occurred and had a major effect: these two references are good evidence and some archaeologists believe they can deduce a brief halt in the Germanic invasion from about that date (Alcock, 1971, p. 115).

But was Arthur at the battle? This entry in the Annals is unusually long, and one authoritative scholar on early Welsh matters, saw 'a figure of legend' here: he thought the entry out of keeping with the dry tone of the others and felt this was a tendentious insertion of Christian nationalism (T. Jones, 1964, p. 8; for support of this view, see Hughes, 1980, p. 92). The entry has a British and Christian point to make, not just a fact to tell.

This is less clearly the case in the second entry, for 539 AD:

Gweith Camlann in qua Arthur et Medraut corruerunt, et mortalitas in britannia et hibernia fuit.

[The battle of Camlann in which Arthur and Medrawd
perished, and there was plague in Britain and Ireland.]

The fact that the Welsh word *gwaith* is used and that its gender is
correctly recognised as feminine in 'qua' suggests that the battle
was known in native tradition – unlike the 'bellum' at Baddon.
There seems little reason to doubt the historicity of this reference –
other similar ones in the 'Annals' are real enough. Here the
compiler's interest lies not in Christian amplification, but in this
as a major British event, presumably when Arthur died fighting
against Medrawd – they are not specified as opponents, but later
tradition about Medrawd (to become Mordred) suggests this.
The *mortalitas* is also presumably a real event – others are similarly
recorded in the annals. So the 'Annals' apparently record
Arthur's death, and they certainly find his great achievement at
Baddon ideologically fruitful in both Christian and nationalistic
terms.

The ingenious British monk Nennius developed this pattern in
the part of his 'History of the Britons' where Arthurian battles are
listed. That structure itself points to a native source, since the
battle-listing poem is a Welsh genre. (For discussion of Nennius in
general, see Alcock, 1971, pp. 29–32; Chadwick, 1958; Dumville,
1975–6.) To glorify Arthur, Nennius lists the locations of twelve
battles – and a Welsh source poem is again discernible because
the number twelve is only achieved by having four battles in the
same place, in 'Linnuis'. Nine events, usually presented in three
threes, would be natural to Welsh art, where triune events, heroes
and deities are very common, but Nennius contrives the Christian
number of the twelve apostles. There is no doubt a similar native
pattern behind the number of enemies Arthur kills at Baddon;
nine hundred and sixty is a very familiar Welsh number; it would
have been given as three times three hundred and three score.

The place-names provided by Nennius themselves suggest a
historical tradition rather than ideological innovation: they are
mostly obscure, but the few that have been even tentatively
identified show a wide spread – 'Coed Celidon', the Caledonian
forest, is in Strathclyde in south-west Scotland; 'Linnuis' is very
likely the Lindsey district of Lincolnshire on the east midland
coast; 'Caer Legionis' is probably Chester, perhaps Caerleon,
conceivably Gloucester. The obscurity of the names is itself
credible because they were apparently not modernised or

rationalised by Nennius. The wide scatter of the identified places is also historically credible: the Celts did travel long distances to fight, as a war was only won and profitable if the enemy's base was sacked.

Within that probable historicity there is, as in the 'Annals', a clear Christian pressure. At 'Castellum Guinnion' (some unidentified Caer Gwynion, no doubt now bearing a Germanic name) Arthur 'carried the image of St Mary, ever virgin, on his shoulders'. To this element of devotion Nennius adds a distinctly Roman touch in calling Arthur 'dux bellorum', while specifying that he was not a king. Titles like that were used in Roman Britain, such as *Comes Brittanorum*, 'Count of the Britons', but the closest thing to it is the title given Arthur in a Welsh poem to be discussed below, where he is called *llywiadur llafur*, 'guider of labour': a battle may in Welsh be called *gwaith*, 'work', or *llafur*, 'labour'. The Latin and Welsh phrases are virtually identical, and Nennius may well have drawn Arthur's title from his Welsh source.

More than anybody, Nennius shaped Arthur as the patriotic British Christian warrior, the victor of Baddon, the defender of his nation. This nationalistic, historical tradition is strong within the Latin and church context and indicates the viewpoint of the clerics. Their sense of continuity through time produced a grasp of historical change foreign to pagan Celtic culture. In addition, the remarkable mobility and sense of identity of the Celtic church, working together, seem to have made its members nationally self-conscious.

Neither history nor nationalism was part of the secular British world. Welsh tradition knows of Camlann, where Arthur died fighting a fellow-Celt, but not of Baddon or any defence against the Germanic invaders (T. G. Jones, 1926, pp. 42–3; Bromwich, 1978, pp. lxxiii–lxiv). For the Welsh secular tradition, Arthur was a great warrior and his heroic development was based on native models. Nennius, a Welshman as well as a Latinist and cleric, knows this material and includes two items among his *Mirabilia*, the 'Wonderful Things' that occur in Britain. He tells of the stone that bears the print of Arthur's dog as they hunted the great boar Troynt, and how after Arthur killed and buried his son the grave kept changing shape.

Many other fanciful and mythical details were associated with Arthur by the secular and largely pagan British tradition, and

those details, non-historical and non-nationalistic, have been
much more fruitful in the legend than the Arthurian sketch offered
by the Latin clerical writers of early Britain.

III

Within early Welsh tradition the versions of Arthur range from an
ideal soldier to a supernatural super-hero. The reference that
seems the earliest uses his name as a model of the martial glory
which is the central value of the text. This is *Y Gododdin* ('The
Gododdin', Aneirin, 1938). The poem is essentially a loose series
of stanzas which lament and glorify the warriors who marched
south from the land of the Gododdin, a tribe settled around what
is now Edinburgh. In about 600 AD they went to attack the
Germanic Northumbrians at Catraeth (now Catterick) in Yorkshire. Each stanza praises a hero, telling how splendid he was,
how many enemies he killed, how he kept to the death his promise
to fight for the Gododdin's chief.

This authentic heroic context provides the first Welsh reference
to Arthur. Stanza 102 of *Y Gododdin* praises Gwawrddur; he is a
great hero, but not the greatest:

> He glutted the black ravens on the wall
> Of the fort, though he was not Arthur.

Arthur may well be mentioned here principally because his name
rhymes with Gwawrddur, but for that to be possible he must have
been known as a pre-eminent hero, an integral part of the heroic
tradition. That reference comes in the oldest stratum of the poem,
which is generally held to have been a contemporary composition,
handed down orally from about 600 AD until it was written down
in the ninth century (Jackson, 1969, pp. 57–67). Here Arthur
represents a major value in the highly developed and directly
functional heroic ideology of the warrior aristocracy of the British
Celts.

Another early reference is similar in context and function. A
poem about Geraint, a hero connected with the south-west of
England, describes in crisp stanzas a battle at Llongborth –
perhaps Langport in Somerset (text ed. Roberts, 1978a,
pp. 289–96). Geraint himself does with honour, and Arthur is
again a superior figure:

> In Llongborth I saw Arthur,
> Brave men struck with steel,
> Emperor, guider of toil.

This is a real battle, at a named place, with the certainly historic Geraint present. There is a brief Christian ending, it is true, but only in the last stanza: the rest seems fully in keeping with the heroic ideology of *Y Gododdin* (which itself has Christian touches). The two poems relate back to the Iron Age Celtic heroic culture that is most fully seen in the riches of Old Irish literature. But this strict military realism and heroic ideology is only one secular version of Arthur. A figure of more general power is shaped in two other early Welsh poems, where fabulous, even supernatural, powers and values augment the great hero.

A thirteenth-century manuscript, *The Black Book of Carmarthen*, preserves a poem in which Arthur describes his followers to the gatekeeper of some unnamed fortress. It is usually called by its first words *Pa Gwr* ('What Man', Roberts, 1978b, pp. 300–9). Two major figures are Cai and Bedwyr, those lieutenants of Arthur who survive in the later legend as Sir Kay and Sir Bedivere.

Much of the poem is like a heroic lay, as when Arthur says:

> Before Emrys's lords
> I saw Cai on the move,
> Spoils he carried off,
> The tall man was in anger,
> Heavy was his vengeance,
> Bitter was his anger.
> When he drank from a buffalo horn
> He drank for four men;
> In battle when he came,
> For a hundred he would kill;
> If god did not cause it,
> Impossible would be Cai's death.

The passage might come straight from *Y Gododdin*. This sort of exaggeration is common in heroic poems just as it is in reports of modern heroes. But as the poem goes on it does stretch a little beyond heroic probability. Cai has fought the nine witches of Ystafanion, and with great difficulty he has killed the 'Cath Palug' (Palug's monstrous cat who is, with French and Creole intermediaries, the ultimate source of that more modern feline fiend, Cat Ballou, the female gun-slinger).

The poem moves away from the strictly human context of heroic poetry into the wider field of fable and folklore. And at least some of the heroes Arthur names among his warband are undoubtedly fully formed Celtic gods. Mabon fab Modron means, in early Welsh, 'Son, son of Mother', and his status as a figure representing the fertility of the Mother Goddess is well-known in Welsh. Manawydan son of Llyr is here as well; possessing supernatural wisdom and on some occasions associated with the sea (especially in Irish as Manannán), he is brother to Bran the Blessed, a major god in British tradition. Llwch, an even more potent figure, also travels in Arthur's warband. He is the powerful and benign Celtic god known as Lugh in Irish and sometimes in Welsh as Lludd. His name lies behind that of places like London, Lyons, Laon and Leiden.

These gods are not shown in action; they seem to be there to add glory and mystical strength to Arthur and his men, just as royal genealogies went back frequently to divinities, pagan and Christian, for greater authority. Nor is anything said about Arthur's own powers and feats. Rather, he is the supervisor of warriors, the *dux bellorum* as in Nennius. The battle Nennius mentions on the river 'Tribuit' is probably the same as Bedwyr's briefly described fight on the banks of the 'Tryfrwyd'. But even if there is a link with Nennius, the two battle-lists differ greatly: this one magnifies Arthur's glory from pagan religious sources and wonder-tale, elements which Nennius recognises but restricts to his *Mirabilia*.

The native development of Arthur is even more marked in another early Welsh poem, usually called *Preiddeu Annwfn* ('The Spoils of Annwfn', Evans, 1915). Apparently of great age, this poem may not have been written down until the eleventh century, and oral transmission seems to have added obscurity to its intrinsically allusive nature. Only four stanzas have been translated with any confidence, but it is clear enough that the poem celebrates a glorious and costly raid on the otherworld. The most revealing stanza is the second (the translation is still speculative in places):

I am famous, splendid if the song is heard:
In the fortress, four-cornered, four-sided,
In poetry from the cauldron it was spoken,
By the breath of nine maidens it was set ablaze.
The very cauldron of the Lord of Annwfn, what is its nature?
Very strong, and a border with pearl:
It will not boil the food of a coward, that was not destined.
For the sword of Llwch Lleawc it was heated,
And in Lleminawg's hand it was left.
And before the door of hell's gate, lamps were burning,
And when we went with Arthur – glorious hardship –
Save seven, none returned from the Fortress of Carousal.

A specifically heroic ideology is still present: the cauldron will not boil food for a coward; Llwch Lleminawg's sword seems to have come from the cauldron – perhaps has been magically tempered there. The hardships of the assault were glorious and few lived to bear the honour; there was great carousal, as in all heroic halls. But it is equally clear that these heroic values are supernaturally magnified.

Preiddeu Annwfn shows Arthur winning for his people the cauldron, this special totem of heroic power. It is a culture-hero story, like the classical one that tells how Prometheus stole fire from the gods – another 'glorious hardship'. The poem creates a mythic projection of the great hero Arthur was known to be. It symbolises the martial values of early Wales, and it also confirms Arthur's status as more than human, so he can bear that intensely condensed value.

The power and early date of *Preiddeu Annwfn* helped to persuade Sir John Rhys that Arthur must have been in origin a Celtic God (1891, ch. 1). But early Celtic myth knows of no Arthur, nor does Celtic genealogy (which is larded with gods) record his name before the sixth century. The evidence is clear that the name suddenly emerged, probably from history itself, and was realised as great through several different ideological frameworks. For the clerical writers Arthur had national and historical importance; in the restricted world of pure heroic ideology he was a token of value.

But outside those two specific and specialised contexts, Arthur began to develop as a special and superior hero. The semi-mythical poems and the *Mirabilia* in Nennius are part of the process and its widespread impact is clear. Among the stanzas which list the graves of famous men there is one exception:

> A grave for March, a grave for Gwythur,
> A grave for Gwgan Bloody-Sword,
> An enigma for ever a grave for Arthur.
>
> (Jones, 1967, p. 121)

To say merely that there is a generally magnified and mythicised legend about Arthur is to indicate no social basis and function for this non-clerical, non-heroic Arthurian legend. But that vague generality is imposed by the brief and fragmentary nature of the texts that have just been discussed. When *Culhwch ac Olwen*, the major example of the wider development of Arthur in Welsh, is examined, it becomes clear that this version of the legend realises sharply a set of social and historical attitudes which amount to nothing less than a coherent ideology specifically related to Welsh tribal life.

IV

Culhwch ac Olwen is the earliest major story about Arthur (Evans, 1887). It has survived only in two fairly late medieval manuscripts, but the language suggests it was put together by the year 1100 at the latest, and perhaps a good deal earlier (Foster, 1959, pp. 32, 38–9; Bromwich, 1954, p. 106; Loomis, 1956, pp. 191–2). That date is important, refuting Tatlock's opinion (1950, pp. 194–9) that this is a Welsh version of the French and Latin development of the Arthurian legend.

As a fully Welsh Arthurian story *Culhwch ac Olwen* has crucial importance in the history of the Arthurian legend, giving access to the society and culture where it first flourished. The story tells how Arthur's cousin, Culhwch, is cursed by his stepmother when he refuses to marry her own daughter. His side will never beat against woman, she says darkly, unless he wins Olwen, daughter of Ysbaddaden Penkawr. The point of the curse is that 'Penkawr' means 'Chief Giant': in the well-known folktale pattern called 'the giant's daughter', the father always resists vigorously because he will die if his daughter marries. The stepmother intends Culhwch will either die or live without wife and children.

However, Culhwch has important connections. On his father's

advice he seeks out Arthur, his first cousin, to enlist his help and that of his warband: its members are invoked by Culhwch in a stunningly long list that contains over two hundred names and many details of the heroes who bear up Arthur's glory. With specially skilled helpers Culhwch is able to locate Olwen, but they discover that before he will agree to the marriage the giant demands a series of *anoetheu*, 'difficult things'. These are grotesquely designed to prepare for the wedding feast the giant hopes to avoid – such as obtaining the blood of the Black Witch from the Uplands of Hell to dress his beard, and stealing the comb and scissors from between the ears of the Twrch Trwyth, the terrible Chief Boar of the Island of Britain. The allies achieve a series of tasks (though by no means what the giant has required), but Arthur himself is needed to obtain the most perilous articles, especially the two just mentioned. Finally the giant is beheaded, his daughter is married to Culhwch, and his lands are seized by Goreu, another of Arthur's cousins.

So ends a story both dramatic and memorable, and also relating directly to the hopes and fears of Welsh tribal society, particularly those of the dominant class who would have sponsored the performance and the recording of the story. To establish this relationship it is necessary first to sketch briefly the character of early Welsh tribal society and its economic structure. The major features of that world are represented in *Culhwch ac Olwen*, though they are presented in a way favourable to those who actually controlled the socio-economic structure, the contemporary models for Arthur and his warriors.

Early Celtic society was 'tribal, rural, hierarchical and familiar,' said the Irish scholar Binchy in an important essay (1954, p. 54). That description rose from early Irish material, but it applies with equal strength to the Celts on the continent of Europe and in Britain itself. Binchy's four categories each have force and interest. The Celts saw the largest social unit as the tribe, not the nation: an attitude visible in Celtic areas to the present day. The towns in modern Ireland and Wales were created, or developed from some humble Celtic settlement, by non-Celts – Norsemen and English in Ireland, Normans and English in Wales. Even today rural communities in both countries still tend to treat the local town more as a crossroads than a community.

The fact that Celtic society was hierarchical is clear enough from the early burials of princes and princesses. A stage of tribal equality for all was abandoned very early (Cunliffe, 1974, p. 305) and the literature that survives deals with kings and nobles and their conflicts with each other. The most crucial of Binchy's four categories is the importance of the family. The central fact of Celtic social life was the kin-group, extending as far as second cousins, that is to all who shared one great-grandfather – the line of descent is patriarchal, at least within recorded tradition. The family was the land-holding unit and the basis for legal action on behalf of members: a person only had status, in a sense only had existence, as a member of a kin-group.

The family units were themselves grouped, somewhat loosely, into three classes or perhaps more accurately into three castes – basically those of ancient Indo-European society, that is priests, warriors and farmers (Martin, 1970). The priestly caste appears little in the surviving Welsh texts, presumably because the influence of Christian composers and copyists excluded them from the transmission process. Priests are powerful in the early Irish texts where the wisdom and influence of the druids often guides and sometimes opposes the leaders of the warrior caste. The farming caste is also absent from the texts in general, and this is because its viewpoint is inherently contrary to that of the warriors who own the land. Because we have no surviving records from this period which give a voice to the farmers, we simply cannot tell whether there were in early Britain peasant disturbances like those in Gaul which the Romans called risings of the 'bacaudae' (Lindsay, 1958, ch. 11). If they existed, which they probably did, they are lost to history. The texts sponsored by the warrior caste realise many threats, but none so ultimately disturbing as revolution.

It was families of the warrior caste who held the ascendancy, through their sheer physical power, and this dominance extended to the economic sphere. In early times property had been tribally collective: the land was the tribe's, and the ruling family merely administered it for general use. In time, the land became the property of the dominant family (Filip, 1977, p. 112). The warrior families originally operated as a self-protecting military aristocracy, with the male members of the kin being trained in war from childhood. However, this was a chancy process: a shortage of sons would soon mean weakness, whether caused by low birth rates, death in war or disease. In time the leading families came to defend their property by assembling a warband, that is admitting men to the family in order to protect it. In Welsh law the leader of the *cenedl*, the kin, had the right and duty to make such admissions (Lloyd, 1939, p. 386). The warband was itself known as the *teulu* – which was and still is the Welsh word for 'family'.

So the warband-supported élite families historically dominated tribal life in Wales and in particular owned the land, which was the major source of economic power, partly through agriculture, though that was restricted in medieval as in modern Wales because of a difficult terrain and climate. The major activity was cattle rearing, with some sheep and horse breeding in suitable areas.

The warrior élite did not work their land; that was the role of the farmer caste. But they did involve themselves in two other activities which were effectively economic processes in this period. Raiding and pillaging the lands of a neighbouring tribe were not only ways of increasing the security of the home tribe: they were also ways of adding to one's own stock of wealth. The cattle-raid is a major feature of early Irish texts and is often mentioned in Welsh as well. It was a way of increasing the tribal herds and so boosting economic activity. Another practice with an economic as well as a military side was hunting. As was normal in many cultures this was a suitably splendid form of relaxation which also kept men and horses trained for war, but here it was in addition an important means of providing meat for the table. Especially sought was the giant wild boar, whose great courage and rich flesh were doubly prized, both as a test of honour and as a festal reward for it.

Both cattle-raiding and hunting are intrinsic to the world of *Culhwch ac Olwen*, and the story centres on the land-owning warrior family with a warband to support it. The threats the story realises are those that would have been perceived by members of that group; the values offered and the results achieved are ones which would have seemed both real and consoling to them. There can be little doubt that such a family would be the patrons for an extended prose story of this sort, and the fact that it was recorded in writing well before other Welsh prose stories indicates it was held in special esteem by its audience. As well it might be: *Culhwch ac Olwen* is not a ramshackle, whimsical, Celtic ruin, as ill-informed readers might think. Rather, it is a wide-ranging and complex narrative, a central ideological text for the tribal élite in Wales between the two invasions of Britain by the Saxons and the

Normans. As a means of access to that obscure period, the text deserves close analysis.

V

The threat represented in the essential plot of the story is the failure of the family to reproduce itself. The stepmother's curse means Culhwch will either go childless or be killed by the giant. And so he would if he were truly alone in the world. But he has family connections: he is Arthur's first cousin.

Culhwch is not the only focus of the fear that the family will fail to hold and extend its position. Another of Arthur's cousins appears: Goreu is the last of twenty-four brothers. The rest have been killed by the evil giant who is also Culhwch's enemy. The motif of the last of twenty-four children is a traditional Celtic way of realising the near-extinction of a once populous family line: the children of Caw mentioned above are one of many examples. But like Culhwch, Goreu both survives and succeeds. He wins the giant's lands at the end of the story when Culhwch wins his daughter: two forms of fertility are appropriated by the Arthurian family.

Before this can happen Arthur must welcome Culhwch into his *cenedl*. The boon Culhwch asks on arrival is for Arthur to cut his hair, a traditional act of intimate grooming between kin. As Arthur does it he says 'My heart grows tender towards thee: I know thou art sprung from my blood' (p. 100). Then he discovers Culhwch is his cousin; Arthur, as *pencenedl*, family chief, has recognised Culhwch as a member of the *cenedl*. From now on their interests are common, and so the marriage of Culhwch is of prime importance.

Arthur's *teulu*, his family-army, is the effective force in obtaining Olwen for Culhwch, though the dominant social structure, and the social unit that is strengthened, remains the family. The power of the warband is recognised partly by the fact that it is in their names that Culhwch invokes his 'claim' on his kinsman Arthur, and partly by the enormous size and impact of the list of warriors itself.

Culhwch's long invocation of the heroes of Arthur's warband ranges right through Welsh tradition and wanders away from it at some points – Cnwchwr mab Nes is Conchobar, King of Ulster, one of several mighty visitors to the list. There are other even more surprising members, including William the Conqueror as 'Guilhenin King of France', evidently a late insertion. But the emphasis is on the brave men of Welsh story and some of them at least are mentioned elsewhere, such as Gereint mab Erbin, whose elegy has already been discussed, and Rhuawn Bebyr from *Breudwyt Ronabwy*. The supernatural heroes Manawydan and Llwch are still with Arthur as they were in the poem *Pa Gwr*. An even better-known warrior is here too: Drwst Iron-Fist is the original Welsh name of the hero known throughout medieval literature as Tristan.

The list symbolises not only the numbers and skill of the warriors, but also their unity and their loyalty to Arthur. That positive force is itself very much a hopeful dream. Warbands were not always loyal, and one of the traditional triads records that fact in the 'Three Faithless Warbands of the Island of Britain' (Bromwich, 1978, p. 61). Such a possibility is not even considered in this text, but there are some traces of the tension and disunity that always occur when armed men gather together. The trouble Arthur had with Huail is glanced at twice: when he is first mentioned in the warrior list the comment is added: 'he never submitted to a lord's hand' (p. 101). Later in the list Gwydre mab Llwydeu provides the occasion for explaining the Huail–Arthur hostility in a way distinctly favourable to Arthur: 'Huail his uncle stabbed him and thereby there was feud between Huail and Arthur because of the wound' (p. 103).

Cai is also recognised as a troublesome figure; he may well be the bearer of historical tension between warband and family. He is named first in Culhwch's list, and is in early tradition Arthur's lieutenant, in action and vigour apparently senior to Bedwyr. Here he opposes Arthur's wish to let Culhwch in against the rules of the court (p. 99) and then repeats his hostility when Culhwch complains that Arthur's men have not yet found Olwen (p. 107). Later on the mighty Cai, apparently his warband leader, actually separates from Arthur. They fall out because Arthur makes fun of Cai's distinctly cautious method of obtaining a hair of Dillus's beard. Here too the feud is reported in Arthur's favour – 'neither for Arthur's lack of help nor for the slaying of his men, did Cai have anything to do with him in his hour of need from that time forward' (p. 128).

The possibility of trouble arising among the warband is only raised to be controlled from Arthur's viewpoint. Essentially, family unity and warband support are a basic force in the text as they would be in the dreams of the tribal élite. As a result of those qualities, the threats are dissipated. Culhwch can marry and produce children with Olwen, Goreu takes the lands of her father after his death. The feared weakness in fertility and land is thwarted, property and fertility are wrenched from the threatening giant.

The central fear of a sterile generation and of reproductive power lying in enemy hands, whether giants or stepmothers, is not only presented through the story of Culhwch and, less prominently, Goreu. In the way of myth and folktale, it is twice repeated in the text in a reinforcing way. On both occasions a brief but telling story meshes with the major anxiety of the tale.

One of the 'impossible tasks' Ysbaddaden sets Culhwch before he can marry Olwen is to find Mabon (who was with Arthur in *Pa Gwr*). Arthur's men enlist the aid of the oldest animals – ouzel, stag, owl, eagle and salmon, in order of age. The salmon alone knows the answer, and Cai and Bedwyr ride on his shoulders up the River Severn to Gloucester and Cai breaks into the dungeon where Mabon is kept. This is obviously a fable about fertility freed from the 'prison' of the womb: Mabon the 'Son', salmon, river and the breached dungeon are patent and potent elements of the mystery of conception and birth.

Another brief story realises with similar force the struggle to recover fertile beauty from the control of dark powers. In the middle of the quest to achieve the tasks is inserted a story telling how Creiddylad, daughter of Lludd Silver-Hand, went willingly with Gwythyr, a human hero, but was suddenly carried off by Gwyn ap Nudd, a dark lord of the otherworld. Lludd's daughter is a valuable prize of fertile beauty, and it is Arthur alone who can bring order to the conflict – but not an easy resolution. Under his command, every May Day Gwyn and Gwythyr fight for her hand and will do so till judgement day, when the winner will keep her. That mythicises the unending battle between dark winter and bright summer for the control of fertility. But ideological texts present consolations as well as threats and there is hope to be found here: she originally chose Gwythyr, after all, and his name is the Welsh version of the Latin 'Victor'. A triumph for the forces of Arthurian light is at least implied. In this way the story of the quest for Mabon and the fight for Creiddylad add dream-like strength to the Arthurian family in its quest for fertility and security.

VI

The triumph of the dominant family is the major ideological feature of *Culhwch ac Olwen*, but the detailed mechanism of that triumph is full of meaning and to study it reveals what the warrior families feared and what they saw as their greatest strength. First the exact threats need to be examined; then the values employed against those threats can be scrutinised.

The immediate and overt essence of Ysbaddaden as an enemy is that he is a true, raw giant, not a culturally trained warrior with culturally fine weapons. In person he is huge and slothful – his servants have to raise his eyelids with his eye-forks so he can see his visitors. He is very hard to fight against because of his great natural resilience. He can absorb terrible punishment and laugh it off: a spear through his eyeball will merely make the eye water when the wind blows. Initially Ysbaddaden represents wild nature, that huge and forbidding force against which the Celts had to pit their collective cultural efforts.

The hostile terrain and climate of Wales not only made agriculture largely unprofitable; pastoralism itself was very difficult. The Welsh lived perilously and close to their treasured animals, especially through the bitter winter. Most beasts were not killed off, as was once thought, but people shared their life with them so enough breeding stock would survive till the spring. Human and animal survival in the face of the oppressive force of nature were intimately interwoven (Harding, 1974, pp. 85–7).

If wild nature threatened severely the animals who sustained human life, inanimate environmental pressures constantly imposed restrictions and dangers upon the Welsh. In particular, the bleak geography kept settlements small and profoundly isolated, always aware of the neighbouring forces – mountain, river, sea, forest – all of which might suddenly bring disaster (J. G. Evans, 1975, ch. 6).

But nature also had its beneficent, summer-like side. This is represented by the giant's daughter Olwen. If his wrath can be faced successfully, her rich fecundity can be possessed. A formal description makes her essence richly clear:

Yellower was her head than the flower of the broom; whiter was her flesh than the foam of the wave; whiter were her palms and her fingers than the shoots of the marsh trefoil from amidst the fine gravel of a welling spring. Neither the eye of the mewed hawk, nor the eye of the thrice mewed falcon, not an eye was there fairer than hers. Whiter were her breasts than the breast of the white swan, redder were her cheeks than the reddest foxglove.   (pp. 110–11)

The threat of wild nature and the promise of nature's fertility in one way bore equally on all members of Welsh tribal society, but they also had special relevance to the anxieties of the élite who owned the land and appropriated the bulk of its productivity. Their authority itself depended on their control of those who actually controlled nature, the farmer caste. To stress the threat of nature itself and ignore the actual power-relation within the tribe's response to nature is an effective piece of ideological writing, like the way in which modern politicians make use of nationalist distractions to conceal internal strains.

The giant represents at a less immediate level another force which operates in a very similar way, being both a general tribal danger and a specific threat to the power of the ruling family. As well as representing wild nature, he is also a symbol of a fearsomely powerful neighbour, the chief of the next tribe. Ysbaddaden's land is hard to find and far away, but when the heroes arrive there it lies right next to the home of a distressed part of Arthur's extended family. A sister of Culhwch's mother, another of Arthur's aunts, has not only married a shepherd (a member of the farmer, not the warrior caste) but has also seen twenty-three sons destroyed by the giant: only Goreu survives. Her descent in class has left her, however fertile, not only nameless but without warriors to defend her, vulnerable to the force of the neighbouring giant.

In real contemporary terms the chief of the neighbouring tribe, given the opportunity and signs of weakness, would raid across tribal borders, killing farmers and rustling cattle. In order to defeat him a raid would need to be mounted on his own base: that would have been a hill-fort deep in his territory, requiring a long journey just like that undertaken by the heroes. The fact that Goreu's house is next to the giant's fort is a symbol of his threatening propinquity, not a realistic detail. It also enables

Olwen to be already in contact with the family which will embrace her, in both metaphorical and literal terms.

Once he is encountered, Ysbaddaden's overt role as nature is exploited to make his threat as a neighbour more confidently faceable: by being nature, he has no culture, and that is the value that Arthurian society consciously brandishes against him, the essence of the self-consciousness of the tribal élite. In following the course of the story, it will become clear that this is also a surface structure with a more potent and disturbing reality beneath it: culture here and in later Arthurian stories is a major part of the self-definition and the self-legitimation of the audience.

Ysbaddaden has no society at all. He and his daughter apparently live alone in his fortress, with no more than a few guards and servants. There are none of the splendid social arrangements of Arthur's court and the heroes fight their way in briskly because there is no complex gate-keeping ritual as at Arthur's court. Like the giant himself, his fortress is slovenly, unmilitary, in spite of its awesome size. A striking detail with considerable resonance is that Olwen must go to Arthur's aunt's house to wash her hair. Ysbaddaden's fortress lacks cultural grooming facilities – the very means by which Arthur and Culhwch sensed and cemented their bond. Grooming is also a means of controlling hirsute nature, a part of attaining the glamour associated with culture and honour – and ultimately with tribal power. When the heroes attack Ysbaddaden's fortress they go 'with pomp and brave combs set in their hair' (p. 112).

Celtic military culture went further than hairdressing. When Culhwch and his helpers fling iron spears at the giant he catches them and flings them back – but they return as stone spears. The Celts were the bearers of the Iron Age into northern and western Europe, and their iron weapons were much superior to the bronze of their predecessors, let alone the stone weapons that may still have been used in areas such as Wales. It seems unlikely that the Welsh in about the ninth or tenth century would have been really perturbed by the few pockets of pre-Celtic people who had survived. The 'stone age' attribution of Ysbaddaden's force is more a belittling and containing of his power than a truly fearful element of it.

The converging threats that the giant poses to the powerful family are partly general and indirect (even obscuring real power relations in the tribe) and partly specific and painful, threatening directly the continued dominance of the warrior élite. Against these disturbing forces the story has assembled a whole set of values which finally contain and frustrate the giant and his multiple threats.

VII

The unity of family and warband is a positive force in the story, overriding the traces of friction that have already been discussed. The plot acts out this collective security on several occasions by making the warriors travel in parties on their various quests. To find where Olwen might be Arthur picks a group of specially skilled warriors to go with Culhwch (pp. 107–8). He does the same in order to find Mabon (pp. 123–4), and the hunt for the Twrch Trwyth, the Chief Boar of the Island of Britain, is a markedly collective matter, with all heroic hands involved. The underlying plot pattern of the whole text has been likened to the folk-tale pattern called 'Six Go Through the World' an essentially group-ethos story (Jackson, 1961, pp. 71–5).

Arising from this collectivity is the value of honour, which is a powerful force in the story. It is not easy to grasp at once the functioning force of honour in earlier texts and earlier life. The topic has been well discussed in the context of Malory (Lambert, 1975, pp. 176–94). Honour is not, as it might now be regarded, a matter of fustian rectitude or cardboard titles. It is an operating system of interrelated duties and values. A person's role is externally known, not privately decided. A person's value is also publicly realised as face, honour, fame, not inwardly constituted as innocence (in the religious context) or self-fulfilment (in the secular world).

A failure in duty towards the collectively secure society brings shame, the dreaded opposite of honour. Celtic bards were believed to have the power to satirise a man to death – Dafydd ap Gwilym, the greatest Welsh poet and a contemporary of Chaucer, was credited with doing just that when another poet insulted his mother (Parry, 1963, pp. xl–xli). Such a fatal exclusion from the honour-bearing and security-bringing collective social unit is still known, if not practised, in tribal Africa and Aboriginal Australia. Poems and stories are a prime source of honour or shame – hence the battle-listing poems, heroic fables and satirical missives of Celtic tradition.

This whole structure was an assumed feature of Celtic society, and so does not need to be broadcast throughout the text to have force. But the power of honour is evident at times. When Arthur has not found Olwen for him, Culhwch feels unrecompensed for his place in the family and threatens to damage it: 'I will away and take thine honour with me' (p. 107). The importance of honour and the need to cultivate it constantly have already been stated by Arthur. Cai does not want to let Culhwch into the hall against custom, but Arthur says they must be flexible, for their own good: 'We are noble men so long as we are resorted to. The greater the bounty we show, all the greater will be our nobility and our fame and our glory' (p. 99). It is also Cai who reveals the power of shame: because Arthur mocks him in verse, Cai is his bitter enemy for life (p. 128).

Like Cai, each hero has his personal honour, to be carefully tended, and each of the major warriors who joins in the collective quest for Culhwch's future wife has his own special quality, explained when Arthur sends out his first search party. Many of the heroes in the warrior list also have distinctive features. These are all unique, but they are not individualistic because they are collectively employed. Sometimes this is literally so: Cai's colleagues can shelter up against him in bad weather because his heroic heat keeps the rain away. More generally they are special skills which are employed in turn in the action to make progress in the collective project, such as Gwrhyr's mastery of languages or Cynddylig's power as a guide.

The skills are all cultural masteries of natural limitations. They conquer, for example, cold, rain, the multiplicity of languages, the mystery of different terrains – in general, the limits of natural human power. Just as the social collectivity of the family and the warband is a cultural unification against the isolated ferocity of enemies red in tooth and claw – human and animal, typified by Ysbaddaden in his lonely fortress – so the sheer skill and the interactive work of the warriors promote the notion that human culture can overcome the problems of nature. This is a recurrent topic in many early texts, offering the combined skill and will of human beings against the overawing forces of nature. The fact that the aristocratic land-owning families are themselves the leaders in culture, the most skilful warriors, the most sophisticated in customs and possessions, enables them to exploit this pattern as a subtle means of legitimising their power.

The way in which the élite family has assumed the leadership of the cultural opposition to nature and the ideological value of cultural display itself are both summed up in the brilliant formal description of Culhwch as he leaves for Arthur's court. The effect is both subtle and forceful and the whole passage needs to be quoted:

> Off went the boy on a steed with light-grey head, four winters old, with well-knit fork, shell-hoofed, and a gold tubular bridle-bit in its mouth. And under him a precious gold saddle, and in his hand two whetted spears of silver. A battle-axe in his hand, the forearm's length of a full grown man from ridge to edge. It would draw blood from the wind; it would be swifter than the swiftest dewdrop from the stalk to the ground, when the dew would be heaviest in the month of June. A gold-hilted sword on his thigh, and the blade of it gold, and a gold-chased buckler upon him, with the hue of heaven's lightning therein, and an ivory boss therein. And two greyhounds, white-breasted, brindled, in front of him, with a collar of red gold about the neck of either, from shoulder-swell to ear. The one that was on the left side would be on the right and the one that was on the right side would be on the left, like two sea-swallows sporting around him. Four clods the four hoofs of his steed would cut, like four swallows in the air over his head, now before him, now behind him. A four-cornered mantle of purple upon him, and an apple of red gold in each of its corners; a hundred kine was the worth of each apple. The worth of three hundred kine in precious gold was there in his foot gear and his stirrups, from the top of his thigh to the tip of his toe. Never a hair-tip stirred upon him, so exceeding light his steed's canter under him on his way to the gate of Arthur's court.   (p. 97)

The splendid weapons, the horse-trappings, the perfectly matched performing dogs, the highly trained horse, the surplus riches evident in the battle gear – this is the height of cultural splendour. The underlying motif here is the elegant control of nature. Culhwch's hair, soon to be trimmed even finer by Arthur, is immobile even as the horse canters – the most controlled of gaits, as well as the showiest. Four clods of earth are always in the air, the counterparts to the four daisies that spring up in Olwen's footprints. These earth clods, though, are not natural: they are taken out of nature, suspended in the air like swallows by the horse's perfect action and its fine-trimmed, culturally perfect, shell-shaped hooves. Most potent of all, the sharp edge of Culhwch's axe will 'draw blood from the wind', a metaphor both intriguing and ideological. The axe can weaken nature. The wielder of it in his skill can outdo nature, for the axe will fall more swiftly than the swiftest dewdrop from the stalk in the ground when the dew would be heaviest in the month of June.

If Culhwch is the symbol of cultural mastery, the tasks he is required to achieve embody the conflict of culture and nature. Ysbaddaden specifies a whole series of *anoetheu*, 'difficult things', which are directly related to the sophisticated splendour of a bride-bestowal. He requires a splendid feast, a perfect veil for his daughter, the finest bragget to drink, the best cups; and hampers, horns, bottles, music, cauldron, all at the height of Celtic sophistication. Then special stress is laid on grooming Ysbadda-den's hair and beard. To some modern readers it may seem merely bizarre and Celticly quaint that the heroes have to obtain toilet equipment from between the ears of the fearsome Twrch Trwyth in order to dress Ysbaddaden's hair and beard. But it is part of a pattern; the giant stipulates the terms of his own defeat as enemies do in wish-fulfilling stories. He nominates the painful creation of a collective and intricate cultural system, typified by careful grooming, and culminating in a great feast, just the sort of occasion in which the cultural and honoured society displayed its orderly self in secure and sophisticated glory.

Yet the list of tasks required and the list of tasks performed are not the same. Nor will there be a bride-bestowing by the giant. At the end Cadw performs a grotesque and cruel version of the giant's toilette, shaving 'his beard, flesh and skin to the bone, and his two ears outright' (p. 136). This typifies the difference between the two lists, tasks required and tasks performed. The first are cultural, with the giant in charge: the second are violent, performed by heroic will and at the expense of the giant. The lists are not different because the text has been garbled in transmission, as has been thought (Foster, 1959, p. 31 and 1974, pp. 71 and 79). The fact that the tasks performed are not those the giant required expresses the fact that the ruling family extends its power in its own terms, at its own will, not dancing to the tune of its opponents. As Ysbaddaden says when Culhwch claims his daughter, 'thou needst not thank me for that, but thank Arthur who has secured her for thee' (p. 136).

More importantly, the nature of the tasks performed is not in fact at all cultural. The ruling family may claim cultural legitimation and revel in its sophistication, but their power actually rests on their ability to do violence with heroic force, skill and trickery – and with the assistance of animal helpers direct from the world of nature, not human culture. In its crisis the text enacts a central, truth about power in the world of its audience, a truth carefully concealed and ideologically mystified by the stress laid on culture. That is a pattern which will recur many times in the Arthurian legend, as the critical action will reveal the fissure between the sophisticated and false self-consciousness of the sponsoring class and the naked power lurking within that structure of euphemism and self-legitimation.

VIII

Just as the list of tasks required has a consistent concern with cultural materials, so the list of tasks performed has its own violent logic. To analyse this is to recognise the inner fears and the real values and practices of the warrior élite in tribal Wales. First comes the Wrnach Gawr episode: Cai kills him by pretending to be a highly cultured craftsman, and while polishing the giant's sword he takes advantage of his relaxed state to plunge it into his head. This episode was the last request by Ysbaddaden and the first task performed. This odd positioning may suggest that a separate story has been inserted into *Culhwch ac Olwen* (Foster, 1974, pp. 72–3). Yet whatever its origin and authority, the episode has a clear function that may indeed have motivated its insertion. As the link between the two lists, it demonstrates the essence of their difference: Cai assumes a cultural role and displays cultural skills merely in order to exercise against an unsuspecting victim his warrior violence and cunning. That, the text implies, is *really* how you handle giants.

The episode foreshadows with optimism the end of Ysbadda-den, another giant with a fearsome fortress, also defeated by violent cunning in a distinctly emasculating way: Ysbaddaden is debearded before death, Wrnach's sword and scabbard are removed by Cai. Another minor task shows the same heroic brutality, when in order to get the culturally required hair from the beard of Dillus, Cai and Bedwyr kill him first by savage trickery.

The episodes that follow Wrnach's death and initiate the series of performed tasks all involve animals. To trace Mabon, the oldest animals aid Cai and Bedwyr; then God himself helps Arthur find for the Twrch hunt the two bitches of the whelp Rhymni, she who while a culturally trained hound goes in the violently natural shape of a wolf. Then because Gwythyr has saved their ant-hill from fire with a skilful blow of his sword, the ants gather the flax seed Ysbaddaden has concealed in a heap of soil. The three sequences are of different length and weight but have convergent meaning, demonstrating a unity between warriors and animals, a reliance in crisis on the forces of the natural world as against the showy front of cultural splendour.

There are animals, however, beyond the possibility of making common cause with the warrior. In reality the wild boar was the fiercest surviving animal in Britain, and Ysgithrwyn is hunted as one of the performed tasks. His death, like that of Wrnach, is a predecessor and good omen for a more serious conflict later: if one giant boar can be killed then the conflict with the Twrch may be faced with greater confidence. But there is also, again as with Wrnach, meaning in the manner of Ysgithrwyn's death. Cadw kills him with the help of Arthur's dog Cafall, not with the hounds Ysbaddaden had specified: the narrator is firm on this point (p. 129). The heroes who act under Arthur's leadership win in their own terms, with their own chosen powers and support, not meekly fulfilling the requirements of some alien giant.

In spite of this optimistic preface, the Twrch is a formidable opponent and though he loses his toilet articles, he is not killed or even wounded. Nor is he any ordinary giant boar. He was formerly a king 'and for his wickedness God turned him into a swine' (p. 131). He is now in Ireland causing trouble and when Arthur goes there to seek his comb and shears he in return attacks Arthur in Wales. One by one his loyal pig-warriors are killed – they are his own family, not a warband, it is interesting to note: his power is antique in structure as well as fearful. He and his kin cause great havoc as they crash through parts of south Wales. Finally Arthur, Osla Big-Knife and Manawydan close in on the giant boar after driving him into the Severn. These are mighty heroes indeed. According to *Breudwyt Ronabwy*, Osla led the Saxons at Baddon, but Arthur has absorbed his strength and hostility. Manawydan here seems to retain some of his sea-god characteristics. As they brawl in the river Mabon and Cylydyr ride in and seize the desired objects. But unabashed, undamaged, the Twrch charges on through Cornwall and escapes west to the open sea.

In part this is just a huge hunt, so realising in story that central activity of the warrior caste and that important economic function. But there is more here than martial exercise and the quest for a royal meal. The Twrch is a prince turned pig, the violent creature from whom the vestiges of culture are plucked in a difficult conflict. In one direction he represents the unrestrained savagery of man, a violence beyond the accepted violence of Arthur and the tribal family. In both ancient and modern times stories have realised the danger of the quite uncontrolled warrior. The Twrch represents in fullest form the extreme of martial vigour which even the heroic warrior society cannot tolerate, just as modern films and novels in post-war periods ponder the problem of what to do with trained killers in a time of peace.

There is also a figure in the story who represents the correct socialisation of the violent warrior, the opposite of the Twrch. That is Culhwch, who is pig turned prince. He was born in a pig-sty, and his name, according to the text, means just that. The interpretation is fanciful, but is in line with the meaning of the figure. In fact his name is more likely to be a Welsh version of Cuchulainn, the great warrior of Ulster, also married to the daughter of a reluctant and finally slaughtered giant (see 'The Wooing of Emer', Kinsella, 1970, pp. 25–39). Even more to the point, Cuchulainn was himself a figure of violent warrior fury, who was nevertheless acculturated into the social court of Ulster, as Culhwch the pig-warrior is accepted as a true prince of the Welsh tribe.

But the threat the Twrch bears is not only one of animal violence and human beastliness. It is also more historic, more specific than that. He comes to Wales from Ireland and is last seen heading in that direction. It is not often recognised that the most serious threat to Wales between the Saxon and Norman invasions was from the Irish. There were large settlements in the north: the Lleyn peninsula takes its name from the men of Leinster, and other Irish groups settled in north-east Wales. The Mabinogi story of *Branwen* at one point deals fictionally with these invasions.

The Twrch attacks the south, however, and this is a fictional treatment of Irish invasions in that part of Wales. His route is still almost completely identifiable (Rhys, 1894–5; Foster, 1935, pp. 246–65; see Plate 3 for a map of his rampage). He enters Wales near St Davids, devastates the cantref of Deugleddyf in what was then, and is now again called Dyfed. Then he heads north into the Preseli mountains, to descend south-east to ravage with special care the fertile valleys east of Carmarthen and north of Swansea. Then his route goes north-east along the ridge above the valleys of Morgannwg (Glamorgan) to come into the old kingdom of Brycheiniog (Brecon). There Arthur brings him to a halt. With forces gathered from as far as Cornwall and Devon, Arthur drives the Twrch into the Severn and across.

This is an intriguing itinerary and more will be made of it shortly. But in the context of the Twrch's Irish origin it is striking to notice how the beginning and end of his invasion and destruction overlap very clearly with the two parts of south Wales where the Irish settled. The route he takes from Dyfed to Brycheiniog was indeed the way they travelled along the Roman road (Bowen, 1954, pp. 21–5). The clearest indication of the Irish force in these areas is the survival of standing stones with writing on them in Irish ogham script (marked on the map in Plate 3). The standing stones and the history of Irish settlements also indicate why it is appropriate for the Twrch to leave through Cornwall and why Arthur gathers a host from there against him. It is not just that Arthur was lord of the south-west, with a court at Celliwig, near modern Wadebridge (Ashe, 1980, pp. 129–31 and 223). Irish settlements were also quite common in Cornwall and some ogham stones survive there as well. The places the Twrch visits and the threat of the Twrch himself are linked with the Irish presence in Wales: in the ninth and tenth centuries there no doubt remained vivid memories of a real threatening force from Ireland.

If the Twrch represents that threat as well as others, and since at the end he is as alive as was the Irish threat, it is the less surprising that among the other tasks performed is a triumphant attack on Ireland. Arthur had after all attacked the Twrch in Ireland to stir him up, in some way rationalising his threat and making Arthur a less passive victim of Irish aggression, but the quest for the cauldron of Diwrnach the Irishman is a fuller and more satisfying containment of the threat from the fellow Celts across the water. Arthur and a selected band raid Ireland for the cauldron and bring it back full of 'the treasures of Ireland'

(p. 130). The story is told just before the Twrch hunt, immediately after the killing of Ysgithrwyn. These two violent Welsh triumphs over a giant boar and over Ireland provide a chauvinistic and preliminary compensation for the stern threat about to be posed by *the* giant boar, the biggest in *this* island, who nevertheless arrives from Ireland.

After the Twrch hunt, only one episode remains in the tasks-performed list. That is to find the blood of the Black Witch, needed to complete the dressing of Ysbaddaden's beard. In part this extends the 'grooming' motif present in the hunt for the Twrch's comb and shears and so makes the final savage shaving of the giant a suitably violent reversal of the expected giant-controlled ceremony. But just as culture itself was a mask for the truly violent practices of the warrior élite, so here too the cultural reason for shedding the witch's blood rationalises a more savage reason for wanting to kill her. Arthur is shown in conflict with one more of the forces of threat in the Celtic world, this time a threat to the male sex rather than simply the warrior class.

The trouble with the witch is that she is a formidable warrior. First she deals severely with Arthur's servants and then disposes of two heroes big enough to have earned the cognomen *Hir*, meaning 'Long' or 'Tall'. She is clearly out of the same mould as the women warriors Aife and Scathach who trained Cuchulainn in arms and who also appear in 'The Wooing of Emer' (Kinsella, 1970). The warrior woman, sometimes dignified as a queen, sometimes vilified as a witch, is an important part of early Celtic tradition, a distinct threat to a patriarchal order and power. It seems that in *Culhwch ac Olwen* the warrior woman is not as severe a threat as the giant and the pig-prince. But her defeat is still the last victory, one that only Arthur can achieve, and one of stark violence, with no trace of the much-valued culture. Arthur stalks into her cave (a consistent symbol of the female mystery and threat to men in folklore) and splits her into two bloody halves with one blow of his great knife.

So the list of tasks performed is a survey of threats to the warrior élite, and their violent control. That violence is the climax of the task-achieving: the bride is seized, not bestowed by her father in spite of his earlier very proper invocation of the family council, accurately extended to the great-grandparents (p. 112). Nor is she bestowed by herself, the other method of marriage possible among the Celts. (On bride-bestowing see Williams, 1969, Vol. I, p. 13).

The warrior élite imposes its own will on all opponents, even finally and with difficulty on the Twrch Trwyth – its own worst-case realisation. At last the giant is killed, in humiliating mockery of his own cultural requirements. Goreu takes the lands, partly in recognition of his own bloodlinks with the farmer caste – though the text has insisted, perhaps a little nervously in the light of his declassé birth, that he is the best of warriors, and so he is named *Goreu*, 'best'. Culhwch himself takes the daughter and so resolves the threat of sterility imposed by the alien mother in Arthur's extended family.

Finally, 'the hosts of Arthur dispersed, every one to his own country' (p. 136). That suggests that the forces gathered have been more than one tribe's élite, even more than its professional warband. It might be said that warriors like Cadw of Prydein, Guilhenin of France, Cnwchwr of Ulster are only there by courtesy of the exaggeration of story, like Glewlwyd's stirring account of Arthur's world-conquests (pp. 98–9). And yet in reality Mynyddawg Mwynfawr's warband in *Y Gododdin* was collected from all over Britain, without apparent exaggeration or mythic elements (Jarman, 1967). Between the liberty of fantasy and the restrictions of contemporary realism there is still some space, and here it is occupied by a quite unusual magnification of Arthur and his position. The extent of his power, the way he is built up to be a great warrior and a great king – these extend beyond simple tribal leadership, however fictionally glorified, and suggest a relation between the figure of Arthur and political developments concerning kingship in Wales which occurred at just about the time when this story was apparently first developed and even first recorded.

IX

Pen teyrnedd yr ynys hon, 'Chief of the princes of this island': the grand title deserves a closer examination. Arthur is not only the model of a tribal king, but of a king of Wales – even of Britain as well, to look into the British past. Towards its end the story emphasises Arthur's supremacy, his ability to do things that are beyond other heroes. This is not merely a physical quality. True, he alone can kill the black witch and he leads with verve the hunt for the Twrch. But his powers go further: he is the decisive, army-organising aggressor against Ireland to win Diwrnach's cauldron, he is the judge over human and otherworld figures who settles the conflict between Gwyn and Gwythyr.

In Arthur the story creates a figure with more than merely tribal power. The huge and widespread warband itself suggests that, and the final dispersal of Arthur's host confirms it. The idea of an over-king is basic to the final events in the story as it is to the title 'Chief of the princes of this island'.

The emergence of an over-king was not easy in the essentially tribal Celtic system. Ireland had them in practice only from the ninth century onwards (Byrne, 1973, ch. 12; Binchy, 1970, p. 72). In Wales the development was equally slow, but by the ninth century the figure of an over-king was appearing, probably as much influenced by English developments as by those in Ireland. Rhodri Mawr, who ruled from 844–78, attempted to unite Wales from his northern base in Gwynedd. The over-king model that is relevant to *Culhwch ac Olwen*, however, is Hywel Dda, who ruled from before 918 to 950. Like Rhodri he extended his power well beyond his original base in Seisyllwg. He came soon to control the two adjacent areas, Dyfed and Brycheiniog. He eventually held authority over Gwynedd as well, and at least some control over Powys in mid-eastern Wales. After 942 he was accorded the title of 'brenin Kymry oll', 'King of all the Welsh' (Lloyd, 1939, p. 337).

As his cognomen *Da* ('the Good') suggests, Hywel, was not only a warrior king. Like Rhodri and like King Alfred of Wessex, both of whom were his conscious models, he was well aware of the importance of culture both in disseminating a super-tribal authority and in providing mechanisms for rule beyond the oral and traditional practices of tribal units. Rhodri's interest in culture has been discussed by Nora Chadwick (1958); Alfred's concern with literacy, history, religion and law is well-known. Hywel's efforts in this area are best known in the laws of Wales which bear his name, created when he gathered together tribal lawmen from all over Wales to agree on a national system which would be recorded – the very cement of over-kingship.

It seems highly likely that the creation and the first recording of *Culhwch ac Olwen* itself should be associated with Hywel Dda's period. Hywel is the only credible model for a Welsh over-king based in South Wales. But there are closer resemblances than that between the story and Hywel's domains. The route of the Twrch is not only to be associated with Irish settlements; he goes out of his way, out of the Irish way, to swing south through the rich heart of Ystrad Tywi, southern Seisyllwg. More strikingly still, there is no interest in the Twrch making any entry into Morgannwg. There had been Irish there (Plate 3), and he is presumably driven from Brycheiniog into the Severn across that area, but the text is very vague about his entry-point – somewhere between the estuaries of the Wye and the Lliw, near modern Llanelli. These points are beyond the two extremities of Morgannwg, and the lack of precision and interest in that area may well stem from the fact that Hywel never did conquer it: then as now it was self-sufficient and faced towards England.

Another link between Hywel's activities and this story lies in its formal technique. Hywel's laws have survived only in later adaptations but there is no doubt that their basic structure derives from the code established in Hywel's day (Williams and Powell, 1942). The character of this structure is often a surprise to modern readers. The laws are merely listed, one custom after another. The sorting of them is by no means as rational or as analytic as we would expect. All the court practices are lumped together, so that the famous statement about the duties and rights of a chief poet is followed by the exact value of 'the cub of a king's covert hound'. The structure of the laws is a series of lists of related things, without any serious attempt to order the lists internally. That is also a fair description of the structural basis of *Culhwch ac Olwen* itself. There is a narrative, but it is constituted and given its ideological impact essentially through lists: the list of Culhwch's characteristics; Glewlwyd's list of Arthur's expeditions; the mighty list of warriors; the list of members of the Olwen expedition; Ysbaddaden's list of tasks required; the list of tasks achieved.

Organising things in lists is a common practice in early Welsh literature. *Y Gododdin* is no more than an unsorted and unsortable list of elegaic stanzas. Elsewhere there are lists of the fortresses of Wales, the graves of the heroes, the horses of the heroes. There are lists of proverbs, of gnomic stanzas filled with natural wisdom. But the laws of Hywel Dda and *Culhwch ac Olwen* alone use lists within a larger framework to realise the power of a lord who is ultimately an over-king. The cultural practice and the political purpose of the two texts seem essentially the same. In both cases a set of detailed tribal materials have been gathered and ultimately superseded, though they still have their tribal force in many respects. The laws work for the tribes but fit together for the

over-king's purposes. The story still outlines firmly the ideology of
the élite tribal families but adds to that the model of a supertribal
king. It seems very likely that both texts stem from the broad-
based cultural programme which Hywel attached to his political
and military attempts to bring peace and unity to Wales. The
traditional date of the text is later than Hywel's period, but that in
part refers to the spelling and grammatical forms of the scribal
version which has survived. A highly technical study of early
Welsh language has shown that *Culhwch ac Olwen* is very much
earlier than any other prose texts and so different from them that
it cannot be dated by comparison with them (Watkins and
MacCana, 1958, pp. 12–13 and 17–18). The distance between the
traditional 1050 for this text and the 950 necessary to connect it
with Hywel is by no means difficult to bridge.

Culhwch ac Olwen, then, is not a ragged and quaint survival of a
boorish yet sometimes entertaining culture – though that is a
common attitude towards it and other early Celtic material.
Rather, it has survived as the earliest full Arthurian narrative
simply because it was so important. The text creates in its
narrative a whole range of alarming threats and then provides
resolutions to them which both console and confirm the position
of the élite who model for the text and support its production.
Today *Culhwch ac Olwen* is still an important text because by
comprehending its function we can bring evidence to bear on the
nature of relations between texts and the society in which they
operate. It is also important because this remarkable story is the
first of a series of ideologically rich and persuasive statements
which comprise the real history, the socially realised history, of
the legend of Arthur.

There was a great mass of Arthurian story that was not
recorded in narrative form in Welsh, but which is briefly
mentioned, especially among the triads. There were also many
other Welsh stories of heroes and kings. The unique feature of the
legend of Arthur in Wales was that it developed the model of an
over-king where all the other British heroes were limited to a tribe,
and that in at least one case, *Culhwch ac Olwen*, it recorded this
development in writing. Both the royal model and the weight of
the literary medium were major features in the further, and much

more extended, dissemination of the Arthurian legend. That took place after the Norman-French invaders made their way into south-east Wales, the home of the first identifiable Arthurian author, Geoffrey of Monmouth.

REFERENCES

Primary Sources
Aneirin (1938) *Y Gododdin*, ed. I. Williams in *Canu Aneirin* (Cardiff: University of Wales Press) trans. J. P. Clancy in *The Earliest Welsh Poetry* (London: Macmillan, 1970).
Evans, J. G. (ed.) (1887) *Culhwch ac Olwen* in *The Red Book of Hergest* (Pwlheli, privately published), trans. T. Jones and G. Jones in *The Mabinogion*, 2nd edn (London: Dent, 1974).
—— (1915) *Preiddeu Annwfn* in *The Book of Taliesin* (Llanbedrog: privately published) trans. R. Bromwich in R. W. Barber, *The Figure of Arthur* (London: Longman, 1972).
Gildas (1978) *De Excidio Britanniae* ed. and trans. M. Winterbottom (London: Phillimore).
Kinsella, T. trans. (1970) *The Tain* (London: Oxford University Press).
Jones, T. ed. and trans. (1967) 'The Black Book of Carmarthen "Stanzas of the Graves" ', *Proceedings of the British Academy*, 53, 97–137.
Richards, M. (ed.) (1948) *Breudwyt Ronabwy* (Cardiff: University of Wales Press) trans. T. Jones and G. Jones in *The Mabinogion*, see under Evans, J. G. (ed.) (1887) *Culhwch ac Olwen*.
Roberts, B. F. (ed.) (1978a) *Geraint* in 'Rhai o Gerddi Ymddiddan Llyfr Du Caerfyrddin' ('Some Conversation Poems in the Black Book of Carmarthen') in *Astudiaethau ar yr Hengerdd* ('Studies on the Old Poetry') ed. R. Bromwich and R. B. Jones (Cardiff: University of Wales Press) trans. J. P. Clancy, see under Aneirin (1938).
—— (ed.) (1978b) *Pa Gwr* in 'Rhai o Gerddi Ymddiddan Llyfr Du Caerfyrddin', see under Roberts, B. F. (1978a), trans. R. Bromwich in R. W. Barber, *The Figure of Arthur*, see under Evans, J. G. (1915).
Williams, I. (ed.) (1930) *Pedeir Keinc y Mabinogi* ('The Four Branches of the Mabinogi' (Cardiff: University of Wales Press) trans. T. Jones and G. Jones, see under Evans, J. G. (ed.) (1907) *Culhwch ac Olwen*.
Williams, S. J. and Powell, J. Enoch (eds) (1954) *Llyfr Blegywryd* ('The Book of Blegywryd') (Cardiff: University of Wales Press), trans. M. Richards, *Laws of Hywel Dda* (Liverpool University Press, 1954).

Secondary Sources
Alcock, L. (1971) *Arthur's Britain* (London: Lane).
Ashe, G. (1980) *A Guidebook to Arthurian Britain* (London: Longman).
Binchy, D. A. (1954) 'Secular Institutions' in *Early Irish Society* ed. M. Dillon (Cork: Mercier).
—— (1970) *Celtic and Anglo-Saxon Kingship* (Oxford: Clarendon).

Bowen, E. G. (1954) *The Settlements of the Celtic Saints in Wales* (Cardiff: University of Wales Press).

Bromwich, R. (1954) 'The Character of Early Welsh Tradition' in *Studies in Early British History* ed. N. K. Chadwick (Cambridge University Press).

—— (1975–6) 'Concepts of Arthur', *Studia Celtica* 10/11, 163–81.

—— (1978) *Trioedd Ynys Prydein: The Welsh Triads* 2nd edn (Cardiff: University of Wales Press).

Byrne, F. J. (1973) *Irish Kings and High-Kings* (London: Batsford).

Chadwick, N. K. (1953) 'The Lost Literature of Celtic Scotland', *Scottish Gaelic Studies* 7, 115–83.

—— (1958) 'Early Culture and Learning in North Wales' in *Studies in the Early British Church* (Cambridge University Press).

—— (1964) 'The Conversion of Northumbria' in *Celt and Saxon: Studies in the Early British Border* (Cambridge University Press).

Cunliffe, B. (1974) *Iron Age Communities in Britain* (London: Routledge).

Dumville, D. (1975–6) 'Nennius and the *Historia Brittonum*', *Studia Celtica* 10/11, 78–95.

Evans, J. G. (1975) *The Environment of Early Man in the British Isles* (London: Elek).

Filip, J. (1977) *Celtic Civilisation and its Heritage* (Wellingborough: Collett).

Foster, I. Ll. (1935) 'Astudiaeth o Chwedl Culhwch ac Olwen' ('A Study of the Tale of Culhwch and Olwen'): (M.A. Thesis, University of Wales).

—— (1959) 'Culhwch and Olwen and Rhonabwy's Dream' in *Arthurian Literature in the Middle Ages*, see under Loomis (1959).

—— (1974) 'Culhwch ac Olwen' in *Y Traddodiad Rhyddiaith yn yr Oesau Canol* ('The Tradition of Prose in the Middle Ages') ed. G. Bowen (Llandysul: Gomer).

Hanning, R. W. (1966) *The Vision of History in Early Britain* (New York: Columbia University Press).

Harding, D. W. (1974) *The Iron Age in Lowland Britain* (London: Routledge).

Hughes, K. (1980) *Celtic Britain in the Early Middle Ages* (Woodbridge: Boydell).

Jackson, K. H. (1961) *The International Popular Tale and Early Welsh Tradition* (Cardiff: University of Wales Press).

—— (1969) *The Gododdin: The Oldest Scottish Poem* (Edinburgh University Press).

Jarman, A. O. H. (1967) 'The heroic ideal in early Welsh poetry' in *Beiträge zur Indo-Germanistik und Keltologie, Julius Pokorny Festschrift* ed. W. Meid (Innsbrück: Rauch).

Jones, T. (1964) 'The Early Evolution of the Legend of Arthur', *Nottingham Medieval Studies* 8, 3–21.

—— (1968) 'Chwedl Huail ab Caw ac Arthur' ('The Story of Huail son of Caw and Arthur') in *Astudiaethau Amrywiol a gyflwynir i Syr T. Parry-Williams* ('Miscellany Presented to Sir T. Parry-Williams') (Cardiff: University of Wales Press).

Jones, T. G. (1926) 'Some Arthurian Materials in Keltic', *Aberystwyth Studies* 8, 37–93.

Lambert, M. (1975) *Style and Vision in Malory's Morte d'Arthur* (New Haven: Yale University Press).

Lindsay, J. (1958) *Arthur and His Times: Britain in the Dark Ages* (London: Muller).

Lloyd, J. E. (1939) *A History of Wales* 3rd edn (London: Longman).

Loomis, R. S. (1956) *Wales and the Arthurian Legend* (Cardiff: University of Wales Press).
—— (1959) *Arthurian Literature in the Middle Ages* (Oxford: Clarendon).
Martin, B. K. (1970) 'Old Irish Literature and European Antiquity' in *Aspects of Celtic Literature* (University of Sydney Press).
Parry, T. (1963) Rhagymadrodd ('Introduction') to *Dafydd ap Gwilym* 2nd edn (Cardiff: University of Wales Press).
Rhys, Sir J. (1891) *Studies in the Arthurian Legend* (Oxford: Clarendon).
—— (1894–5) 'Notes on the Hunting of the Twrch Trwyth', *Transactions of the Honorable Society of Cymmrodorion*, pp. 1–34.
Tatlock, J. S. P. (1950) *The Legendary History of Britain* (Berkeley: University of California Press).
Watkins, A. and MacCana, P. (1958) 'Cystrawennau'r Cyplad mewn Hen Gymraeg' ('Copula Constructions in Old Welsh'), *Bulletin of the Board of Celtic Studies* 18, 1–28.
Williams, A. H. (1969) *An Introduction to the History of Wales* (Cardiff: University of Wales Press).

2 'So great a king':
Geoffrey of Monmouth's
Historia Regum Britanniae

I

It is not at all surprising that the early Welsh had many stories about Arthur and that eventually some were recorded in writing. The remarkable thing is that the legend of Arthur escaped to the wider European world. The direct cause of this, as of so much else that occurred in early medieval Europe, was the wide-ranging military power of the Normans. They encountered Celtic people first in Brittany and then in Wales. In both cases they used translators for military and administrative purposes (Bullock-Davies, 1966) and as a result the exotic and fully developed riches of Celtic story from those areas were available to the Normans.

Like the British fragments discussed in the previous chapter, the Arthurian stories that were disseminated orally across Europe undoubtedly had ideological functions, but these are not traceable in the scanty references to the non-literary legend (Loomis, 1959, ch. 6). Social ideology is clear, however, in the written versions of the legend which were created in the twelfth century, starting with Geoffrey of Monmouth's *Historia Regum Britanniae* ('History of the Kings of Britain', 1929) and then developing greatly through Chrétien de Troyes' verse romances in French.

The striking thing about this new European Arthur is that he is most unlike the Welsh Arthur. His role, his deeds and the values enacted through him and his warriors are clearly those of a medieval world, not those of the heroic age Celtic Arthur. In modernising Arthur, Geoffrey and Chrétien shaped a king and a court of warrior knights who have been the dominant pattern of the Arthurian world right up to the present.

The ideologies they created were quite different: Geoffrey presented royal and national dramas characteristic of the century and Chrétien defined the problems faced by ambitious individuals within that larger structure. But the two models meshed remarkably well and were quite soon combined in the French 'Vulgate' Arthuriad. This huge prose survey of the Arthurian world was created by the 1230s and, in an abbreviated and ideologically reshaped version, has come down in English through the work of Sir Thomas Malory and his many followers. But to see the initial forces which gave the Arthurian legend its European lift-off it is necessary to trace first the determining conditions and ideological core of Geoffrey's pseudo-history.

The *Historia Regum Britanniae* is a largely fictional history in Latin prose of the Celtic British kings from the fabulous Brutus, who escaped from the destruction of Troy to wander across Europe until he eventually found – and founded – Britain, down to Cadwallader, the last independent British king. Geoffrey gives particular prominence to Arthur, who ejects the Saxons and goes on to defeat the Roman imperial army before Mordred's rebellion brings the reign to an end. The sequence from Arthur's birth to his passing (not clearly a death) occupies about a quarter of the text and another quarter builds up steadily to Arthur's reign, an Arthurian prologue dealing with Vortigern, Merlin, Arthur's uncle Ambrosius and his father Uther. The audience readily seized on Arthur as the major figure in the *Historia*, partly no doubt because he was already known, but also because he is structurally and thematically central. The ideological force of the text is primarily communicated through him, but the stories of other kings provide both echoes and clarifications of the latent meaning of Arthur and the text.

II

Geoffrey of Monmouth died in 1154: a birth date around 1100 is usually assumed. The *Historia* was apparently completed between 1136 and 1138, though an earlier simpler version may have existed (Parry and Caldwell, 1959, pp. 86–8). It became famous at once, as is clear from a letter written by Henry of Huntingdon, a leading monastic historian. In January 1139 he was visiting the prestigious and scholarly abbey at Bec in Normandy and was shown a copy of Geoffrey's work. Henry was amazeᴏ by it, especially by the Arthurian material, and wrote excitedly to a friend about its contents (Chambers, 1927, pp. 44–5 and 251–2). Henry's reaction must have been a common one: the *Historia* survives today in over two hundred manuscripts, a staggering number for such an early work, and over fifty of them, a relatively huge proportion, come from the twelfth century itself. It is true that a Latin work, likely to be copied and preserved by monks, has a better chance of survival than a secular and vernacular text, but it is still a sign of extraordinary success.

Since it is written in Latin, the primary audience for the *Historia* must have been clerics. Their number was increasing in the period: it was an economically expansive time because of relative peace, generally good weather and improved farming techniques in northern Europe. Rulers tended to support the church and learning generously, both as a cultural support to their dominance and as a recruiting area for their expanding bureaucracies. The support was so considerable in its effects that scholars talk about a 'twelfth-century Renaissance' which was the springboard for the later Renaissance (Haskins, 1927).

But Geoffrey's work was not limited to clerics. It was also popular with the Norman aristocracy, who were most unlikely to have understood Latin. His book was probably translated orally into French at their gatherings, and it was soon turned into written French. Geoffrey Gaimar's version is now lost, but it was completed in the 1140s and the interest of the Norman élite is obvious. Gaimar was commissioned by a noble Norman lady who had received the book from Walter Lespac, an important magnate in Norman England. He in turn had obtained it from Robert of Gloucester, Henry I's favourite illegitimate son, who was very powerful after Henry's death in 1135 (Tatlock, 1950, p. 208; Griscom, in Geoffrey of Monmouth, 1929, pp. 67–8). By 1155 an extant verse translation of the *Historia* was completed by Wace, a Channel Islander and professional poet of the Norman aristocracy.

Geoffrey's *Historia* is a book ostensibly about British Celtic kings, especially Arthur, which found an enthralled audience among the Normans who ruled England. It seems an unlikely mixture at first sight and the detailed reasons for the relationship will be the main topic of this chapter. However, there was a real basis for the contact of Normans and Celts. There were Breton knights at Hastings, and William I, the Conqueror, gave lands to many of them in Britain, especially in the Celtic parts, Cornwall and Wales, where their linguistic and cultural links would be useful. Geoffrey himself came from an area of major contact. As the Normans rapidly moved into Wales to secure their borders against Welsh incursions, the newly formed marcher lordships, fundamentally autonomous buffer states, called for Norman-Welsh intercourse simply to keep the peace. These contacts developed particularly in the fertile south-east of Wales, where there was a productive surplus to control, not just a border to be patrolled.

Full integration in that area came after Geoffrey's period, but he is nevertheless a clear case of Norman-Celtic connections. 'Geoffrey' is a Norman Christian name, while Monmouth was a predominantly Welsh town, and the probability is that he was educated at a Breton-run priory there. He is one of a number of Norman-Welsh who were quite important in the cultural wing of Norman and Angevin power in the twelfth century – Gerald of Wales and Walter Map are later figures, and a contemporary of Geoffrey's was his friend Walter from whom, Geoffrey insists, he received his major source, 'a very ancient book written in the British language' (Thorpe, 1966, p. 51: all quotations will be from this edition).

No such manuscript exists today. Many scholars have thought Geoffrey made this up as one of the fictional self-authorisations common in medieval writing. J. S. P. Tatlock, the most thorough student of the *Historia*, was particularly sceptical about Geoffrey's Celtic claims, though even he had to admit that Geoffrey did know Welsh (1950, p. 202). Among his sources Geoffrey certainly had Nennius and had also at least read Gildas and the great Anglo-Saxon historian Bede (Fletcher, 1906). But that leaves a lot of the *Historia* unaccounted for. It has long been accepted that Geoffrey used a Welsh genealogical manuscript for some of his names (Lloyd, 1939, p. 527), and the best modern opinion is that he had a reasonable, but not intimate, knowledge of Welsh tradition (Bromwich, 1954, pp. 125–8; Roberts, 1976) – that is, just the sort of knowledge which might come through a learned intermediary like Walter. One small but telling point supports Geoffrey's claim. He mentions his Welsh source in his opening and closing pages as might be expected, but only once in the text does he insist upon the existence of a Welsh source. When he describes Arthur's last battle he says he read in the ancient book and heard from Walter himself about Camblam, as he spells it. It seems a deliberate footnote to indicate that he knew this particular battle was only recorded in the Welsh tradition.

There is a basis of Welsh material in the *Historia*, in some of the events and in many names of people and of places. A Welsh viewpoint is adopted in calling the Germanic invaders *Saxones* and England *Logria* – few English readers realise those are simply Latin versions of *Saeson* and *Lloegyr*, still the Welsh for the English and England. Equally, there is a great deal of invention in the *Historia* and more importantly there is a clear intention to redirect the material to a Norman audience. This chapter will present that pattern in detail, but there is one especially sharp piece of evidence. Geoffrey knew a certain amount about the Welsh prophet-bard-magician called Myrddin when he wrote the *Historia* – and he knew more later when he wrote the *Vita Merlini*, 'The Life of Merlin'. He must have been aware of the Welsh form of the name, because he repeats the tradition that the great man came from Caerfyrddin, known in English as Carmarthen (a fanciful derivation in fact, see Bromwich, 1978, pp. 470 and 560). Why then did Geoffrey change the name? In Middle Welsh orthography it is written Merdin; that would Latinise as Merdinus; to anyone knowing French that could only mean 'shitty'. Geoffrey elegantly changed one letter, to suggest the name of a noble bird. Perhaps that is doubly clever, because part of the Myrddin legend in Welsh was that he was transformed into a bird at one stage, but at all events it is fine evidence that Geoffrey was a Norman-Welsh writer with a Norman audience clearly in mind.

It has been suggested that Geoffrey was of Breton origin (Tatlock, 1950, p. 443), partly because of the known Breton presence in Monmouth, but largely because of the admiring emphasis given to Bretons in his text. There are probably other reasons for the praise of Bretons, that will be mentioned later, and there seems no sufficient reason why Geoffrey should not simply be part-Welsh. His father's name appears to have been Arthur, since Geoffrey signed himself several times as Geoffrey Arthur. That name indicates a family interest in the hero and a probability of Welsh origin, which seems most likely in all other respects, especially from his detailed knowledge of the Monmouth area which has been shown by Tatlock (1950, pp. 72–7) and Hutson (1940, p. 13 and pp. 80–95).

However, Geoffrey did not remain at Monmouth – had he done so there would have been no point in the surname, of course. He appears to have been a member of St George's college of secular canons. Canons were clerical scholars and administrators, not priests, and these particular canons were lodged inside the new Norman castle at Oxford. The very fact that we know so much about Geoffrey from documents shows he was attached to the military and secular world as a small part of the clerical apparatus of the state that the Norman kings so much developed as a part of their new legal, fiscal and administrative sophistication. Oxford itself was a Norman power-base. In the Anglo-Saxon period it was moribund, but was then royally developed and often visited by the Norman kings, especially Henry I (Norgate, 1887, p. 41).

But after recognising the physical contact between Celts and Normans the question remains: what was the ideological function of Geoffrey's Celtic book for the Norman lords? It is common enough to find conquered or allied nationals serving a state, but they do not necessarily use their own culture in the process. The Celtic material must have contained some element which appeared valid to Normans, which could be used to deal with issues new and disturbing in the developing state. The *Historia* should be looked at closely to establish what that essential factor might be.

III

Some commentators have felt that Geoffrey's racial patriotism is the central meaning, that the *Historia* is at once an origin-legend and a messianic text for the British Celts and the Bretons who stemmed from them (Tatlock, 1950, pp. 427–8; Parry and Caldwell, 1959, pp. 74–5). In the 'Prophecies' which Merlin gives before Arthur is born the text certainly does predict that in time the seed of Brutus will again rule Britain. Such a passage and the Welsh traditions Geoffrey uses were no doubt major reasons why the *Historia* was so frequently recreated in Welsh (Roberts, 1976, xxiv–xxi). But that hardly explains why Geoffrey was so acceptable to Latin-reading clerics and Norman-French aristocrats.

One very specific suggestion has recently been made about the purpose and popularity of the *Historia*, arguing that Geoffrey has with detailed and painstaking skill satirised a good deal of contemporary church thought and practice (Flint, 1979, p. 449).

This too, like the Welsh interest, may indeed be valid for a special part of the audience – Geoffrey does seem to include a set of in-group references to clerical matters. But the full ideological impact of the text must be sought more widely: not only churchmen were fascinated by the text, and Arthur is plainly the major source of interest, not clerical practices.

The obvious area to look at is the symbolic relation between the Celtic kings and the Norman ruling group. Geoffrey has been described as 'flattering the Normans by revealing Arthur as in all essentials an Anglo-Norman king' (Brooke, 1967, p. 192). Tatlock gives a great number of specific resemblances between recent Norman details and the activities and identities in the *Historia*. The trouble with these two approaches is that they are no more than reflective, just suggesting that because the life of the Normans was like Arthur's fictional world they therefore enjoyed it. This view seriously understates the interpretive, processing force of ideological literature and ignores its power both to realise and also assuage the disturbing forces operating in a society.

A more sophisticated interpretation, with its own limits, is to suggest that the *Historia* is in some way a legitimation of the Norman conquest. This would refer to a more actively ideological process in the text, an attempt to justify and euphemise the violent and unprincipled nature of the Norman attack on Britain. Evidence for this appears when King Cadwallader says British rule has with him come to an ordained end: 'it is not God's will that we should rule there for all time' (p. 281) and so, he says to the Saxons, 'The door to Britain lies wide open before you'. The implication that God rules the destiny of Britain in itself justifies generally the Norman presence, but their conquests are specifically legitimised by the fact that the Saxons are always perfidious – from Hengist on, they will always be so, according to the saintly Brian, who feeds his own lord on his own flesh (pp. 269–70). A more secular version of this process is suggested by Lindsay (1973, p. 433): 'By making Brutus the Trojan the ancient invader of England, bringing a superior culture, the Norman conquest was justified and put in a new perspective'.

There is force in these interpretations, but they depend on only a few references, and so do not draw on the inherent force of the story as a whole. A more far-reaching interpretation was provided under the refreshing title 'King Arthur and Politics' (Gerould, 1927). This essay argued that while they were still continental dukes the Normans were able without difficulty to accept Frankish heroic propaganda and take Charlemagne and Roland as their figures of royal authority and martial glory – hence the story that William's minstrel, Taillefer, sang *La Chanson de Roland* before the Norman army at Hastings. In the Bayeux Tapestry, which has been aptly described as a *chanson de geste* in fabric (Lindsay, 1973, p. 214), the Normans are usually identified as *Franci*. But then, Gerould argues, when they were kings ('a dynasty become English in sentiment, if not in manners and speech' 1927, p. 45) they could no longer use a Frankish model and so they adopted a non-Germanic British hero.

Gerould does identify an ideological vacuum in the loss of the Frankish heroic model, but he sees both the loss and the filling of it in much too idealistic and purely literary terms. The Normans principally dropped the Frankish heroic model because as a royal force they gave no homage to another royal house, while as mere dukes they had necessarily deferred to – and no doubt aspired to – the kingship symbolised by Charlemagne. And to say that Geoffrey merely 'formed Arthur in the image of Charlemagne' (Gerould, 1927, p. 49) is nearly as idealistic as the view that Alexander was Geoffrey's model (Tatlock, 1950, pp. 312–20). Geoffrey did not tamely borrow a literary model that Normans might like: he did much more to earn his fame. He created from contemporary Norman experience a new literary model, with its own specific ideological function.

IV

Geoffrey alludes, more or less overtly, to his own links with the Norman ruling class. The version of the dedication which is accepted as the earliest honours first of all Robert Count of Gloucester. He, Henry's favourite bastard and senior surviving son, was no doubt known to Geoffrey partly through his elevated position and also partly through links with Oxford, his role as Lord of Glamorgan and his contact with Llandaff, then the seat of the diocese including Monmouth. The other dedicatee in this first full edition of the *Historia* was Waleran of Meulan, son of a major baron in the conquest period and himself close to Henry I and Robert, though Henry imprisoned him from 1124–9 because of rebellion.

These two men were among the most powerful in the country

after Henry's death, but a characteristically rapid change of events and fidelities is clear in the dedication to the 'second edition', where Waleran has been omitted and Robert demoted in favour of the new King Stephen. This edition must have appeared between April 1136 when Robert took an oath to Stephen and June 1138, when he withdrew his fidelity from the king to support Henry I's daughter Matilda – like Waleran's imprisonment, a sign of the inherent disorder of the period. A dedication of the 'Prophecies', which come within the *Historia*, is directed to Alexander, Bishop of Lincoln – he was Geoffrey's superior, as Oxford was then within the diocese of Lincoln. These dedicatees were the central patrons of Norman ideological culture. Both William of Malmesbury and Henry of Huntingdon addressed their histories to Robert and Alexander, and those contemporary historians are mentioned in Geoffrey's epilogues.

There are also signs in Geoffrey's text of covert references to powerful contemporary figures. Robert of Gloucester himself is honoured by the way Geoffrey changes the story about Hengist's slaughter of Vortigern and the Celts on the original 'night of the long knives'. In Nennius all the British are killed, but Geoffrey makes Eldol, Count of Gloucester, survive and avenge his kinsmen on the treacherous Saxon. There are probably many other coded praises of Robert's family and their possessions – some of the more convincing ones are that Geoffrey's emphasis on the port of Hamtoun and its derivation from Hamo honours a name common among Gloucester's kin (Tatlock, 1950, p. 48); that Eldadus, Eldol's brother and Bishop of Gloucester, is a version of St Aldate, a mysterious figure connected with both Oxford and Gloucester (Tatlock, 1950, p. 262); that Brian, the self-sacrificing nephew of Cadwallo, is a tribute to Robert's own son Brian (Tatlock, 1950, p. 169–70).

Geoffrey also includes a wide range of contemporary phenomena. Tatlock and Hutson have identified people and places, both English and Celtic, and while some of their links seem tenuous, many are much stronger. The text lays great emphasis on London and Winchester; while these were important enough in Anglo-Saxon times they were much more significant for the Normans. Their centralised rule used the Tower of London as its major fortress and the normal seat of the Treasury was Winchester, a city dominating the access to and from Normandy via Southampton. Similarly, the towns that are mentioned on the continent, especially Barfleur, are often those well-known to the Normans.

There are also some plain references to contemporary people, outside the circle of patronage. Count Hoel of Brittany is a transparent version of the historical Hoel who helped William I. Arverigus, himself a lord of Gloucester and having a son called Brian, may be a version of Alain Fergaint, another Breton count whom the Normans knew well as enemy and ally (Knight, 1980, pp. 17–18). Sometimes it is events which are recognisable, as when King Guintalacus of Denmark is wrecked in Northumbria, brought to Belinus, and returned home after submitting to the British king. This seems familiar, and the link is clinched when Geoffrey adds 'To this he added that he would confirm the pact by an oath' (p. 93). The resemblance to Harold of England is plain. He was wrecked in Ponthieu in 1064 and brought by his rescuers to William of Normandy. In order to win release from William's informal imprisonment he was persuaded to swear submission to the Duke. As a result, when Harold claimed the English throne on the death of Edward the Confessor, Norman propaganda could make much of the broken oath. This well-known story was used to justify William's attack on England by Norman historians, and is included in the Bayeux Tapestry (Plate 4).

Geoffrey also presents other contemporary threats which were even more disturbing and had to be more carefully concealed than the straightforward military hostility of non-Norman peoples. Essentially, the greatest anxiety to the Norman lords rose from the continual strife that existed within their own world, through the competitive search for property and glory.

An especially important cause of trouble in reality and in the text is disputed inheritance. This problem is recurrent in the narrative before the Arthur sequence. A series of emphasised episodes illustrates the problems caused when the children of a powerful king are at odds, and each sequence seems to bring up not only a general resemblance to the warring sons of William I but also some specific reference to this major example of recent disorder among the power-élite.

After the founder Brutus dies, the British kingdom is peacefully divided among his three sons, who take England, Scotland and Wales. But this custom of partible inheritance is no more than an ancient dream of peace and from then on inheritance, especially among multiple children after a powerful king, is a major cause of conflict. The first instance is the story of Leir and his daughters. As in Shakespeare, Cordelia will not flatter to gain part of her father's kingdom and so is exiled to Gaul. Geoffrey, however, has no tragic end to the story. She is finally reinstated, Leir defeats her greedy sisters and their husbands, Cordelia succeeds to his throne.

In all this Cordelia is a sentimentally euphemised version of Henry I. By the Conqueror's will, Henry's elder brothers had their father's lands. William Rufus, the second son, took England as William II. Robert Curthose, the eldest son, became Duke of Normandy. Henry was left five thousand pounds of silver. Like Cordelia he eventually won his way to the crown of England, though not even Henry's greatest admirer could see any resemblance between his own devious ruthlessness and Cordelia's pure fidelity – but that is how ideology works, with bold distorting strokes, legitimising the realities of power and obscuring its origins.

Soon after the Cordelia sequence, Geoffrey reworks the whole Norman royal scenario in a partly realistic, partly optimistic way. Dunvallo Molmutensis left behind him peace, order and the Molmutine laws – they are apparently Geoffrey's own invention but resemble William's ordering of the kingdom. The following events closely parallel the doings of William's sons. Dunvallo's sons Belinus and Brennius disputed the kingship (as did Rufus, Curthose and Henry). Brennius, the younger brother, is forced to France and seeks help from the Gallic leaders (as both Curthose and Henry did against Rufus). He marries the daughter of the powerful Gaulish leader Segnius (Curthose married the daughter of a Norman Count in Sicily after the death of Rufus). Brennius finally attacks Britain from the coast of Normandy (Robert sent troops to Odo's rebellion in 1080 and came against Henry himself in 1101).

So much is a displaced but realistic account of Norman fraternal strife, seen especially from Henry's viewpoint: but now the consoling, wish-fulfilment aspect of ideology begins. The brothers are reconciled by their mother, they kiss and join forces to conquer Gaul and Rome. Out of the traditions of Beli, a famous Welsh king, and Brennus, the continental Celt who sacked Rome, Geoffrey has woven a striking contemporary fable which realises both fears of internecine conflict and dreams of united glory.

Another lengthy sequence of conflict between brothers follows the rule of Constantine II. He was specifically invited by the British to come from Brittany to help defeat the Germanic invaders. This model of William I leaves three sons, and the scheming Vortigern sponsors Constans as king: he is the eldest but also the weakest. That is just like Robert, but here that weakness is rationalised because Constans was a monk. Vortigern is able to manipulate and effectively supplant him; the other brothers, Aurelius Ambrosius and Uther Pendragon, are exiled. They gain aid from Brittany, and then are themselves called to Britain. They defeat Vortigern, fight the Saxons, and Uther produces Arthur as his heir.

In this sequence Geoffrey has expanded the traditional Vortigern story by using the brother-conflict motif. The rights and powers of younger sons are stressed – a topic dear to Henry I. The theme of being invited to seize power recurs. Royal legitimisation was crucial when thrones were being seized. William I had made a great issue of his right to take England – the Bayeux Tapestry is one of the propaganda texts urging this. Henry himself had a highly dubious rationalisation of his right to rule, claiming that as only he of the brothers was born when their father was actually a king, he, born to the purple, should succeed.

Arguments over inheritance and the right to property were common in the Norman world, but these stories seem to have a specific relevance to Henry's own history. Excluded from inheriting either England or Normandy at his father's death, he achieved the crown of England under circumstances at best suspicious. William II was killed by an arrow when hunting in the New Forest in August 1100; it was said to be an accident and Walter Tirel, the alleged culprit, fled abroad at once. But Henry was nearby, in a position to gallop to Winchester and seize the Treasury; the Clare family, Tirel's in-laws (several of whom were also with William on the fatal day), received remarkable favour from Henry in the next few years. It is a network of circumstantial evidence which must rouse suspicion that Henry was involved in Rufus's death. Then, after years of conflict with his elder brother, Robert, Henry took the Duchy of Normandy from him at the battle of Tinchebrai in 1106. Robert was captured and Henry, with pitiless thoroughness, kept him in prison until his death in 1134. There was much to legitimise and euphemise in Henry's own career, let alone the nefarious and internecine struggles of other Norman lords.

In the later part of Henry's reign, it was not only his past that needed ideological processing: there was the future to worry about. 1120 is the transition year. Henry had done all he could to confirm the succession of his own son William, but he was drowned in the White Ship, sailing back to England from Barfleur in December 1120. Henry's only other legitimate child was Matilda. Again he urged his magnates to accept her as successor, but there were doubts about women rulers. They are expressed about Cordelia herself in the *Historia*, by her nephew (p. 86). Intriguingly, Stephen of Blois, Henry's own nephew, was the threat to Matilda, and after Henry's death he managed to seize the throne – though after *his* death Matilda's son succeeded as Henry II.

So the text deals with some of the problems about uncertain inheritance that worried the powerful in the period, and it also euphemises a good deal of Henry's actions. None of this process is overt, nor even created through one-to-one symbolic narrative. Rather, events keep occurring which seem strangely familiar: threats, values, displacements, euphemisations all interweave in a telling ideological structure, both disturbingly realistic and consolingly optimistic.

Within the general pattern of disputed inheritance are many other features that create local and contemporary tensions. Exile is the normal state of the disinherited and even the Saxons Hengist and Horsa are given a sympathetic reason (overpopulation) for their departure from home (p. 156). In exile the virtues of the disinherited are recognised by a powerful figure – this is a euphemised version of the real processes of gaining allies by bribery and by promising future support after a successful coup, the normal ways of gaining support for an attack on the exile's homeland. And this attack is almost always by invitation of a good-spirited few in a land either empty or occupied by such villainous rulers that it is a positive duty to kill or supplant them.

Sometimes the sins of these bad, supplantable kings come very close to Norman home. Mempricius, who has killed his brother to possess the whole of Britain after the happy reign of their father Maddan, is a tyrant, a wholesale murderer, and finally he 'deserted his own wife . . . and he abandoned himself to the vice of sodomy' (p. 78). This begins by sounding like a dark portrait of Henry, but finally, and no doubt consolingly, seems very much like Rufus, who was reviled for preferring men to women, especially by churchmen who used this as the justification for their real anger at his attacks on their riches. The link with Rufus develops: Mempricius went hunting, was separated from his companions and was eaten by wolves . . . it is a neatly naturalised and so neutralised version of the notoriously odd death of Rufus.

Another major motif in these stories of denied and seized inheritance is betrayal. The wicked break their word, murder the former king, turn on the deserving younger, or often youngest, brother. On the other hand the hero of each story virtuously gains new support from overseas allies or wins people at home to his side through his qualities, his right, his generosity. Both sets of actions are essentially the same – they are merely a bad and good view of the constant side-changing and ally-shuffling that was both common and easy throughout the period. Feudal relations, which the Normans did much to develop and impose on Europe, depended on a man's word – which was very often broken, hence the great fuss about oath-keeping in medieval literature, urging the value of a frequently ignored sanction.

The driving motive of such infidelity, of course, was the constant quest for securing and increasing one's property; there were ready models of a man rising through the ranks to high status – the Dukes of Normandy and Anjou had done so in recent history. In fact a marked feature of the Normans was the brief history of their powerful families: they had made themselves by the sword, and for them honour and word were devices of legitimisation, not instruments of a traditional order (Lindsay, 1973, pp. 135–6; Davis, 1976, p. 37; Douglas, 1969, p. 27). This *arrivisme* in itself explains the Norman concern with mystifying their power through various cultural media, especially literature and architecture.

V

Through the British kings before Arthur, Geoffrey creates a detailed web of Norman ideology. The Arthur sequence is thematically as well as structurally the climax and centre of the *Historia*, being both the most dramatic and the most specific expression of the fears and hopes of the contemporary authorities. After being crowned, Arthur is the model of the Norman kings imposing their will on England by military force, controlling all attempts to challenge his power. And then Arthur symbolises Norman expansionist vigour, adding colonies all around Britain on the continent of Europe. He is also, especially in his court at Caerleon, a figure who adds glory to the reality of naked military power and so moulds a suitably mystified figure of royal power. In this Arthur is to a considerable degree a model of what the Normans felt they might be achieving in terms of power and its cultural accompaniment.

But Arthur also encounters the darker side of the Norman world: some of his actions are organised to mystify and emotionally dissipate some of the central problems of Henry I's royal career. As well as that encounter with anxiety Arthur is, in his sudden and enigmatic end through betrayal, the prime expression in the whole *Historia* of the fear and doubt that is the central anxiety of a power-holding class, whether Norman or not. The glory is suddenly gone – even Arthur is betrayed. After all the confidences and consolidation, the text details that nagging fear of catastrophic civil war in which the Norman military power, so good at intimidating others and appropriating their possessions, becomes a weapon of mutual destruction. So the text is not merely a confident plaster of optimism; it raises the sharpest of contemporary threats and does not really, not fully, resolve them. This summary of the ideological force of the Arthur sequence requires detailed support and elaboration.

As a young king who needs to impose his authority, Arthur inevitably recalls the problems of the young Duke of Normandy, later to be William I. He succeeded his father at sixteen and in any case suffered under the stigma of illegitimacy. From Nennius' structure of Arthur's battles and the account of the Saxon invasions in Gildas and Bede, Geoffrey stitches together a fluent and rapid set of adventures by which the young king asserts his authority. His actions are fully concordant with Norman practices of power. He is crowned by the archbishop with general consent, and his 'outstanding courage and generosity, and his inborn goodness' (p. 212) make this seem correct. At once he gives generously to his followers, and he intends to distribute more when he plunders the Saxons: the fact that this is a common heroic motif does not make it any the less real in the Norman context.

Arthur marches with just cause against the enemies who deny him the throne; 'for he had a claim by rightful inheritance to the kingship of the whole island' (p. 212). The central motif of military power is present, but it is cloaked and made respectable, partly by right of birth and church approval, also by the token of public consent and the promise of wealth, at least to the soldiers. Arthur's coming to power in Geoffrey of Monmouth's account is a much more pragmatic and credibly medieval process than the traditional act of drawing the sword out of the stone, which enters the written legend after the twelfth century.

The activities of the young king are notably like those of William I: 'Besides his imperialism, the actual course of events in his conquest is consciously reflected, it is hard to doubt' (Tatlock, 1950, p. 309). R. H. Fletcher (1906, pp. 109–10) shows how Arthur's movements around the country resemble those William made in the years after the conquest. Apart from that, the ways in which Arthur faces the Saxons mesh with Norman ideas of a strong king. He is personally brave, as at the crucial battle of Bath (where Geoffrey locates Baddon: some scholars now think he was correct, Alcock, 1971, pp. 71–2). But Arthur is also judicious in war, as when he and his advisers agree to withdraw from the siege of York 'for if so large an enemy force were to come upon them they would all be committed to a most dangerous engagement' (p. 214). The king's courage, which can match even that of a berserk warrior, is only applied at the well-judged moment of crisis or in a desperate corner: William I and William II both showed clearly that crucial mixture of violent anger and shrewdness.

There are other familiar features. Arthur is skilled in calling up allies, such as the Breton lords who come with Hoel; he is supported by his own church, as in Dubricius' speech before Bath; his own men are determinedly loyal to him because of his virtues and the rewards he brings them. All these are vigorously Norman characteristics. Arthur is as greedy for land and power as the Norman kings were: he drives on to pacify the Scots and the Picts. But then his ferocity is, in an intriguing and ideological moment, contained. After he has treated them 'with unparalleled severity' (p. 219) the bishops and clergy beg Arthur for pity. Because 'their patriotism moved him to tears' (p. 220), he rebuilt the churches in the north, especially York.

This episode shows clearly how Geoffrey reworks disturbing events from the past and presents them in an acceptable, value-ridden way. It is the mention of York that reveals the hidden impact of the sequence. William I conducted a notorious raid on the north, culminating in his presence in York at

Christmas 1069. Because the northern counties had continued to resist the Norman power, William simply destroyed their lands. Contemporary chronicles and archeological evidence speak bleakly of his aggressive scorched-earth policy, meant as a terrible warning. It was a grand-scale version of William's preference for mutilation over execution as a penalty. The maimed or blinded man was a living, or partly living, reminder of the king's terrible power: a hanged man was soon forgotten.

In Geoffrey's story, William's scourging of the north is at first displaced into acceptability by being shifted against the Scots and Picts, those long-term harriers of northern Britain whether it was Celtic, English or Norman. A common enemy is found, to euphemise the savagery a little. And then the 'royal mercy' motif is brought in, and made to operate at York itself. The real brutal despotism of William is absorbed into a legend of authority, capable of moderating itself with pious pity. A place of haunting memories, a Hiroshima or Dresden of the period, is transmuted into a legend of justified authority – just as military and political memoirs often represent those modern war-crimes as exemplars of stern, unsentimental leadership.

Another sort of threat is even more delicately handled by Geoffrey. It was much more fearsome because it came from within the Norman power structure itself. There were serious rebellions of Norman lords against William I, William II and Henry I on a number of occasions: Odo, the Conqueror's half-brother led them in 1082 and 1088, Robert attacked his brother Henry's newly established power in 1101. All three Norman kings faced the threat that their powerful barons would find a leader, especially from the royal family, and use their military power to unseat the king just as he had unseated others.

This fear, covertly present in the 'betrayal' motif already discussed, is made overt in the Arthur story through the terrible betrayal by Mordred. And when Geoffrey relates that episode he immediately indicates the delicate nature of the topic, saying 'About this particular matter, most noble Duke (i.e. Robert of Gloucester), Geoffrey of Monmouth prefers to say nothing' (p. 257). The moment reveals the strain of urgently ideological writing: the topic is too real a threat to be ignored, yet too real a threat to be fully faced. And in that apology, Geoffrey invokes the leader of the power structure whose emotional health requires that threat from within to be both expressed and repressed.

The hunger for power that led to such dissension also created the urgent imperialism of the Normans, and this is embodied in Arthur. He takes Ireland, Iceland, Norway, then attacks Gaul. The newly conquered Anjou is given to Kay and Normandy to Bedivere. They were Arthur's seneschal and cup-bearer, his household officers: the fiction enables the Duchy of Normandy and the powerful province of Anjou, which the Normans greatly coveted, to be brought into the king's household and his own power. They are not delegated to some former ally, who as a result would become nearly as powerful as the king himself: the text neatly avoids one of the structural weaknesses of feudalism. This detail also points further inwards to the major, and covert, meaning of the sequence. Although this first assault on Gaul is officially against Rome because Frollo is Tribune for Gaul, the effect is very much that of a personal vendetta with Frollo; it culminates in single combat between him and Arthur and the winning of Anjou and Normandy.

The latent meaning is the hostility between the kings of England, both William II and Henry I, and their older brother Robert, the Duke of Normandy. The appropriation of Anjou and Normandy indicate that Normandy is the true seat of the conflict, and the name Frollo must bring to mind Rollo, the first Duke of Normandy. This enemy is a new version of him. In the subliminal manner of symbolic names he suggests the combined hostility of Normandy (Rollo) and France, a connection especially threatening to Henry I. The fact that Arthur's generous gifts bring many of the Gauls to his side is a respectable version of the normal bribing process by which the Norman kings drew both Norman and French lords out of the line against them – Henry was particularly adept at this, but Rufus was also famous for the practice.

The single combat between Arthur and Frollo is the major ideological distortion here. Duke William challenged Harold to battle at Hastings and might have meant it; when Louis VI of France challenged Henry I in 1113 their champions did battle. Henry's won, but nothing came of it. Here, the text offers a dream of firm, military and honourable treatment of a thorough pest like Robert. The whole encounter, especially the end, as Arthur splits Frollo's helmet and head in half, is a grandiose euphemisation of the distinctly unheroic and unchivalric way in which Henry I finally neutralised Robert: he schemed and bribed his way to victory at Tinchebrai in 1106 and then locked his brother up for life.

After Arthur has conquered the north and Gaul there comes the famous display of royal splendour at Caerleon. This is itself a feature of Norman rule and deserves examination, but for the moment it will be logical to continue to trace the inner meaning of Arthur's military exploits. Indeed, these intrude on the splendour itself, because the great ritualised scene at Caerleon is interrupted when the Roman emperor sends envoys demanding tribute and threatening war, and in response Arthur and his men set off to overthrow the Roman empire itself.

There is traditional Celtic support, of a general kind, for the notion that Arthur defeated the Roman empire. *Culhwch ac Olwen* included Glewlwyd's speech about Arthur the world conqueror, and Welsh tradition certainly cherished the idea of some heroes who had gone from Britain to imperial power (see Bromwich, 1978, under Custennin and Maxen, in 'Notes to Personal Names', pp. 314–5 and 451–4). Both Arthur and Hoel refer to this idea in the discussion about the Roman demand for tribute. But the tradition seems no more than surface rationalisation for a story with deeper and more contemporary meaning. The immediately evident piece of contemporaneity is the fact that the battle is fought in France – Lucius is not the Emperor of Rome as later versions, including Malory's, have it, but the Procurator. This makes the displacement easy: the effective enemy is not Rome but France.

That hostility is a reality of the Norman world in the twelfth century. The Kings of England and Dukes of Normandy, whether the same person or not, were constantly in conflict with the power of France in its border areas such as the Vexin, as well as with other neighbours like Maine, Anjou and even Flanders; France could be relied on to support the enemies of the Normans. The terms of the Roman complaint are themselves familiar: Britain has not paid tribute and has alienated Roman lands. The overt grounds of French hostility to the Normans were failure to pay homage in oaths, men or money, and a related continual nibbling at French territory. Apart from the long-standing Norman dislike of the kings of France, Arthur's war with Lucius relates specifically to the series of wars, skirmishes, truces and disagreements that Henry I had with Louis VI of France in the years up to 1124, when Louis finally got the upper hand. The crucial difference between this campaign and that against Robert, represented by the Frollo sequence, is that it was a failure. Henry conducted no more than a series of 'endless, indecisive campaigns . . . on the borders of the French domains' (Brooke, 1964, p. 127).

There is a broad resemblance between the two wars. Battles, prisoner escorts, parleys and provocations occur in the text and similar events swung to and fro across northern France during the intermittent hostilities. And also as before, specific details are the visible tips of the covert material – Barfleur, where Arthur's forces land, was the natural Norman entry-point to fight against France, but by no means an obvious place from which to tackle Rome. The name Lucius has itself not been traced to a source, and it is suspiciously like an oral anagram of 'Louis six'. The great battle in which Arthur confronts and defeats Lucius takes place in a carefully described area that Tatlock doubtfully and Thorpe confidently have identified as Saussy, between Langres and Autun in eastern France – and Arthur was coming from the north-east, from beyond Langres in Haute-Marne. That may seem highly unlikely as a direction from which Henry might confront Louis – yet history can be surprising. Henry's final effort was to enlist the aid of his son-in-law the Emperor Henry V against Louis. But the strategy was a major failure: Matilda's husband turned back at Metz when marching on Reims because he heard Louis was waiting for him there with a large force. The apparently surprising route Geoffrey gives to Arthur is a literal displacement down the Moselle-Meuse valley of the path of the recent attack on France.

But it is also, of course, an ideological displacement – a reversal of what happened. Where Henry's new attempt after the disasters of 1120 was an abject failure, Arthur triumphs against Lucius. Here the text strains towards wish-fulfilment, and there is a striking formal indication of this optimistic fantasy. In the previous battles and wars the detail has been remarkably credible in military terms. The weapons, numbers, deployment and conduct of battles are all contemporary, revealing the full Norman panoply of sieges, ambushes, manoeuvres with cavalry (which only Arthur possesses, p. 235), encirclement, tactical reserves, the exploitation of hill-tops, rivers and ports, Norman armour (the nasal by which Eldol caught Hengist) and Norman tactics (the oblique charges at Saussy and Camlann, actually used at Tinchebrai).

Realistic as those early battles are, there is a remarkable change in the war against Lucius. Some aspects of strategy and fighting details remain but the overall shape and detailed tone is markedly literary. Faral, one of the most scholarly commentators on the text, noticed the change and thought it derived from a deliberate reference to Caesar's campaigns (1929, pp. 291–2). But the effect is ideologically specific, not merely literary: to create this wish-fulfilment war, to bolster up Henry's actual failure, Geoffrey has to go beyond Norman reality simply because that military power had not managed to master France.

A similar wish-fulfilling use of a literary tradition occurs when Arthur kills the giant of Mont St Michel. As soon as he reaches Barfleur on his trip to fight Lucius, Arthur goes off to kill this monster who is oppressing his Breton subjects, and has raped and murdered one of his own relatives. Significant details in this sequence are that Arthur takes with him only Kay and Bedivere, but then leaves them behind; in the fight he tries to prevent the monster reaching his club, then kills him; finally he remarks this was his strongest opponent since the giant Retho, who had seized the beards of many kings and wanted Arthur's as well.

The episode is clearly based on a Celtic monster fight, and is broadly reminiscent of some of the encounters with giants in *Culhwch ac Olwen*. So the essence of the scene is quite familiar, and there is a similar episode earlier in the *Historia* when Corineus, Brutus' lieutenant, kills Goemagog. But this Arthurian giant-killing has a distinct historical reference and a specific ideological function.

Mont St Michel, a rock pinnacle just off the north coast of Brittany, had a particular meaning in Henry I's life, which would have been well-known throughout the Norman power-structure. When William I died, Henry was left no land, no castles – only silver. Fairly soon he bought the Cotentin peninsula and the fortress of Mont St Michel from the impecunious Robert, who was then at odds with Rufus. As usual, Robert was defeated by Rufus and not only ceded to him the lands already sold to Henry but also agreed, malleable as ever in his weakness, to help Rufus seize them. Henry took refuge in Mont St Michel, but was eventually forced to march out in humiliation. He was stripped of his lands and left without even the money he paid for them. Once again he was no more than a weak and property-less youngest brother.

The giant is a rapist, carries a huge club and inhabits a

sky-scraping peak. He is a model of phallic aggression and male dominance, perceived through the eyes of a smaller man: the mention of beard-stealing Retho deepens the castration anxiety in the scene. Geoffrey has used a Celtic story (which may or may not have been previously told about Arthur) to exorcise a particularly shaming and emasculating event in Henry I's life, a special disaster in his often uncertain progress towards the potent possession of property.

After this, as has already been argued, the text goes on to dissolve in fiction Henry's other major weakness, his inability to deal decisively with Louis VI. And for all the dream-like success of the campaign against Lucius, this too is set in the context of uncertainty. The whole trip to Gaul is prefaced by Arthur's dream, which he takes as an omen of the destructiveness of the conflict with Rome. Geoffrey implies that the king fears failure in the coming war, but the text sets that fear aside in triumph – only then to raise a truer fear, that of rebellion from among the power-holding class.

The treachery of Mordred is undiscussable, as Geoffrey states; the reference to Guinevere 'who had broken the vows of her earlier marriage' (p. 259) is enigmatic, suggesting she might not have been entirely unwilling to go with Mordred. These betrayals make possible the successful grab for power by a powerful relative left behind when the king and the army are away – still an obvious time for a *coup d'état*. The final battles with Mordred realise that central fear of the Normans, bitter man-to-man fighting among trained warriors of the same nation with no political mediation, no quarter asked or given. The leadership of the two sides, king and his nephew, makes the force of the conflict clear, especially when Henry I's only credible male successor was his nephew Stephen of Blois.

The narration dramatically enacts the idea of war escalating out of control, bitter civil war to the death: 'While the two commanders were encouraging their men in this way in both the armies, the lines of battle suddenly met, combat was joined, and they all strove with might and main to deal each other as many blows as possible' (p. 261). Mordred is killed and Arthur is at least close to death. He is 'mortally wounded and was carried off to the Isle of Avalon, so that his wounds might be attended to' (p. 261).

The idea of the undying Arthur, certainly current before Geoffrey's day (Loomis, 1959, p. 64–71), may well have influenced the phrasing of that remark. But for the non-Celtic audience, the main thrust of the story will be the terrible sudden decline of royal grandeur and extensive power. Both the means and the circumstances of the disaster would seem quite credible, even possible, for the contemporary Norman warlords. The message is not just that the Celtic British power has waned, but that all splendid power based on arms and tenuous human fidelities must be likely to fail when infidelity sets the military power into internecine conflict.

VI

The sudden pitiless ending is all the more severe because it brings down the edifice of grandeur, the elaborate cultural superstructure which Geoffrey tells us Arthur was able to construct on the basis of his military power, and which the Norman kings themselves were anxious to create. The Caerleon episode is the centre of Geoffrey's representation of cultural splendour. That was the means by which medieval rulers both consumed the productive surplus they had alienated and, by the grandiose figure they cut in the consumption, established themselves as having a natural right to their appropriations.

Caerleon was, of course, a Roman city and Geoffrey, from nearby Monmouth, presumably knew well its imposing ruins. While that gives the fiction a certain historical credibility, there can be little doubt that the reference is to the splendid 'crown-wearing' occasions that all the Norman kings arranged (Thorpe, 1966, p. 226; Tatlock, 1950, p. 271). These were only the high-water marks of the Normans' remarkably lavish cultural display. It is not often realised just how rich the Normans were in England, where their total control of a fertile and relatively unravaged country made them much more wealthy than they had been in Normandy. William I is thought to have had a personal yearly income of about £12500 (Davis, 1976, p. 114). Such wealth was largely spent, of course, on military equipment, especially on the provision and training of the superb horses which were the prime source of their military supremacy, so lovingly portrayed by the Norman designer of the Bayeux Tapestry (Plate 5). Geoffrey, however, finds little place for them in his battle-scenes.

In spite of their expenditure on equipment the Norman lords were still very wealthy, and building was another great charge they undertook with enthusiasm. Castles, initially wooden but increasingly stone, were a major and military feature, but the Normans were also great builders of churches, as the countryside still testifies. This too had a function, apart from the awe-inspiring and legitimising force of sheer splendour. The Normans derived great support from the church's moral and spiritual authority. William I had good relations with Lanfranc, the distinguished man he made archbishop. William II was less able to bend to his will Lanfranc's successor, the saintly Anselm. Church-state tension did exist under Henry I and exploded in the later twelfth century between Henry II and Beckett. In Geoffrey's story the firm support the state church gives to Arthur is partly reflective of the ideal situation and partly an ideological hope that it will continue.

The close church-state links that greatly helped the Norman kings developed from the unusual fact that the borders of the duchy of Normandy and those of the archdiocese were more or less the same. Geoffrey shows such rare unity at work: the archbishop Dubricius crowns Arthur, encourages the British before the battle of Bath and lends all his prestige to the great doings at Caerleon. Yet this optimism is not all; the reality of church-state strain, felt in particular through Anselm, is recognised when Dubricius, at this point called 'saintly' (p. 230), resigns to become a hermit. There are solutions for such problems, and nepotism was one much favoured by the Normans. Accordingly, Arthur's uncle David follows Dubricius to the archbishopric. This is an elegant absorption of the major Welsh saint into Arthur's family and power, but it is also an accurate detail: Henry of Blois, Henry I's nephew and King Stephen's younger brother, held the very rich bishopric of Winchester from 1129 until his death in 1171.

The Caerleon episode does more than show the smooth relationship of a military power and its supportive church. The major impact of the sequence is the realisation of Norman cultural splendour. Geoffrey creates for the first time in the Arthurian legend the medieval monarch as we know him, at the centre of a complex, static and glorious court. It is far from the mobile hubbub of Arthur's entourage in *Culhwch ac Olwen* or his representation in the Welsh romance *Owein* where the king sits on rushes and Cai goes to the cellar for a pitcher of mead to accompany chops on a spit. At Caerleon honour arises not simply from physical power but from complex rituals and notions of genteel behaviour. Here is the full emergence of 'the code of courtliness' (p. 222). This is recognised as an edifice based on sheer wealth: Geoffrey praises Britain's 'general affluence, the richness of its decorations, and the courteous behaviour of its inhabitants' (p. 229).

This last feature is immediately elaborated as something like courtly love, for the women 'scorned to give their love to any man who had not proved himself three times in battle. In this way the womenfolk became chaste and more virtuous and for their love the knights were ever more daring' (p. 229). The code of *fin amor* is not acted out in the narrative as it will be in Chrétien's romances, but the fact that the notion itself was relatively new in France indicates the radically contemporary nature of Geoffrey's world of Arthur. This passage is the most sophisticated part of the whole model of culture which Geoffrey creates. It will be greatly developed in the later Arthurian legend as a central part of the cultural mystification by which the essence of military power – the appropriation of property and surplus productivity – is euphemised for those who practise it, and concealed from those who suffer its oppressions.

All of this splendour leads directly back to the king, just like all the planning, motivation and profit of war. Where in *Culhwch ac Olwen* heroes could dissent from the king and act without his presence or interest, here the king is abolutely central and omnipresent. Even when he is not active, characters think and talk about the king, especially how he will judge and reward their actions. A model of royal despotism is constructed. At times of crisis the true savagery of a military despot, and especially a Norman one, breaks out from beneath the cultural legitimisations. In particular there is the recurring motif of the king's rage, the iron fist in the cultural glove. At the battle of Bath, against the giant, in the final encounter with Lucius, King Arthur becomes very angry. He loses control, he feels his own settled order has been disturbed, he senses dishonour facing him – these are all rationalisations of the fact that his will has been crossed, his property affected. The royal rage always unleashes the most extreme moments of martial fury, the physical violence that was the inner core of Norman power-holding.

Great rage and great splendour are the two sides of the Norman concept of royalty, the essence of what it is to be 'so great a king' as

Arthur (p. 217). He rules the centralised feudal state, where all power runs back to the king's personal pleasure, where 'all those who in the office which they held had done Arthur any service were called together and each rewarded with a personal grant of cities, castles, archbishoprics, bishoprics and other landed possessions' (p. 230). The personal character of the service and the grant, the propertied nature of the senior church appointments – these features delineate the feudal state as the Norman kings would have liked it to be, rather than the complex of religious dissent, multiple loyalties, sub-infeudation and even cash substitutions for service which they could not prevent developing and which would be the structural weakness, from a despot's viewpoint, of the medieval state.

VII

In many ways the author's own position is convergent with that of the Norman hierarchy. His learning and skill are themselves aspects of cultural splendour. Both his Latin style and his narrative structure are a sophisticated development of Norman historical writing (Thorpe, 1966, pp. 24–5; Tatlock, 1950, p. 395). There are cross-references, especially in the earlier part of the *Historia*, to classical and biblical events which further dignify the narrative. And Geoffrey is well aware of the elegant shape he gave to his work: he suggests that the 'very ancient book' he allegedly used as a source was 'attractively composed to form a consecutive and orderly narrative' (p. 51). If he did indeed have a Welsh source it would have been at best like Nennius's simple compilation: the values Geoffrey praises and recreates in literary form are those of the rising tide of twelfth-century scholarship and rationalism.

That phenomenon was both fostered by and helped to develop the newly wealthy and newly organised secular powers of the period, and as a part Celt, a churchman and scholar, Geoffrey is a classic example of the marginal figures who are so often found realising the ideological requirements of a newly dominant class. Yet marginality does also mean a certain separation from the prime interests of those holding power, and the ideologue will at times indicate that fact by a certain (though often implicit) withdrawal from the ideology he creates. For instance, Geoffrey's lack of interest in horses is a telling sign of his difference from the horse-empowered feudal lords. But his marginality goes further. In the *Historia* Geoffrey apparently withdraws to some degree from the values he has made so forceful.

The fact that he represents the fall of Arthur and the decline of those quasi-Norman values need not suggest he wants that to happen: it can, as was argued above, be seen as a tragic ending, effectively realising the weight of threats of treason and misfortune. In any case that ending is fully aligned with and fictionally recognises the severe problems faced by the Norman élite in the 1120s and 1130s. But Geoffrey nevertheless seems to project the catastrophe beyond that and he does so in the only place where he makes clear reference to the Norman present. In the 'Prophecies of Merlin' Henry I is mentioned, as 'The Lion of Justice' (p. 174), and so is the White Ship disaster – 'The Lion's cubs shall be transformed into salt-water fishes' (p. 174). Well after this comes the return of Cadwallader and Conanus: 'Then the foreigners shall be slaughtered and the rivers will run with blood' (p. 175). That comment seems unequivocally pro-Welsh, to say the least.

The fact that Geoffrey is so critical of the Welsh need not stem, as Tatlock thought, from a pro-Breton attitude (1950, pp. 396–402). The favouring of the Bretons may well be merely a tactful restriction of Celtic praise to the only Celtic group allied to the Normans, as Parry and Caldwell have suggested (1959, p. 73). The Welsh are criticised for their inefficient dissension and divisiveness, which might well be the frustration of a covert nationalist – similar views are often heard today. In the 'Prophecies', and perhaps in the general approach to the Welsh and Bretons, there appears to be a private Welsh-supporting interest of Geoffrey's, one that cannot look forward to any return from patronage, but which might well have been shared with others of his private circle. And for that interest, of course, the Celtic nature of so much of the material is not a displacement of the Norman interest, but has direct force.

Other signs of private interests are partly convergent with this one. Geoffrey provides quite a few jokes in the text. Tatlock refers to two comic Roman names, which apparently mean 'Puppy-Face' and 'Undershirt' (1950, p. 124–5). It is by no means uncommon to find this sort of jesting in medieval texts, even of the most serious sort – medieval psalters have droll and even obscene drawings in the margins, and the Bayeux Tapestry has its share in the friezes above and below the action. One piece of apparently private comedy enters the tapestry proper (Plate 6). But a lot of Geoffrey's jokes seem to have more specific point than those comic reversals. They are rather academic, depend on a multilingual wit and tend to privilege Welsh figures and to mock Normans. One of these jokes is made obvious, when Geoffrey says that a certain Boso is lord of 'Rhydychen, that is Oxford'. He translates the Welsh name to draw attention to the play on Latin *bos*, 'an ox'. So the character is really called 'Oxo of Oxford'. The etymological play is perhaps a harmless joke but it does make fun of the Norman name of the lord of a city where Geoffrey lived and worked.

Another of these oddities is sharper in its implication. Geoffrey has invented a character called Anguselus, of some importance. He is King of Albany and speaks in Arthur's debate over the Roman envoys: he is 'bloodthirsty', all for war. This name has often been wrongly represented in a quasi-Roman form, as Auguselus, but the authentic form is clear and anyone familiar with Middle Welsh will immediately recognise a Latinised name based on *angusel*, negative of *cusel* (Modern Welsh *cysul*), meaning 'council, counsel'. So *angusel* is an exact translation of 'Unrad', the famous epithet for Ethelred. Often mistranslated as 'Unready' the name really means 'of bad counsel'. Geoffrey's involved joke finally points to Anguselus' bloodthirstiness as 'bad counsel' – it is a neat anti-militarist point.

Though complicated, this reference seems beyond an accident, and must suggest there are many other scholarly jokes buried in the text. Perhaps they are buried forever if, like this one, they have been distorted by scribes and unrecognised by editors who knew no Welsh. There are certainly other Celtic in-jokes, like making Nennius appear as a warrior whose brother has the doubtful name of Androgeus – perhaps a reference to the bizarre nature of Geoffrey's source? There can be little doubt that Sulgenius, often wrongly Latinised to Fulgenius, is a reference to Sulien, the famous eleventh-century cleric and father (in the celibacy-scorning Celtic church) of a dynasty of scholars who survived into Geoffrey's own day.

These are not large points, and the research necessary to excavate more of them from the manuscripts of the *Historia* is probably not cost-effective in terms of the value of the evidence. But in these jokes there lies support for the national feeling indicated in the prophecies themselves. They are fine examples of the inward-looking, face-saving ironies by which a member of a marginal group justifies to himself and his peers the ideological work he does for another, more powerful group on whom he depends for a living. Present-day works have no shortage of such responses.

Whatever the private effect of these face-saving ironies, the outward effect of the *Historia* was entirely ideological and almost entirely successful. There were those who mocked the book for its fantastic creations. William of Newburgh put his dissent in a historian's prose (quoted by Fletcher, 1906, pp. 101–2). Gerald of Wales mocked Geoffrey with characteristic verve, saying that a certain man was possessed by demons and when St John's gospel was laid on his chest they all left, but when the *Historia* was placed there they flocked back in greater numbers (1978, p. 119).

They were rare dissenting voices. The *Historia* was much copied, much revered, much used – Henry II in particular found Arthur a politically helpful model of a king as great as he felt himself to be, not without reason. And the text soon moved out of its Latin limits; Gaimar and Wace quickly made translations public, and they worked directly in the aristocratic connection, widening the audience for this central work of Norman ideology. The model of a powerful royal despot who in spite of his success, his personal power and his excellent organisation still faces threats both military and personal was a potent image for this period, and among the Normans and their French neighbours and relatives the figure of Geoffrey's Arthur was taken for the model of what everyone powerful would like to be – 'so great a king'.

Into that royal structure Chrétien de Troyes, a French writer of extraordinary imaginative power, was to fit the orally disseminated Celtic stories which Geoffrey had largely by-passed. Chrétien would use them to express the anxieties not of kings, but of those beneath that rank who had less extensive ambitions, especially the knightly youth of northern Europe who were themselves faced with specific historical pressures in that period. Chrétien's work meshed with Geoffrey's political structure to create the Arthurian legend as it has come down to us, with the full exotic mixture of royal power and knightly quests for glory. Studying Geoffrey's *Historia* has revealed the ideologies connected with kingship. Chrétien's texts will reveal the threats faced and the values cherished by those who aspired to an honoured, rewarded and secure place within that power-structure.

REFERENCES

Primary Sources
Geoffrey of Monmouth (1929) *Historia Regum Britanniae* ed. A. Griscom (London: Longman), trans. L. Thorpe (London: Penguin, 1966).
Gerald of Wales (1868) *Itinerarium Cambriae* ed. J. F. Dimock (London: Rolls Series), trans. L. Thorpe (London: Penguin, 1978).
Roberts, B. F. ed. (1971) *Brut y Brenhinedd* ('*Brut* of the Princes') (Dublin Institute for Advanced Studies Press).

Secondary Sources
Alcock, L. (1971) *Arthur's Britain* (London: Lane).
Bromwich, R. (1954) 'The Character of Early Welsh Tradition' in *Studies in Early British History* ed. N. K. Chadwick (Cambridge University Press).
—— (1978) *Trioedd Ynys Prydein: The Welsh Triads* 2nd edn (Cardiff: University of Wales Press).
Brooke, C. (1964) *Europe in the Central Middle Ages, 962–1154* (London: Longman).
—— (1967) *The Saxon and Norman Kings* (London: Collins).
Bullock-Davies, C. (1966) *Professional Interpreters and the Matter of Britain* (Cardiff: University of Wales Press).
Chambers, E. K. (1927) *Arthur of Britain* (London: Sidgwick and Jackson).
Davis, R. H. C. (1976) *The Normans and Their Myth* (London: Thames and Hudson).
Douglas, D. C. (1969) *The Norman Achievement 1050–1100* (London: Eyre and Spottiswoode).
Faral, E. (1929) *La Légende Arthurienne: études et documents* (Paris: Champion).
Fletcher, R. H. (1906) *The Arthurian Material in the Chronicles* (Boston: Harvard Studies and Notes in Philology and Literature, 10).
Flint, V. I. J. (1979) 'The *Historia Regum Britanniae* of Geoffrey of Monmouth: Parody and its Purpose. A Suggestion', *Speculum* 54, 447–68.
Gerould, G. H. (1927) 'King Arthur and Politics', *Speculum* 2, 33–52.
Haskins, C. H. (1927) *The Renaissance of the Twelfth Century* (Cambridge, Mass: Harvard University Press).
Hutson, A. E. (1940) 'British Personal Names in the *Historia Regum Britanniae*', *University of California Publications in English* 5, no. 1, pp. 1–160.
Knight, S. (1980) 'Ideology in "The Franklin's Tale" ', *Parergon* 28, 3–35.
Lindsay, J. (1973) *The Normans and Their World* (London: Hart-Davis MacGibbon).
Lloyd, J. E. (1939) *A History of Wales* 3rd edn (London: Longman).
Loomis, R. S. (1959) 'The Oral Diffusion of the Arthurian Legend' in *Arthurian Literature in the Middle Ages*, ed. R. S. Loomis (Oxford: Clarendon).
Norgate, K. (1887) *England under the Angevin Kings* (London: Macmillan).
Parry, J. J. and Caldwell, R. A. (1959) 'Geoffrey of Monmouth' in *Arthurian Literature in the Middle Ages*, see under Loomis, R. S. (1959).
Roberts, B. F. (1976) 'Geoffrey of Monmouth and Welsh Historical Tradition', *Nottingham Medieval Studies* 20, 29–40.
Tatlock, J. S. P. (1950) *The Legendary History of Britain* (Berkeley: University of California Press).

3 'Prowess and courtesy': Chrétien de Troyes' *Le Chevalier au Lion*

I

Chrétien de Troyes wrote five Arthurian romances. Here are first set out the noble and lofty king, the beautiful and distant queen, the Round Table which brings together knights famous both for their prowess – physical power – and for their courtesy – the ethical qualities that especially distinguish Chrétien's world. The basic apparatus of the Arthurian legend as modern readers know it, absent in *Culhwch ac Olwen* and barely suggested in the *Historia Regum Britanniae*, is suddenly present in Chrétien's work.

He wrote in the later twelfth century, in the 1170s according to most scholars. At this time Henry II of England had collected authority over much of what is now France. Through his mother Matilda he ruled Normandy and claimed Brittany; Geoffrey of Anjou, his father, passed on control of Anjou, Touraine and Maine; his queen Eleanor brought him the rule of her huge province of Aquitaine, with its claim on Toulouse. Henry's Angevin empire stretched from Scotland to Spain and dominated France. In particular it combined the wealth of England with the sophistication of Aquitaine and this whole area has been described as 'the base of French-speaking culture' in the period (Heer, 1961, p. 157). Chrétien's patroness, Marie de Champagne, was the daughter of Eleanor of Aquitaine by her first marriage. He has clear links with the military, economic and cultural monolith of the Angevin state, which disseminated the new ideologies of chivalry and the courtesy of love, and especially used the Celtic stories, including those of Arthur, as a structure for those ideals (Benton, 1961).

Henry II and the later Plantagenet kings were as interested in the legitimising myth of the legend of Arthur as the great Norman

68

lords had been. The legend was nourished at court; Arthurian material and events were sponsored, though they were carefully diverted to the royal interest. Henry's part in the 'discovery' and exhibition of the bodies of Arthur and Guinevere at Glastonbury in 1191 was very likely intended to assure the Welsh that *their* glorious king really was dead (Barber, 1973, pp. 59–64). Some scholars have gone so far as to suggest that the Plantagenet royal power was the direct source of Chrétien's material (Hofer, 1954, pp. 49–50; Köhler, 1974, pp. 64 and 69). Chrétien may well have had British contacts: Henry I of Champagne, Marie's husband and so Chrétien's patron, was nephew to both King Stephen and his powerful brother Henry, the Bishop of Winchester. Chrétien may have worked for the bishop (Holmes and Klenke, 1959, pp. 23–4), and it is certainly clear that Champagne (like Flanders for whose Count Philippe Chrétien wrote his last work, *Le Conte del Graal*) was in close political and cultural contact with Britain, a natural ally against the King of France. A British link may have partly provoked Chrétien's use of Arthurian material, but the meanings he created from his sources were fully related thi his own world.

Only Chrétien of the authors studied in this book produced more than one major Arthurian text and the extraordinary richness of his material in social and ideological terms makes it necessary to choose only one of his poems for detailed discussion. *Le Chevalier au Lion* (1948) has been nominated by Frappier, the doyen of recent French Chrétien scholars, as the 'chef d'oeuvre' (1969, p. 12), and the major British expert has found it 'the most characteristic' of the romances (Reid, 1948, p. v). It is also the text which most patently uses British material and the one which makes most plain the extensive relations between Chrétien's work and the socio-economic forces of his period and environment. A synopsis of the romance is necessary before it can be discussed in detail.

II

Chrétien introduces his story by saying that Arthur's bravery (*proesce*) teaches us to be brave (*preu*) and courteous (*cortois*). The king held court one Pentecost at Carduel in Wales, in the olden time before love and courtesy were debased to their modern state. While Arthur slept with Guinevere, his knights talked among themselves. Calogrenant told how seven years ago, seeking adventures, he came to a vavasour's wooden castle where he was welcomed; he was sent on to an ogre who directed him on to a spring where, if he spilt water on the adjacent stone, he would first face a terrible storm and then find adventure. Calogrenant did this; after the storm a fierce knight appeared to fight him because of the disturbance he had caused. The knight unhorsed Calogrenant easily and he returned to court by way of the hospitable castle, deeply shamed.

Immediately, his kinsman Yvain (the son of King Urien) says he will avenge him. Kay, Arthur's seneschal, mocks Yvain but is rebuked by the queen. The king wakes and having heard the story swears he and his knights will seek out the marvellous spring at midsummer. Yvain is annoyed; he wants the honour to be his alone and so leaves secretly that night. He follows Calogrenant's steps exactly, but defeats the spring-knight who flees, fatally wounded. Yvain pursues him so he can have a token of victory to prove his triumph. The knight gallops to the gate of his town; this is cunningly built, for as the knight passes through the gateway a portcullis falls very close behind Yvain. It cuts in half both his saddle and his horse and even slices off his spurs before it hits the ground. Then another portcullis falls in front of him, after the wounded knight has left the gateway.

Yvain is trapped. A maiden appears and says that Yvain was once the only knight at Arthur's court to be courteous to her. She gives him a ring of invisibility, then she feeds him. Soon people come to search for their lord's killer, but they cannot see Yvain. He observes the lady of the town and falls in love with her; the maiden restrains him from rushing to her, and agrees to go wooing for him. Yvain is love-struck.

The maiden asks the lady who will defend her spring when Arthur comes, now that her lord is dead: she offers to provide a better defender than him. The lady sends her away in anger. The maiden returns, to argue that the man who killed her lord is the better man. Again she is sent away angrily.

The lady thinks it over; her own defencelessness and the maiden's known loyalty change her mind. She recalls the maiden and says that if her candidate is an acceptable person she will take him as husband and lord of her realm. The maiden says she will send to Arthur's court for him. She needs a period for this notional errand, during which the lady will consult her men for advice. The maiden teases Yvain that the lady will make him her prisoner; he accepts this, as he is already a love-prisoner.

After five days, they pretend Yvain has come from court. He and the lady are married after her men give consent because of the need to continue the custom of the spring. She is named as Laudine de Landuc, daughter of Duke Laudunet.

Arthur comes to the spring and pours water on the stone. Yvain arrives in arms. Kay encounters him and is humiliated. Yvain welcomes Arthur to his lands; great festivities follow for a week. Gauvain invites the helpful maiden, Lunete, to be his 'demoiselle'. Then Arthur prepares to leave and Gauvain urges Yvain to accompany them, lest he degenerate in his married state. His lady unwillingly permits him to go for a year and a day. She gives him a ring to protect him from harm. He leaves, weeping bitterly: his heart remains behind.

Yvain and Gauvain pass the year in jousting and winning honour. Yvain forgets to return to Laudine. He suddenly remembers and is ashamed: at once a maiden appears, berates him publicly and seizes back the protective ring.

A storm breaks in Yvain's brain: he tears off his clothes and runs into the forest, seizing a bow and arrow on the way. He eats raw meat until he encounters a hermit, who leaves bread and water out for him and then cooks the venison Yvain catches.

One day the Lady of Noroison and her maidens see Yvain; she recognises him and sends a maiden with a precious ointment obtained from Morgan the Wise. Ordered to use a little to bring back his senses, she uses it all then throws away the jar to pretend she has lost it. Yvain returns with the maiden and fights Count Alier, who is oppressing the Lady of Noroison. He defeats Alier and his men; the lady would marry him and give him her lands, and her people expect this, but Yvain leaves hurriedly without explanation.

In the woods he sees a lion and a serpent fighting. He kills the serpent because the lion is a noble beast, but has to cut off the tip of the lion's tail in beheading the serpent. He is ready to fight the lion if need be, but it kneels before him weeping and then follows him. It helps Yvain hunt.

They wander until they come to the wonderful spring. Yvain swoons in grief and his sword cuts his cheek. The lion thinks he is dead, and is about to fall on Yvain's sword in suicide when Yvain wakes, to reproach himself for his fault. He is in despair.

A maiden imprisoned in the chapel by the spring calls on him. He feels he is more wretched than her. But she is about to be executed; only Gauvain and Yvain would dare to fight for her. It is Lunete, accused of treason by Laudine's seneschal. Yvain agrees to fight for her tomorrow, because Gauvain is away seeking the abducted queen Guinevere, but he insists on being incognito. He and the lion leave, to seek lodging for the night.

They come to a castle where live Gauvain's sister and her husband. An ogre called Harpin oppresses them. He has killed two of their sons, captured the other four, and will give their daughter to his underlings for their sport. Yvain agrees to fight him tomorrow. Harpin does not arrive, and Yvain frets about his agreement to help Lunete. He says he must leave at prime, but nevertheless he waits, out of pity for the oppressed people. Harpin comes; Yvain and the lion kill him. Yvain asks the people to report to Arthur's court that 'The Knight with the Lion' has helped them, and hurries away.

He arrives just in time to fight for Lunete, who is already at the stake. He has to immobilise the lion first, and fights alone against the seneschal and his two brothers. The fight goes against Yvain, and the lion breaks loose to help him: they win, but are both wounded. Laudine thanks him, as 'The Knight with the Lion'. He says he cannot stay in spite of her invitation, for his beloved is angry with him. She prays that God may bring him joy with her. Only Lunete has recognised him. He and the lion go off and are healed at a castle.

Meanwhile, conflict has broken out between the two daughters of the dead lord of Noire Espine because the older has seized all the property. At Arthur's court the younger seeks help, a knight to fight in judicial combat for her part of the property. The older sister has already engaged Gauvain on her side: he will only fight if he is incognito. The younger sister hears of the prowess of 'The Knight with the Lion' and goes off to seek his help. She falls sick and another maiden takes up the quest. She discovers Yvain's track, and comes at last to the wonderful spring; Lunete is at the chapel and points her in Yvain's direction. She finds him, and the lion, and he accepts the fight.

They come to Pesme Aventure. The townspeople say only shame awaits Yvain here, but he presses on. In the courtyard are three hundred maidens in filthy rags working at embroidery. They are from the Isle of Maidens: their young king was imprisoned here by two evil men and his ransom was thirty maidens a year. Yvain passes through the splendid, new hall into the garden where the lord and his family relax in the greatest luxury. They welcome Yvain, and regretfully tell him he must, to fulfil the custom of the castle, fight the two evil *netuns*, half-devils, and that if he wins he will marry the daughter and own the property.

The champions make Yvain lock up the lion. The fight goes badly for Yvain, and the lion digs his way out. They defeat the champions comprehensively. Yvain refuses the daughter, saying he cannot marry her but will return if possible. The lord sets free the three hundred maidens as Yvain demands, but gives him a churlish farewell.

Yvain hurries to court, arriving just in time to fight for the younger daughter of Noire Espine, whose messenger has been with him at Pesme Aventure. Of his own accord he leaves the lion behind, and then he and Gauvain, who truly love each other, fight with great ferocity and hatred since neither knows the other. They battle all day, and finally, seeing neither can win, they exchange compliments, then names. They try to give each other the victory, for the sake of each other's honour. The king steps in and tricks the elder sister into admitting her bad behaviour; he makes her give her sister feudal tenure over part of the lands.

After their wounds are healed, Yvain feels love for Laudine and leaves for the spring, where he makes the storm rage worse than ever. Lunete tells Laudine she must find a knight to defend the spring, and suggests 'The Knight with the Lion'. To achieve this end, Laudine swears to do all she can to bring him peace with his angry beloved. Lunete sets off to look for Yvain and, to her surprise, finds him at the spring. She brings him to Laudine and her oath forces her to take him back. They are reconciled, and there is peace between Yvain *le fin* and his beloved *chiere et fine*.

III

It is an intricate and exotic story. Much has been said about its sources and about the varying attitudes it has aroused. But the most striking and most relevant thing about *Le Chevalier au Lion* is that practically every detail in that synopsis has some specific ideological force, and to expose these patterns is the purpose of this chapter.

Before examining the text it will be helpful to give an account of the relevant historical and social contexts. These have been described by a number of scholars, some with specific attention to Chrétien. His role as a creator of ideology was outlined by Bloch, with *Le Conte del Graal* seen as one of the first codifications of knighthood (1961, p. 317). Bloch also described the gulf between that ideology and reality: 'It is hardly surprising that the realities of knightly life, with its frequent trickery and deeds of violence, should have been far from conforming always to these aspirations' (1961, p. 318).

The word 'aspirations' suggests Bloch thought the values had at least some real positive force. Other scholars have identified the oppressive core of chivalry: *'cortois* behaviour patterns and attitudes of "romantic" love . . . served these people to define themselves as socially superior' (Moller, 1958–9, p. 143). Bloch himself recognised the exploitative basis for this superiority; he quotes a chillingly dispassionate remark from Ramon Lull's influential thirteenth-century work, *The Order of Chivalry*: 'Lull did not think he offended Christian sentiment by saying that it was conformable to good order that the knight should "draw his well-being" from the things that were provided for him "by the weariness and toil" of his men' (Bloch, 1961, p. 319).

Erich Köhler has summed up the situation: 'The courtly romance, particularly the Arthurian romance of Chrétien, represents the literary expression of this self-consciousness of the "second feudal age" of which M. Bloch has brought out the essential traits' (1974, p. 394). Köhler and other scholars have established the material basis of the ideology of romance, which it seeks both to conceal and resolve: in order to approach these urgent distortions of reality it is necessary to trace the lineaments of reality in the period.

In social terms, it is clear that in the twelfth and thirteenth centuries the aristocracy was expanding in times of peace and prosperity, that is, in the absence of large-scale war, famine and plague. Salter has described the *prima facie* relation between romance literature and the physical context of sheer prosperity, especially in the Angevin empire (1973, pp. 407–9), but she does not recognise the conflicts which this prosperity and expansion created, and which the literature both realised and ideologically resolved.

In this period the aristocracy was notably an 'open class'. To defend its newly elaborate castles and to staff its increasingly sophisticated systems of rule, finance and defence it employed large numbers of non-aristocratic people skilled in war and administration. Moller (1958–9) outlined the basic patterns of an augmented nobility, with a surplus of males; he did not, however, relate the resultant ideals of chivalry to a specific and material class tension, but merely to personal ambition.

Köhler, on the other hand, has traced the essential rise of ideals of chivalry and *fin amor*, that is, elegant courtly love, to 'the permanent state of tension existing between the upper and lower nobility in their common life at court, and the historical necessity of neutralising by an ideal of class unity the divergent interests which existed in the existential plane between the two groups' (1964, p. 28). The fact that the upper nobility, the barons, and the lower nobility, the knights, came together in Champagne itself during the period in which Chrétien was writing has been exemplified in great detail by a close study of the Champagne nobility from 1152–1284 (Evergates, 1975, especially ch. 5).

Köhler explains the function of courtly romance in the context of this social development and its attendant tensions. The higher aristocracy offered chivalry and a selfless, refining *fin amor* as an ideal of behaviour to be shared by nobles of both levels; that is, a false consciousness of unity was tendered to the lower nobility and it obscured any consciousness they might have had of the exploitation of their skills and vitality by the higher nobility. This lower nobility accepted such neutralisation and its idealist medium as a means of ideological integration into the ranks of the aristocracy (Köhler, 1964, pp. 36–7).

Köhler has also described another dynamic determining force in romance, which also involves the upper nobility, but which operates in another direction. The higher nobility who patronised the romances were baronial, not royal; they were typically the Counts of Champagne and Flanders, not Louis VII or Philippe II of France. Although the barons did pay feudal homage to the Kings of France, they were in fact at odds with him. In the period when Chrétien was working, the Capetian kings, especially Philippe II, were attempting to curtail the power of the barons. In particular they fostered relations with the new professional and administrative classes, that lower nobility whose loyalty the barons sought to appropriate. The kings also patronised the mercantile classes, those townsfolk whom the romances usually deride as being *vileyn*, unchivalric (Köhler, 1974, pp. 16–22). This process gave a greater urgency to the effort to weld together the lower aristocracy and the old nobility against the royal attempt to create a centralised state; there are clear signs in the romances of the baronial need to believe they can be independent of the king.

It is also easy to see, though Köhler does not make this point, that the ideal ethics of chivalry and generally *fin* behaviour also act for this higher nobility as a false consciousness to conceal from themselves both the aggressive and often brutal character of their dominance and also (an intriguingly dialectical feature) the fact that much of their real wealth came from the rise of mercantilism. Champagne largely owed its great riches to its position at the meeting of two trade routes, and the town of Troyes each year had a prosperous mercantile fair which the Count controlled through his 'sergeants', also called his *ministeriales*, typical new members of the upper class (Holmes and Klenke, 1959, p. 10). And naturally, the idealised ethics of chivalry and courtly behaviour gave to the *arriviste* members of the upper class an even more urgently attractive false consciousness, covering their aggressive profes-sional skills – the personal *proesce* by which they won their way upwards – with a pleasing mystification of *courtoisie*.

There is another important dynamic to be added to the social tensions observed by Köhler. Georges Duby (1977) has related the development and the audience of chivalric romance to a change in inheritance practices from partition of the estate (at least among brothers) to primogeniture. This became established by the late twelfth century, and its effects were remarkable. Duby writes of bands of errant *juvenes* who, being without patrimony, had to seek their way in the world by fighting, sometimes joined or even led by elder brothers waiting for their fathers to die. Many, of course, went on crusades or to the Norman states outside France, but their impact as a disorderly force at home was well-known at the time. Chrétien offers a specific and extremely potent piece of wish-fulfilment for such men, the dream of marrying a woman who owns a large property.

Duby has shown that this was a real contemporary possibility: 'All *juvenes* were on the look-out for an heiress,' he remarks firmly (1977, p. 119). And it was real because in the absence of sons a daughter would inherit her father's property and a widow would retain her husband's rights. Twelfth-century records show many women holding the right to property, though they seem to be a diminishing number (Herlihy, 1962, p. 108; Gold, 1977, pp. 299–303), probably because of the increased number of propertyless men keen to snap up such prizes.

Wealthy unmarried women were treated in an extremely peremptory way. When Eleanor of Aquitaine was separated from Louis VII he returned her Duchy (by his own choice, he could have kept it). As she rode home to Poitiers from Paris, her men fought off two abduction attempts – and not by brigands. One was by Theobald of Blois, younger brother of King Stephen, the other by Geoffrey of Anjou, younger brother of Henry of Normandy (who was later to be Henry II, her second husband). Both men would have seized and married her, by force if necessary, and so held the great duchy.

In this context it is hardly surprising that the knight errant, the classic member of the lower nobility, sees marriage as a path to success, and that Chrétien's dream-like representation of this process is a crucial part of his ideological power.

In the discussion that follows, specific passages of the poem will be analysed to show the conflicts that arise on the one hand from the difficult relations between the barons and the king and, on the other hand, from the more extensively treated tension between the old and the new members of the aristocratic class. In each case Chrétien manages to provide ideological resolutions which work both for the new members of the aristocratic class, the knights errant, and for the barons themselves. That skilful balancing act has much to do with the great impact of *Le Chevalier au Lion*; it works as a totality to weld together ideologically the clashing interests of the expanded nobility.

IV

In terms of the hostility between king and barons in late twelfth-century France, *Le Chevalier au Lion* has some clear anti-royal elements. Yvain becomes the owner of a land outside Arthur's power: when the king comes to the spring he is welcomed as a distinguished visitor, not a liege-lord, and his champion receives a humiliating defeat. Yvain rules in his own right and the audience would have been very sensitive on this point, for the dream of an inalienable territory was strong. A similar effect is suggested when Yvain refuses to enter the royal city of Chester, just before the moment of his disgrace for forgetting Laudine.

Some critics have taken this as a sign of Yvain's rudeness, part of a generally poor chivalric performance in the first half of the poem (Ferrante, 1975, pp. 156–7; Diverres, 1973, p. 99) but they over-moralise the position. The point is that even when in high honour Yvain chooses to remain outside Arthur's embrace, just as he deliberately left court and breached etiquette in order to win both honour and, as it turns out, a land.

In spite of this distancing of the king, the presentation of Arthur's court is not negative: in general it is a model of honourable life and a powerful source of acclaim. That was true enough of the contemporary royal court: while the barons might fear the king, they did not despise kingship. Indeed, to dream of attaining that status was not ludicrous in a country where it was still well-known that Hugh Capet had personally established the Capetian dynasty and where a number of counts and dukes had recently founded kingdoms, notably in England but also in the mediterranean area from Sicily to the Holy Land. This tension between valuing kingship and fearing the power of the real king is elegantly resolved by Chrétien through the fact that Arthur does not rule forcefully. His familiar role as a *roi fainéant*, a 'do-nothing king', is the product and the image of these conflicting feelings.

Geoffrey of Monmouth's Arthur was nothing like that, but Chrétien's king merely presides over knightly adventures even when, like Yvain's, they are basically hostile to his interests and power. The instrument of this reduced kingship is, of course, the Round Table itself. It is first recorded in Wace's French version of Geoffrey of Monmouth, and his source is unknown. The Round Table realises the idea that all knights are equal and that the king himself is no more than first among equals: the importance of the feeling embodied in this symbol is indicated by its prevalence. It is a focal point of ideology and works both for those barons who feel equal to a king whose role is still honoured, and also for those knights errant who, in joining the noble class, wish to feel equal to all those already in it.

Uneasy feelings about the king are also the basis of the treatment of the figure of the seneschal. Realising this provides the proper explanation of a feature which (like the Round Table itself) is new in French, has been part of the legend ever since, and has intrigued many Arthurians. The problem has been why Kay is so bad-tempered with other knights and so ineffective. He was fiery in Welsh, but also very powerful and led the warband, even against the tribal ruling family in *Culhwch ac Olwen*. In Chrétien, however, he has become an ill-mannered, hot-tempered enemy of good knights. His dismal lack of success in arms seems to avenge the humiliations he presses upon the heroes. The key to the matter is that Kay is now the king's seneschal, his chief administrative official. The Capetian kings used seneschals as a major instrument of their centralising effort, as did Henry II (Köhler, 1974, p. 19). From the baronial viewpoint it would be pleasing for seneschals to be represented as aggressive and incompetent troublemakers, like Kay himself and like Laudine's seneschal who, with his two brothers for support, accuses Lunete of treason. There are many other bad seneschals in the literature of the period, and a useful article has surveyed their malign but ultimately ineffective activities (Woledge, 1969).

But in this case, as with the Round Table, Chrétien's ideology does not only work from the top down. The anti-royal feeling may belong to the baronial patrons of the texts, but Chrétien incorporates the anxieties of the knights errant as well. It is they who are abused by the seneschals. Those in authority at court mistreat a young knight in his effort to enter the world of the upper nobility: Kay provides a focus for the acceptance anxiety of the *juvenes*.

That anxiety does not only show itself in negative form: there are court personnel who benevolently ease the hero's path to acceptance, seneschal-substitutes of a sort. These are always women, and women below the highest rank. Lunete is one of the many maidens who befriend Yvain, help him escape from crises and achieve his goals. The maiden who serves the Lady of Noroison is another, and the maiden who helps the younger Noire Espine daughter is similar in many respects. In Arthurian romance there are squadrons of these busy but humble maidens who resolve the knight errant's fears and problems. They always act without reward and confirm the markedly narcissistic male viewpoint in the texts.

Royal power, then, whether in the person of the king or the seneschal, is distinctly reduced by the text, and at the same time the personal anxieties of the upwardly mobile young man are assuaged. The same pattern is found in the treatment of the institution of 'customs' in the poem. It was Köhler (1960) who first observed the structural character of these customs, showing that they are not merely plot devices, but that they embody the traditional rights of territorial princes, to which a centralised and statutory royal law is inherently hostile. The king does have his own customs, like waiting for a marvel to appear before eating (not exhibited in *Le Chevalier au Lion*, but very common elsewhere), but these tend to be festal, at dinners or tourneys, and so are linked to ways of honouring or initiating the individual warriors. Property-linked customs do operate, but only outside Arthur's court. Many of them are evil, such as the one at Pesme Aventure or those in other romances where a rogue knight will contest a bridge or ford against all comers. These bad customs the hero will defeat and abolish. But his own profitable customs, like Yvain's right to fight the disturber of the spring, remain unchallenged, as does (at Pesme Aventure in this text) the potentially rewarding custom that he who defeats the evil custom will marry the daughter and the land.

Here Köhler has uncovered an intriguing pattern of ideology in events that seem merely quaint to an inattentive and underhistorical modern reading. There exists a basic baronial assumption that customary rights have force, provided they are controlled from the viewpoint of the individual lord or baron. So customs that prove hostile (that is, inconvenient or contrary to the hero's interests) are cancelled; those favourable to him or exploitable by him are validated; and the king, that annoying but ineradicable and even partly admirable presence, is given customs which have no socio-economic force and which in fact tend to privilege the baronial and knightly figures of the Round Table.

The three socio-historical areas of conflict discussed so far belong primarily to the royal-baronial conflict and are then projected by Chrétien so that the interests of barons and knights are convergent. The areas of conflict that remain to be discussed illustrate interests common to the upper and lower nobility, without specific anti-royal features. They tend to deal primarily with threats perceived by the knights errant and to resolve them by a wish-fulfilment achievement of a baronial level of life, but there are also elements which deal with the same threats from a baronial viewpoint – whether one actually held, or one achieved in youthful dreams.

V

The clearest link with the genuine situation of the wifeless and landless young warriors in the period is the problem of inheritance. This emerges overtly in the struggle between the daughters of the lord of Noire Espine – the name 'dark thorn' implies the gloomy and intractable nature of the problem for those who face it. The elder sister demands her primogenitural rights; in response the younger sister demands her rights in equity to a partition of the property. The text has dramatised at some length the problem that sent younger sons on the road to find a living and dream of an inalienable property, as Duby has shown.

The contemporary relevance, even the legal accuracy, of the inheritance sequence has been clearly established (Jonin, 1964, pp. 47–50). This is plainly the source of the episode and not even the most devoted Celticists have been able to find an Irish or Welsh version of it (Loomis, 1949, p. 325). But the force of the sequence is not merely wish-fulfilment for younger sons. The whole chain of events firmly recognises that primogeniture is now the dominant pattern of inheritance. Arthur cannot act legally to interfere with things (another feature which reduces the royal power). He is only able to 'advise', 'recommend' and 'urge' the elder sister to surrender part of her property; he cannot compel her. He finally tricks her into admitting a moral, not legal, wrong, and so she is persuaded to make her sister her vassal: that structure acknowledges fully the elder's right but seeks a compromise for the moral right of the younger.

The tenuousness of that solution is made more acceptable, or less disturbingly noticeable, because the whole text centres on an essentially wish-fulfilling answer to the same problem: the knight gains power and property through a woman. The dream of marrying a lady and a land is central to the drama of Yvain's fight at the spring and its consequence, but it is found elsewhere in the poem as well. After Yvain's fight against Count Alier he is expected to marry the Lady of Noroison whom he has saved, and rule her property as 'lord of all her possessions' (p. 223, 3332: references are to Comfort's translation and Reid's edition). At Pesme Aventure he is offered daughter and lands, even though the father is still living.

A number of details in the text make it clear what is happening. Beneath the legitimising fictions of noble Ovidian love between Yvain and Laudine, and unobscured by the helpful busy-ness of Lunete, there can be discerned the lineaments of gratified ideology, the young knight's lust for property. When Arthur comes to the spring he is welcomed by Yvain, not Laudine, and Yvain's ownership is specified: 'whoever wished to see the land which had come into the hand of my lord Yvain with the lady whom he had married, could go to enjoy himself at one of the castles which stood within a radius of two, three or four leagues' (p. 212, 2470–5). This is not a fantasy land of springs and enchanted forests where a lucky knight lives in fairy luxury: this is a well-defended border area like that between Normandy and France in the Vexin or between Normandy and Anjou in Maine, bristling with castles and held firmly by a powerful baron only too glad to demonstrate his power to a neighbouring king who does not hold his allegiance.

The fact that the woman and her lands come into Yvain's hands with marriage is of considerable importance. It is stressed by the treatment and nature of her name. In medieval romance the moment when characters are named has particular importance, because a person's 'name' was the epitome of honour and so of social status and even existence. Laudine de Landuc is only named once in the whole romance, at the moment of her marriage (p. 208, 2151). Loomis has argued in convincing detail that Laudine is a French version (with overtones of 'praise') of the place-name Lothian, an area south of Edinburgh in south-eastern Scotland. This is also true of her father's name, Laudunet (Loomis, 1949, pp. 302–3).

The territorial nature of the heroine's name confirms what is clear from the general shape and obvious source of the bulk of *Le Chevalier au Lion*, that at its heart there is a reshaped Celtic sovereignty fable. A number of these have been identified, both specifically in Welsh (Goetinck, 1975, ch. 4) and in Celtic generally (Lovecy, 1977–8). An important essay (Bromwich, 1961) has shown their extension into the Breton lay, a form written in French, in Chrétien's period, by Marie de France, who was almost certainly an illegitimate half-sister to Henry II. Three of her lays, *Graelent*, *Lanval* and *Gugemar* have a sovereignty element in the 'fairy mistress' structure. It seems highly likely that Chrétien would have had access to the story-type.

The essence of a sovereignty story is that a man gains the kingship of a land through the power or right of a woman who has supernatural abilities or connections, often associated with a spring or a river. It is probable that the source Chrétien shared in some still unclear way with the Welsh prose romance *Owein* (Thomson, 1968) was originally a legitimising myth about the power the historical Owein extended, or wished to extend, over Lothian. He lived in the late sixth century and ruled over Rheged, an area centred on Carlisle – the original of Chrétien's Carduel. This story about dominion over Lothian, itself perhaps no more than a dream, may well be what Bromwich calls a 'dynastic theme' (1961).

That structure belongs to the past of the story, but Chrétien has modernised and Gallicised it, seeing the rich possibilities for his own period of the Celtic sovereignty story. The basic idea was by no means dead, however, nor confined to the Celts. The Doges of Venice were ritually married to the sea, and there is a startling parallel much closer to Chrétien: in 1170 Eleanor wanted to arrange for her favourite son's confirmation as the future Duke of Aquitaine. Among other events a ceremonial symbolic marriage was held in the church of St Stephen at Limoges, between Richard and St Valery, the legendary martyr and patroness of the region (Heer, 1961, p. 170).

It is clear enough that the sovereignty story, as Chrétien handles it, as it appears in Marie de France's lays and in the 'fairy mistress' romances, is a comforting dream of security for landless, wifeless men. But these stories also operate in the other direction, to calm the fears of those who are already in control of property. The motif in *Le Chevalier au Lion* which is the key to this is Yvain's own background. He is the son of a king; a far-off king, it is true, but royalty all the same. This is no doubt why Owein is one of the very few characters who bears his patronymic from Welsh into French. Yvain in *Le Chevalier au Lion* fills the role of the 'fair unknown' in many medieval romances, and this story-structure is held by Luttrell to be basic to Chrétien's poems (1974, ch. 6). In this pattern the hero is at first alone and humble; he is criticised at court, often by Kay, but is finally triumphant and – the crucial point – revealed to have been all the time an unrecognised member of a noble family.

That richly ideological story is a reproduction myth: the society knows that it must find new blood to replenish its forces, but it

fears that the new members of the class will have different values –
an especially urgent anxiety in a time of class expansion. One way
of dealing with this is to impose a class morality, and chivalry is
that imposition in this period. Another less functional but more
immediately consoling response is to have a dream that the
unacceptable incursion never actually happens, that rough and
strange though they might seem, the new men are really all right
all the time. The medieval version of this ideological formation
has been well described by Wittig, who aptly calls the 'fair
unknown' structure the 'male-Cinderella' pattern and specifies its
ideological duality:

> In one sense the romance serves as an apparent vehicle for
> mobility; it offers the hope to the lower class that even a princess
> can be won by a worthy man, whatever his economic and social
> status. But at the same time, it endorses the upper-class belief
> that worth and birth are synonymous, that only a nobleman
> can be a noble man, fit by nature to gain the princess and the
> kingdom and rule over both.   (1978, p. 189)

Yvain does prove his physical right to seize the spring, the lady
and the kingdom, firstly by beating Esclados (who is also only
named once, after he is dead) and secondly and more conclusively
by establishing a great incognito name for himself in the second
part of the poem where he is openly a fair unknown with a *nom de
guerre*, the Knight with the Lion. His success in both parts is based
on violence, as was so often true in reality, whether it was
professional violence in the employ of a lord, or the violence of
heiress-abduction, or sheer opportunistic theft. But Yvain's
innate aristocratic, even royal, blood at least partly euphemises
his force; that point is made at a crucial moment in the text when
Laudine must know his familial quality before accepting him for
his proven power (p. 203, 1802–6). It is clear that his strength is
the true reason. If he was good enough to kill her husband he will
be an even better defender of the spring: but his lineage and his
love mystify into acceptability this archetype of aggressive
advancement, removing the spectre of a crass, murderous *arriviste*
from the text.

So in satisfying both the insecurity of the knights errant and the
anxieties of the barons, the sovereignty motif is highly effective in
ideological terms. And yet, not all is calm. Texts of great impact

are never quite truly settled nor fully confident, for that would be a false response to a dynamically disturbed context. A strain emerges from the dream of sovereignty in that it makes the hero dependent on a woman, and this threatens both the general patriarchal structure of contemporary society and the personal male narcissism of those for whom the hero models. This conflict is overtly enacted in the narrative and deserves a detailed scrutiny.

VI

Masculine neurosis pervades Yvain's arrival at Laudine's castle. In this amazing and memorable scene he pursues Esclados into the fortified gateway of the town. Yvain is trapped there, in the entry to his future lady's dominion's. His horse, saddle and spurs are all slashed in half by the descending outer portcullis. If this is not an image of the male fear of castration in entering the vagina, it is hard to know what might symbolise that. The prevalence of this image in masculine fears has been amply recorded in terms of modern oral 'humour' (Legman, 1978, pp. 489–542) and it is found in this context in other medieval romances (Knight, 1980, p. 15). Another potent image of the same sort is Lancelot's self-mutilating journey across the sword-bridge into his lady's territory in Chrétien's *Le Chevalier de la Charrete* (Plate 7).

The propertied heroine is necessary for the wish-fulfilment dream of landless knights; but that property becomes condensed with a woman's physical nature and her feared demands on, even control of, a husband. This condensation creates fear of emasculation and of losing the cherished masculine freedom, impoverished though it might have been. The whole passage satisfies the dream of knight errantry, provides a suitable model of baronial independence: and then – the crucial aspect of strain that makes the poem so dialectically potent – this consoling and historically credible wish-fulfilment generates new tension at the personal level. The individual is exposed as the basic unit of interest, but is equally exposed as very vulnerable, both physically and psychically.

There is another area of tension in which Yvain operates, and that is his relationship with Gauvain, an uneasy contact rich in ideology. As Arthur's nephew and defender of the elder sister's right Gauvain represents the established power, the *haute noblesse*, primogeniture – three forces hostile respectively to barons, *petite noblesse* and landless knights. In the fight with Harpin, Yvain shows himself able to fill a princely role, acting on behalf of Gauvain's family while he is absent. So Yvain becomes a peer of Gauvain, and that is enacted by their drawn fight over the Noire Espine inheritance. Arthurian romance has traditional patterns of proving for a young knight, a conventional series of deeds which he performs to establish publicly that he is a man of worth, deserving a seat at the Round Table of the *haute noblesse* (Benson, 1976, pp. 70–3). An even combat with a major Round Table figure is a common final event in the proving sequence, and the better the young knight is, the more notable the hero will be: here Gauvain is 'the best knight in the world' (p. 242, 4791).

Equating the royal nephew and the leading hero is obviously an appealing feature of the poem's ideology from both a baronial and, by projection, a knight errant viewpoint. But there is more than this in the relation with Gauvain. In the case of sovereignty it was plain that a pattern acceptable to both knights errant and barons had been constructed but also it had certain residual anxiety. This is true here too. Royal princes have special threatening powers from a baronial viewpoint, and Gauvain is also feared enough to be diminished in the text by a little sleight of hand.

When Gauvain comes with Arthur to visit Yvain's lands he forms a relationship with Lunete, offers her his love and places himself at her disposal (pp. 211–2, 2418–40). But she has already said that only Yvain showed her kindness on her visit to Arthur's court (p. 193, 1012), and when she is in distress later she says that Gauvain is unavailable to help her. This is rationalised through a reference to the quest for Guinevere in *Le Chevalier de la Charrete* – that is where Gauvain has gone. Such rationalisations are often used to conceal ideological strain, and the essential point is that Gauvain's value and presence is elided from the text, just as he is from the relationship with Lunete, which is not heard of again: she is loyal to Yvain, even as his unrequited lover. The basic threat Gauvain poses, as king's nephew, rival at court and with women, is resolved with untidy urgency.

A topic of even greater ideological complexity is the spring. There Yvain's success is first gained, and finally regained. It seems plain that Chrétien was referring to the wonderful fountain near the forest of Brocéliande which Wace mentioned in his *Roman de Rou*, a history of the Normans (lines 1160–74). Celticists have traced Irish sources in a spring from the story of St Brendan and a storm-knight in *Fled Bricrenn* (Loomis, 1949, pp. 278–85 and 289–93), but neither of these sequences is much like what happens in Chrétien's text. Hamilton's world-wide survey of storm-making springs and lakes (1911 and 1914) suggested that there is a potent archetypal force in the scene, and an 'anthropological' interpretation has been offered, that Yvain is killing the king of the sacred grove and spring to take up his perilous role himself (Nitze, 1955, pp. 172–4). That certainly brings in a sense of property, and envisages a nymph of the wood as its tutelary spirit. Two other interpretations at least deserve a mention, the notion that this was a Celtic otherworld story (Frappier, 1969, p. 101; Haidu, 1972, p. 38) and Luria's opinion that the spring scene represents a 'symbolic baptism' (1967, p. 581).

The problem with all these interpretations is that they look externally to other texts, other springs, to see what light they might cast. As a result, such accounts of the episode fit ill or not at all with the other events in the poem and their meaning. There is, however, a connection to be found among all the events, and it can even be found in the Celtic sources if structures, not specific details, are considered. In his thorough book on the material culture of the early Celts, Filip remarks on the connection in Irish tradition of an ogre, a spring and the idea of sovereignty (1977, p. 178) and it is quite clear that the Celtic sovereignty stories often make the fairy mistress a water-nymph. That is certainly a better account of the ultimate source of the spring and the heart of the poem for Chrétien, but it is still without vitality and operative meaning: the function of the scene in the text still needs elaborating in its full context.

To look first at the contemporary historical meaning: Esclados accuses Calogrenant of having made an improper challenge, without notice, without provocation. The incursor has destroyed his woods and damaged his towns and from now on 'there shall be neither truce nor peace between us' (p. 186, 515–6). The language is straight from the register of feudal war as it was in the previous attack: Calogrenant is addressed with contemptuous aggression as *vassaus*, he has not made a formal *desfiance*, he has made *guerre* ('war', not an 'attack', as Comfort says) and Esclados has the right to *plaindre*, to make formal complaint and military response, not just neutrally 'complain' as Comfort has it (p. 186, 491–505). The same register is used when Laudine's seneschal says Arthur is coming to confront them with *guerre* and 'to ravage our lands'

(p. 207, 2084), and so 'all will have been laid waste unless some valiant defender shall appear' (p. 207, 2085–6). When Yvain finally activates the spring with great ferocity there is terrible destruction and the people feel desperately unprotected.

One of the things represented by disturbing the spring is the feudal warfare that was endemic in Normandy and northern France during the eleventh and twelfth centuries. If a dispute existed and was not solved by agreement, the normal step was harrying the enemy's lands – destroying his crops and killing his peasants and beasts, so liquidating his productive capacity. This is what Esclados charges Yvain with and what later it is feared Arthur will do. A further stage in this neighbourly conflict was an attack, often with allied forces, on the offending neighbour's fortified towns and castles. Esclados suggests Yvain almost does this, and when at the end the townspeople curse the man who built their city in this place they imply that it is not capable of proper defence against such a full siege.

The implied reality is that if a property can be gained by thorough war across its borders, the real purpose of defending a borderland is not simply to keep its spring pure but to cut off harrying raids before they can do too much damage – attackers normally turned back if it became clear the assault would be costly. The text cannot describe directly this very common behaviour: it is too simply aggressive, too unchivalric, too lacking in *cortoisie* and too revelatory of the real nature of *proesce*. But as a dominant form of property-seeking masculine self-realisation it cannot be ignored, so it is created by displacement, and in a way that enables the single knight to dream of attaining the level of such activities, binding the knight errant and the baronial interests together. To use a spring as the core of such a displacement does have considerable credibility, since to damage or deny water has always been a potent way of discommoding an enemy. There is in any case a long tradition of fights beside water, that is, at places where passage may be refused – fords and bridges, or where water itself may be denied – springs, wells and streams. But Chrétien's language plainly puts this encounter into the field of feudal war, the quest for masculine self-assertion through winning and extending one's property by sheer *proesce*.

VII

There remains one series of specific episodes to consider before drawing together the motifs of the poem into a general account of its ideological patterns. A number of encounters seem to bear on the distinction between the lower and upper layers of the nobility and the hero's transition from one to the other.

Calogrenant and Yvain represent the knight errant; the former is unsuccessful in his quest for more than a lowly and humiliating position at court, the latter is able to break out of that socio-economic cocoon to become Arthur's equal. Both leave Arthur's court on the same adventure, both go through the same stages, meeting first the Hospitable Host and then the Giant Herdsman, as these figures are usually called in Chrétien studies.

The Hospitable Host is not hard to interpret. He is a *vavasour*, one of many in medieval romance. Their appearances are described in the essay referred to above which also dealt with seneschals (Woledge, 1969): that was an intelligent pairing because one is a reflex of the other. The Host is an unthreatening member of the *petite noblesse* who launches the two knights errant on their quest to surpass the status all three share; he gives them comfort, praise, guidance and above all a courtesy that already implies their superiority. He welcomes them before they can greet him, a definite sign of respect in medieval manners. His castle is not stone, just the old-fashioned and easily stormed timber; he remains a *vavasour*, that is a 'vassal of a vassal', one of that class which romance urgently links in to the upper nobility but which the pretension-baring genre of fabliaux reveals as social upstarts (Pearcy, 1973). From the knight errant viewpoint, the Host scene represents the beginning of the hero's social ascent from the marginally noble class, and the Host's values are the essence of that courtesy which is both the medium of incorporation for the upwardly mobile man and also the means of cementing these *arrivistes* into the baronial interest: the scene works from both viewpoints.

But the Hospitable Host is curiously inoperative in the plot: it is the Herdsman who directs the knights to the spring. He is huge, dark-skinned, one-eyed, one-footed, animalistic – more than man and less than man. He is surrounded by animals whom, in his rough way, he has under complete control: he uses a stag as a gong to assemble his herd in a droll and memorable assertion of his power. But there is more than comedy in this: it points to the ultimate source of the figure. He is a descendant of Cernunnos, the 'Horned One', who in Celtic myth is Lord of Animals. The famous silver cauldron from Gundestrup represents him as uncannily like the Herdsman in the Welsh *Owein*, who has stag, serpents and lions ready to hand (1968, lines 130–5, see Plate 8). As with so many other Celtic motifs, Chrétien developed the figure to create his own ideological concerns. It has been pointed out that the French Herdsman is in important ways like the contemporary archetype of the agricultural labourer (Jonin, 1964, pp. 50–1). He is a symbol of those people who worked with animals and were seen as themselves part animal – he is 'master of my beasts' (p. 184, 355). The plot intimately links him to the Hospitable Host, and the two figures are by implication aspects of the same person.

The Herdsman represents the fertility and prosperity of the rural property holder. He controls the animal means of reproduction that makes figures like the Host so rich. It is ideologically important that the Herdsman should send the hero on to his encounter at the spring because he symbolises a material base for the rise of the lower nobility which is rural, and so acceptably *vileyn*, not truly and threateningly *vileyn* by drawing his power from the mercantilism of a *ville*. At the same time his animal vitality and imposing physical presence imply the dynamic vigour of the knights who combine sheer and skilful prowess with Hostly courteous behaviour as their passport into the noble and propertied life.

This dual sequence, however, is not the only relationship the text has with the *petite noblesse*. In the sequence of adventures in the second part of the poem Yvain has two experiences which match and reverse the effect of the Hospitable Host and the Giant Herdsman.

The first is his encounter with Harpin of the Mountain. He has severely harassed the family of Gauvain's sister; he has killed two sons and captured the other four, so is about to extinguish their male line; he is threatening now to take their daughter as a hostage and defile her by giving her to his scullions for their pleasure. There are plenty of ogres in Arthurian romance, and they suggest threatening, unchivalric forces. But Harpin is not just a generally gross ogre. His name appears to mean 'Hooked' or 'Having claws', implying a means of hanging on rather than destroying: the Old French word 'harpin' means a boat-hook. If the detailed action is juxtaposed with the idea of clawing at for the sake of attachment, Harpin's ideological meaning becomes discernible even through the displacements and coding processes that have obscured it.

Harpin has neutralised the sons of the aristocratic family and will now defile the daughter. The uncivil mountain man represents the threat of insurgence from the lower orders into a weakened upper nobility: these *arrivistes* are indistinguishable from *vileyns* when seen from a lofty viewpoint, and to describe them as churls is itself an emotionally satisfying response to their threat. The details make it clear that Harpin's threat is more complex than the real class-confrontation of the Jacquerie-type risings that were common throughout medieval France. There is a striking analogy to Chrétien's use of Harpin in the poems of Marcabrun, who reviles social upstarts and uses a wide range of sexual and class invective to contain what is patently an incursive threat of some force (Lawner, 1973). The threat that Harpin will defile the daughter is the knight errant's dream of a property marriage seen from the other side, from the viewpoint of those whose daughters and lands are to be snapped up.

The intriguing thing, of course, is that Yvain is now against this figure, when he was on such good terms with the Giant Herdsman who was a positive representation of this uncouth *arriviste* vigour. Since he attained lady, land and comradeship with Gauvain, Yvain's position (like that of many recently ascended people) seems to have radically changed: his viewpoint and actions are now favourable to the upper nobility whom he has just joined.

In both the Giant Herdsman and the Harpin episodes a good deal of interpretation is necessary, since the disturbing forces at work require considerable displacement before they can be confronted, either positively or negatively. But just as the Hospitable Host scene was fairly straightforward in its meaning, so is its reflex, Yvain's experiences at Pesme Aventure.

In the castle Yvain finds a bizarre mixture: a yard full of ill-clad, ill-treated maidens sewing away; two 'half-devils' who supervise them and attack knights errant; a very suave lord who lives in the height of luxury and apologises for the two *netuns* who administer the castle and its evil custom.

Through the maidens Chrétien refers to the sweat-shop conditions of the clothing industry in his own part of France (Jonin, 1964, pp. 53–4). It has been argued that this is impossible, because no factories large enough to employ three hundred yet existed so Chrétien must be thinking of the Middle East (Hall, 1941). This reductive and neatly foreigner-blaming argument overlooks the fact that poets can exaggerate to make a point. A better piece of scholarship leads firmly to the meaning of the scene: Loomis (1949, pp. 323–5) showed that the word *chanpion*, used for the *netuns* as they prepare to fight (5575) is a technical term, and they are accordingly dressed and armed just as non-aristocratic sergeants would be if fighting in judicial conflict. Together the maidens and the 'champions' represent the physical and economic reality of urban mercentilism. They are much more forcefully present at Pesme Aventure than in any of Chrétien's other towns, and they were of central importance at Troyes itself, where the lucrative cloth fair was run by the count's officials and sergeants (Holmes and Klenke, 1959, pp. 9–10).

Supported by these forces, and also shamefully controlled by them, are the lord and his family. They live in a luxury that seems brand new and artificial. Their hall, which Yvain enters straight from the open-air workshop, is wonderful and new (p. 248, 5190) and their garden is not only lovely and made by artifice: they are listening to a romance in it. This is Chrétien's only mention of such an activity, a telling moment of self-awareness from the creator of a literary ideology which works towards concealing the strains that this very scene partially exposes. Finally, when the victorious Yvain is offered the maiden and declines, the lord responds with rudeness: 'Now go about your business. For it is quite the same to me whether you go or whether you stay' (p. 255, 5769–70). Yvain's own promise to return 'if possible' is the height of white-lie politeness, most unlike the elegant but churlish lord; Yvain retains the obscuring value of courtesy, as he hurries away from Pesme Aventure, this 'bad encounter' with the truth.

The whole sequence is a striking exposé of the *nouveau riche*, of a nobility which is, from a conservative viewpoint, improperly based. Pesme Aventure is a negative reflex of the vavasour's house. They are linked by a luxurious garden (Haidu, 1972, p. 37), but here the wealth is embarrassingly exploitative and mercantile; there the cause of wealth was at first invisible and then suggested to be the natural productivity of the Herdsman and his charges.

However, the two scenes are not merely negative and positive analyses of the forces inherent in the *petite noblesse*. Because of their

arrangement in the text, before and after Yvain's access to
property and nobility, and because the negative treatment is a
part of his recovery of his lost land and nobility, it becomes clear
that the upwardly mobile knight errant first uses and then rejects
the essence of his originating class. That is by no means an
unfamiliar pattern today, and Chrétien has embedded it with
great skill in the ideological ensemble of his poem. Once again the
impact is equally consoling for knight errant and for baron. The
text realises and tries to contain the fact that there were many
hookers-on and many bad encounters to disturb the precarious
edifice of chivalric and courteous aristocratic ideology.

VIII

Throughout the specific scenes which have now been analysed,
there have run a number of recurring ideological threads. These
have not been developed so far because they can only be com-
prehended in a more general overview of the poem. Essentially,
the dynamic of the whole text is *proesce* and *cortoisie*, that dialectic
relation between sheer knightly bravery and skill on one hand and
social and ideal values, or mystifications, on the other. It is
because of the central importance of this complex relationship
that it has been used in the title of this chapter.

In social terms the dominant ideological tension of the poem is
between an individual acting for his own ends and a collectivity.
To fight at the spring Yvain leaves the court in urgent secret.
Comfort's translation moderates this a little: he has Yvain's
squire wait with his horse 'one side of the road in a place apart',
but Chrétien writes 'far from the road in a detour' (p. 190, 757).
Comfort also softens Yvain's attitude, saying he 'yearns eagerly'
for the path to the spring and 'great is his desire' to see the
herdsman, but Chrétien says he is *trop cusanconeus*, 'over anxious'
to find the path and that *Li veoirs li demore et tarde* from seeing the
herdsman, an idiomatic way of saying 'he is impatient to see' him
(p. 189, 700 and 710).

   There is important meaning in this note of over-anxiety, of
unbridled *proese* on Yvain's part. It isolates what he is doing as
odd, distinctly anti-social and not *cortois*. This is the more evident

because from Pentecost to St John's Eve (that is from Arthur's feast to his promised arrival at the spring) was a period traditionally free from military activities, devoted to campaigning for honour and profit: it was set aside for knight errantry (Heer, 1961, p. 171). In the action of the story this was only a fortnight, which has led some positivist commentators to date the poem in a year with a very late Easter such as 1169 (Holmes, 1970, pp. 104–5). That is a reductive misinterpretation of the point: Chrétien employs a very short period to make more urgent Yvain's self-imposed task of literally stealing a march on Arthur. The text does give another reason for Yvain's private departure. If he went to the spring with the collective knight errantry, Arthur would surely give the challenge at the spring to Gauvain or to Kay ahead of him (p. 189, 682–8). To be *cortois*, Yvain would have to defer to them, and so his *proesce* could not achieve advancement in the euphemising guise of honour. The explanation of Yvain's departure, the secrecy of his journey, the distinctly pejorative trace of over-eagerness, all these factors point inwards to a crucial conflict in the romances and the character of feudalism generally, and one that has been misinterpreted by recent critics as an admiring realisation of an individualist hero.

On the contrary, the essential point is that when the text emphasises individualism it is seen as a critical state, dangerous to the individual himself and to the society he eludes. When Yvain sneaks away, the primacy of the public social world is recognised in his very secrecy. And as with other lone adventurers in chivalric fiction, his journey is a fantasy. A knight never rode alone. He needed someone to lead his war-horse, which was too valuable to ride all the time, and he needed someone to arm him for battle, because his armour was too uncomfortable to wear all the time, too awkward to put on by himself. The lonely knight, riding through the forests ever-ready for self-proving and profitable combat is a dream-like projection of the state of anxious isolated manhood, hoping to gain honour and property by deeds of arms. This extreme individualism is both a fantasy and a perilous state.

Nevertheless, one forceful trend in criticism has been to treat *Le Chevalier au Lion* and Chrétien's other poems, even *Le Conte del Graal*, as if they are novels dealing with the consciousness of an individualist hero – one study is even called *Chrétien de Troyes: Inventor of the Modern Novel* (Guyer, 1960). Literary individualism in the twelfth century has been isolated from its social context and approvingly displayed by Hanning (1972 and 1977) and Dronke (1970); its religious equivalent has been canonised by Morris (1972). There is, however, a book on medieval individualism which is not special pleading and which gives the key to the conflict of hero and class in *Le Chevalier au Lion*. This is Ullmann's *The Individual and Society in the Middle Ages* (1966). He points out that the institution of feudalism was in its structural operations markedly individualised. The fief was handed to a liege by a lord, and the fidelity was personal, not to the country or the family; nor did the fief descend to the liege's heirs without the creation, at the Lord's pleasure, of a new personal bond.

This reality was culturally obscured. Homage was performed publicly to collectivise the feudal relationship; the dominant sense of reality and value remained public. Similarly, an oath was a single person's word, which was ratified collectively by a variety of means – confirmed by other individuals, or performed in public, or empowered by holy words and relics. However, homage-giving and oaths are not especially important in *Le Chevalier au Lion*. The clearest and most fully developed sign of the disturbing character of individualism in this text, as in other Arthurian romances, lies in the area of honour.

Honour was an idealisation of great scope and considerable contemporary authenticity – after all, a fief was called an honour, and oaths were sworn by a person's honour. The elements of honour-based social values have already been discussed (see Chapter 1). It is usually said that in an honour-based society, honour and shame are the operative and public evaluations and that in a guilt-oriented society, as ours is now said to be, punishment must be personal, by pain (financial or physical) or by restriction of liberty, and the positive value is held to be self-satisfaction, a sense that one has fulfilled or even discovered one's individual being. A moment's thought suggests that matters are less simple than this, and that the alleged 'modern' structure of values incites individualism as much as the 'medieval' one promoted collectivity. And since it is evident that peer-group approval is very important in our society in spite of the individualist set of its values, it is likely that the earlier period also had a structure both public and private, with an ideological drift towards collectivity. Both history and fiction show this is so: knights whether real or Arthurian actually won honour as they won property, by fierce competition against other knights. But the mystifying aura of fraternity and the ideals of chivalry were used to obscure and collectivise this individualist aggression.

For example, the fight between Yvain and Gauvain ends in mutual honour and fraternity. But this is a perilous balance achieved from fierce competitiveness, and they only draw by trying to give each other the victory, that is, by reversing the dominant competitive structure. They only stop to exchange compliments, then names, when each realises that in spite of all his efforts he cannot win. The scene, like the formal tournaments in Arthurian romance, stylises and so makes acceptable the innate individualism of the aggressive heroes.

The Yvain-Gauvain fight also clarifies the importance of the incognito motif as a mechanism in this whole process; it is very common in proving sequences, and its impact is to enable knights to fight the hero without recognising him, as he is either bearing unblazoned arms or those of some other knight (often the unpopular and incompetent Sir Kay). Without his name publicly known the knight can exercise the individualist ferocity which was in reality basic to feudal society: once his name is known his public honour and concomitant social duty emerge and he must exercise the collective ideology of the aristocracy, presented in fiction as the ethics of the Round Table. To avoid the constraints of *cortoisie*, his *proesce* must be nameless; having achieved its objects it can relax in the mutual security of *cortoisie*.

In presenting that individualist aggression the text enacts the grasping, brutal acquisitiveness of knights and lords in the period, by which they actually won and defended their honour and the material power it symbolised. Henry II of England and his unappealing sons are good examples of such naked *proesce*; Louis VII of France is a notable exception. At the same time the text enacts in *courtoisie* the cultural overlay that asserted all was for the best in the best of chivalric, publicly conscious worlds. This too was real; the ideal of chivalry provided various forms and rituals which could bring Henry II to meet with Louis VII and swear allegiance to him for Anjou and Maine, though the two kings were bitter enemies. More sharply still, these public forms were substitutes for sheer aggression. Henry again provides a good example: as Count of Anjou he held Touraine, but it was held from the Count of Blois, not from the King of France. So to keep a small but strategically valuable county this king of awesome power would happily kneel and swear faithful service to a relatively minor count. Nobody ever expected him to serve anything other than his own interest, certainly not to obey Blois or go to war for him. The county was worth a lie; the ideological superstructure both permitted and concealed such profitable private actions.

Yvain, to fulfil the acquisitive dreams of the knights errant and realise the independent self-consciousness of the great lords, must journey alone, away from the others like Kay and Gauvain who would have preference over him by public right. He must later avoid that collectivity by not camping within Arthur's city and power. And after this dream-like individual quest and the equally lonely adventures in the second part of the poem, he is established as lord of a kingdom which, with its ghostly 'knights' and 'townspeople' is quite unlike the threatening reality of Pesme Aventure. Laudine's town and kingdom are only the shadow of a collectivity, an unthreatening token recognition of the cultural dominance of collective institutions over private aggression. To see the dialectic pressure of the *proesce* of the individual and the *cortois* collectivity in *Le Chevalier au Lion* is to see both the text's credibility for the lonely and dispossessed warriors and also the ideological impact of chivalry and *cortoisie*. They concealed those disorderly but real forces of individualistic aggression, and did so in a way that conformed with both the actual and the conceptual institutions of the period.

If *proesce* and *cortoisie* are realised in social terms as a conflict of the individual and the collective, in terms of behavioural practice, the text is uneasily strained between its underlying praise of naked aggression (*proesce* at its barest) and its overt applause of chivalric values – the elaborations of *cortoisie*. When a knight shows courage in single battle against another powerful knight, or against odds, or against an ogre, he exercises the virtue of *proesce*, which has a central meaning of courage, and an attached sense of knightly skills. To show *proesce* makes you a *preud-homme* or in Chrétien's spelling a *prodon*, a man of courage, skill, honour – and also a man of power and property. Etymology and ideology can be close kin, and it is revealing to note that the adjective *prod* is also a noun meaning, quite simply, profit. There is something to be gained by this courage, this superiority in one-to-one combat.

Essentially, *Le Chevalier au Lion*, like other chivalric romances, tells that stark story that the strongest is the richest. Yvain kills Esclados, takes lady and land. Kay cannot kill Yvain, so the land is not appropriated by Arthur, Kay's lord. The simple physical superiority of the well-armed, well-mounted and well-trained knight, that basis of Norman power and of aristocratic dominance in the early Middle Ages, is the underlying structure of power and values in these stories. The most ferocious battles are fought either to appropriate property, as with Esclados, or to defend it, as with Harpin, or to dispute its transmission, as with Gauvain. Many details in the text bear the message of raw physical conflict for power and property.

On his way to the spring Yvain has minor fights, but not being profit-oriented they are not discussed in the story of this *prodon*, this profit-man (p. 190, 766–7). His act at the spring is one of deliberate provocative aggression, and Esclados's death wound is given grisly emphasis. Later on, in the reprise of this scene, the text dwells on Yvain's fury as, still with the lion, he whips up the spring into an unparalleled storm (p. 265, 6535–9). For Laudine and her knights, as well as for Yvain, the matter of the spring is sheer physical necessity – a fighting knight must be stationed there. Or he must be when Yvain is the challenger or the knight: the story elides away the question of who defended the spring when Yvain was away, and why some other did not take it. In accepting Yvain as the spring knight, Laudine has physical power in mind before any legitimation that love or nobility may bring (p. 202, 1737). The fight with Count Alier is similarly a physical matter, all sheer skill and power and endurance (p. 221, 3152–234). After that Yvain meets the lion, who externalises his physicality and his capacity for violence.

The lion is a symbol central to this tension between *proesce* and the euphemising value of *cortoisie*. Chrétien's title to the romance privileges the lion and criticism has engaged with gusto in the problem of its meaning. The more extreme versions see in the noble beast a figure of Grace (Luria, 1967, p. 569), a figure of Christ (Harris, 1949, p. 1163), or the structural opposite of Gauvain as Yvain's companion (Lacy, 1970–1). It is more usual to find some sort of chivalric value represented: fidelity is central for Frappier (1969, p. 21), together with an outer ring of force, nobility and generosity (1969, pp. 213–6). Ferrante surveys the various meanings, including strength, courtesy, courage, gratitude, generosity, but she too comes down in favour of fidelity (1975, p. 114). Haidu, who treats the topic at some length, finds the lion 'polysémique', a symbol referring not only to Christ, but also to Satanic ferocity and to the humanisation of the lion in the Androcles story (1972, pp. 57–71).

Some of these interpretations, especially the Christian ones, derive from what lions mean elsewhere; others have some relation with the text, trying to find what Yvain represents when he is with the lion (courage, nobility and so on), or what the lion does in the story (force, courage), or what the lion feels towards Yvain (fidelity, gratitude). But for a full comprehension of the lion, he must be interpreted in the context of the meaning of the whole poem.

It is clear that Yvain and the lion are closely related: they share many misfortunes and adventures. The *nom de guerre*, 'The Knight with the Lion', privileges Yvain's fighting skill, the *proesce* that is basic to his success and to that of knights errant and barons alike in the period. Yet the lion is a noble beast, hence Yvain's preference for him over the serpent, and that image itself contains the seeds of the 'noble' euphemisation of warrior power. This is developed in the action, where the lion is closely controlled by *cortoisie* and only acts in a crisis: he is free to fight the savage Harpin, but is excluded from the more formal fights, with Laudine's seneschal and with the *netuns* at Pesme Aventure. He breaks out to help Yvain when he is under real pressure and so signifies the final physical resources of a man who is truly *preu*, a force not present in formal fighting until the crisis and not necessary at all in the highly sophisticated and culturally resolved final fight with Gauvain.

The lion and Yvain are a potent realisation and the major focus of the dialectic of *proesce* and *cortoisie* in the poem. There are a number of other occurrences of the tension, often in forms which indicate the inherent strain involved. For example, there is Yvain's sudden love for Laudine, conceived as he sees her mourn over her dead husband. Love, in its full elegance as *fin amor*, is one of the major euphemising and legitimising elements in this and other romances. The poem opened with praise of courteous lovers from the past (p. 180, 21–3), and Yvain, the upwardly mobile travelling murderer, is suddenly transformed into a model of blushing love.

The general function of love as a part of courteous mystification is clear; it is equally plain that in evaluative terms it is secondary to knighthood. When knighthood and love encounter one another, the former is either damaged by love or is given evaluative precedence over it. Gauvain says both these things in his long speech before he and Yvain leave Laudine. First, he urges Yvain that after marriage he will have 'got worse' (p. 212, 2494; not 'grown soft' as Comfort has it). Then Gauvain says that Yvain, as a result, will lose his own friendship – the privileged values of knightly fraternity will be lost to him.

The fact that Yvain agrees to leave, forgets to return and is then both abused and deeply shamed indicates that Gauvain's position is not truly acceptable. Or, to be more accurate, not *overtly* acceptable. In fact, the covert practice of the poem seems to support Gauvain's view and adopt an entirely masculine viewpoint. There is a whole series of references which set the values of knighthood and love at odds, and imply the former have greater weight. When Love comes to Yvain, Love has no care for honour or dishonour (p. 198, 1386–90); love is said to 'sweeten', that is reduce, Yvain's fear of mockery (p. 197, 1356–7); a wound from love is worse than a war-wound (p. 197, 1369–74); love makes Yvain fear the lady (p. 205, 1986–9).

Throughout these references the vocabulary is that of the warrior, not the lover. The linguistic register of language itself suggests that love is disruptive, unnatural. The viewpoint remains that of knighthood, being steadily damaged and destroyed by love. Haidu has pointed out how the very language used as Yvain and Laudine come together is feudal, and that Chrétien has specifically omitted the aspects of feudal allegiance (handholding and the kiss of allegiance) which are shared with love-behaviour (1972, pp. 42–4). In the light of these subtle implications, Gauvain's harangue is not unprecedented, and it seems the less surprising that it goes unanswered.

While the overt plot of the poem indicates that what Yvain does in forgetting Laudine is wrong and not *cortois*, it does not privilege the values of love, and its sub-text tends to contradict its overt opinion. After the breach with Laudine the isolated Yvain acts as a warrior, not a prostrate lover; when he *is* prostrate through grief this threatens to be the death of his *proesce* through the suicide of the lion; when he laments as a lover he hears that Lunete is worse off and as a knight he can save her. In his adventures in the second part of the poem he is a true warrior, showing full *proesce* and, as he thrusts his way in to Pesme Aventure, the warrior's *folie*, the true heroic *élan* and lust for adventure in all circumstances (p. 247, 5176).

In keeping with this structure, whereas Gauvain's company and values separated Yvain from Laudine, his reuniting with her does not breach his relation with Gauvain. That is sealed with mutual respect and affection before Yvain suddenly and conveniently senses that he would die without Laudine (p. 265, 6511-6). Once again it is as a fighting man that Yvain wins her. He goes to 'fight at the spring' Comfort says, making it sound like a normal affair, but Chrétien uses the verb *guerroier*, 'to make war' (p. 265, 6519). This he does so ferociously that Laudine recognises her need of a champion and accepts the fiercely named 'Knight with the Lion' because of his military reputation. From his first secret mission to his final fury of provocative destruction, Yvain represents an admired aggressive warrior who is masked by various processes of aristocratic mystification, just as in reality the classes who depended on military power to appropriate the material basis for that power and their prestigious, honourable lives consistently offered chivalry and courtesy, even *fin amor*, as instrumental values, when in fact they were aspects of a false consciousness, consoling to themselves and concealing to those who were in fact oppressed.

IX

Proesce and *cortoisie* are, the opening lines of the poem insist, both essential and related (p. 180, 2-3). There is tension between them. Medieval illustrations of honourable fighting often show how the bloody deed of the individual is set in the social context with some awkwardness (Plates 9 and 10). Chrétien exploits this tension and treats *proesce* and *cortoisie* to emphasise the strain between the collective social model and the actually aggressive individual in feudal society. At the same time he employs *proesce* and *cortoisie* as idealistic values which mystify away that violent acquisitiveness.

Finally, it is important to see that the poem is not in its impact a meticulous analysis, neatly multi-levelled like an archaeological excavation: rather it is a vital synthesis like the living settlement. Condensed, suggestive, dynamic, it realises together the political and the personal aspects of tension in the period. Chrétien's ability is to develop images and actions as a totality, without succumbing to reductive deformations, whether medieval and collective or modern and only individual. To comprehend that and to see the processes of Chrétien's remarkable achievement is both a necessary and a sufficient explanation of the power of *Le Chevalier au Lion*.

The result of that power is that throughout the Arthurian legend in its many French-derived versions, the motifs and sequences that Chrétien developed here and in his other romances occur again and again. The Vulgate Arthuriad, which set itself both to collect and to rationalise the stories about Arthur and his knights, is enormously longer than Chrétien's poems combined. But in many ways it only amplified the issues which he had condensed into his extraordinarily fertile texts, *Le Chevalier au Lion* being a leader among them for richness and influence. Both the Vulgate's massive elaboration and Chrétien's pervasive ideological imagination are potent influences on the work of Sir Thomas Malory, who in the late fifteenth century wrote the first major English Arthuriad, a text which has since dominated the legend in English.

REFERENCES

Primary Sources
Chrétien de Troyes (1948) *Yvain (Le Chevalier au Lion)* ed. T. B. W. Reid, 2nd edn (Manchester University Press), trans. W. W. Comfort in *Arthurian Romances by Chrétien de Troyes* with Introduction by D. D. R. Owen (London: Dent, 1975).
Thomson, R. L. ed. (1968) *Owein* or *Y Iarlles y Ffynawn* ('The Lady of the Fountain') (Dublin Institute for Advanced Studies Press), trans. G. Jones and T. Jones in *The Mabinogion* 2nd edn (London: Dent, 1974).

Secondary Sources
Barber, R. W. (1973) *King Arthur in Legend and History* (London: Cardinal).
Benson, L. D. (1976) *Malory's Morte d'Arthur* (Cambridge, Mass.: Harvard University Press).
Benton, J. F. (1961) 'The Court of Champagne as a Literary Center', *Speculum* 36, 551–91.
Bloch, M. (1961) *Feudal Society* (London: Routledge).
Bromwich, R. (1961) 'Celtic Dynastic Themes and the Breton Lays', *Etudes Celtiques* 9, 439–74.
Diverres, A. H. (1973) 'Chivalry and Fin Amor in *Le Chevalier au Lion*' in *Studies . . . in Memory of F. Whitehead* (Manchester University Press).

Dronke, P. (1970) *Poetic Individuality in the Middle Ages* (Oxford: Clarendon Press).

Duby, G. (1977) 'Youth in Aristocratic Society' in *The Chivalrous Society* (London: Arnold).

Evergates, T. (1975) *Feudal Society in the Bailliage of Troyes under the Counts of Champagne, 1152–1284* (Baltimore: Johns Hopkins University Press).

Ferrante, J. M. (1975) 'The Conflict of Lyric Conventions and Romance Form' in *The Pursuit of Perfection: Courtly Love in Medieval Literature*, ed. J. M. Ferrante and G. Economou (Port Washington: Kennikat).

Filip, J. (1977) *Celtic Civilisation and its Heritage* (Wellingborough: Collett).

Frappier, J. (1969) *Etude sur Yvain ou Le Chevalier au Lion de Chrétien de Troyes* (Paris: Societé d'Editions d'Enseignement Supérieur).

Goetinck, G. (1975) *Peredur: A Study of Welsh Tradition in the Grail Legends* (Cardiff: University of Wales Press).

Gold, P. (1977) 'Image and Reality: Women in Twelfth Century France', Ph.D. thesis, Stanford University).

Guyer, F. E. (1960) *Chrétien de Troyes: Inventor of the Modern Novel* (London: Vision).

Haidu, P. (1972) *Lion-queue-coupée: l'écart symbolique chez Chrétien de Troyes* (Geneva: Droz).

Hall, R. A. Jr. (1941) 'The Silk Factory in Chrétien de Troyes' *Yvain*', *Modern Language Notes* 56, 418–22.

Hamilton, G. L. (1911) 'Storm-Making Springs: Studies on the Sources of *Yvain*', *Romanic Review* 2, 355–75.

—— (1914) 'Storm-Making Springs: Rings of Invisibility: Studies on the Sources of the *Yvain* of Chrétien de Troyes', *Romanic Review* 5, 213–37.

Hanning, R. W. (1972) 'The Social Significance of Twelfth-Century Chivalric Romance', *Medievalia et Humanistica* n.s. 3, 3–29.

—— (1977) *The Individual and Society in Twelfth Century Romance* (New Haven: Yale University Press).

Harris, J. (1949) 'The Role of the Lion in Chrétien de Troyes' *Yvain*', *Proceedings of the Modern Language Association of America* 54, 1143–62.

Heer, F. (1961) *The Medieval World, 1100–1350* (London: Weidenfeld and Nicholson).

Herlihy, D. (1962) 'Land, Family and Women in Continental Europe', *Traditio* 18, 89–120.

Hofer, S. (1954) *Chretien de Troyes: Leben und Werke des altfranzösische Epikers* (Graz/Köln: Bohlaus).

Holmes, U. T. (1970) *Chrétien de Troyes* (New York: Twayne).

—— and Klenke, M. A. (1959) *Chrétien, Troyes and the Grail* (Chapel Hill: University of North Carolina Press).

Jonin, P. (1964) 'Aspectes de la vie sociale au xiiᵉ siècle dans *Yvain*', *L'information littéraire* 16, 47–54.

Knight, S. (1980) 'Ideology in "The Franklin's Tale" ', *Parergon* 28, 3–35.

Köhler, E. (1960) 'Le rôle de "coutume" dans les romans de Chrétien de Troyes', *Romania* 81, 385–97.

—— (1964) 'Observations historiques et sociologiques sur la poésie des troubadours', *Cahiers de Civilisation Medievale* 7, 27–51.

—— (1974) *L'aventure chevaleresque: Ideal et realité dans le roman courtois* (Paris: Gallimard).

Lacy, N. J. (1970–1) 'Yvain's Evolution and the Role of the Lion', *Romance Notes* 12, 198–202.

Lawner, L. (1973) 'Marcabrun and the Origins of Trobar Clus' in *The Medieval World* ed. D. Daiches and A. Thorlby (London: Aldus).

Legman, G. (1978) *No Laughing Matter: The Rationale of the Dirty Joke* 2nd series (London: Granada).

Loomis, R. S. (1949) *Arthurian Tradition and Chrétien de Troyes* (New York: Columbia University Press).

Lovecy, I. C. (1977–8) 'The Celtic Sovereignty-Theme and the Structure of *Peredur*', *Studia Celtica* 12/13, 133–46.

Luria, M. (1967) 'The Storm-Making Spring and the Meaning of Chrétien's *Yvain*', *Studies in Philology* 64, 564–85.

Luttrell, C. (1974) *The Creation of the First Arthurian Romance: A Quest* (London: Arnold).

Moller, H. (1958–9) 'The Social Causation of the Courtly Love Complex', *Comparative Studies in Society and History* 1, 137–63.

Morris, C. (1972) *The Discovery of the Individual* (London: Society for Propagation of Christian Knowledge).

Nitze, W. (1955) '*Yvain* and the Myth of the Fountain', *Speculum* 30, 170–9.

Pearcy, R. J. (1973) 'Chaucer's Franklin and the Literary Vavasour', *Chaucer Review*, 8, 33–59.

Reid, T. B. W. (1948) 'Introduction to *Yvain*', see under Chrétien de Troyes (1948).

Salter, E. 'Courts and Courtly Love' in *The Medieval World*, see under Lawner (1973).

Ullmann, W. (1966) *The Individual and Society in the Middle Ages* (Baltimore: Johns Hopkins University Press).

Wittig, S. (1978) *Stylistics and Narrative Structures in the Middle English Romances* (Austin: University of Texas Press).

Woledge, B. (1969) 'Bons vavasseurs et mauvais seneschaux' in *Mélanges offerts à Rita Lejeune* (Gembloux: Duculot).

4 'A grete angur and unhappe': Sir Thomas Malory's Arthuriad

I

Sir Thomas Malory finished his collection of Arthurian stories in 1469–70 and since then his work has dominated the legend in English. Almost all later accounts are directly or indirectly based on the structure Malory created, largely from French and English sources but also, too rarely recognised by critics, from his own imagination.

Both the work and the author present some initial problems. Two distinct versions of the text exist. That known as *Le Morte Darthur*, printed by Caxton in 1485, was the only one for centuries and modern versions of it are still widely available. The Winchester manuscript which was dramatically discovered in 1934 (Oakeshott, 1963) and then edited by Vinaver is the earlier and fuller version. However, there has been argument about the status of this text. Vinaver himself thought it was eight separate romances, not one long story, hence his title *The Works of Sir Thomas Malory*. Vinaver's critics have insisted it is one unified, novel-like structure. Both opinions are extreme, as I have discussed elsewhere (Knight, 1969). Malory actually wrote a long narrative which contains both medieval looseness and, towards the end, a more modern type of unity. So it is best to avoid the special pleading of titles like *The Works* and *Le Morte Darthur*, and use the flexible description, Malory's Arthuriad.

The author refers to himself as a 'knight-prisoner', and it was a moment of some scholarly excitement when records threw up a Sir Thomas Malory who had been in and out of jail at the right time. The fullest survey of the life-records is by Matthews (1966, ch. 1). From Newbold Revell in Warwickshire, this Malory was often charged with and sometimes convicted of crimes, occasionally

105

imprisoned, included in a general pardon in 1461 and excluded from one in 1468. He died in 1471. In the past he seemed unusually active in old age both as criminal and writer because he was thought to have served with the Earl of Warwick at Calais in 1414–5, but this connection is now thought unlikely (Field, 1979–80).

Some crimes associated with him include cattle-stealing, criminal assault, robbery and the sack of a nunnery. However, a lot of the alleged crimes have political connections. As befitted a Warwickshire man, the evidence indicates Malory was closely connected with the Earl of Warwick, Richard Neville, known as 'the Kingmaker'. Political activism and dirty tricks mixed with some private score-settling and opportunism seem to account for the whole slate of accusations against Malory. The pattern is by no means improbable or even unfamiliar for a member of the gentry in the middle of the violent fifteenth century.

Doubts have been cast on this identification of Malory. Matthews (1966) argued that the Warwickshire man had neither the right dialect nor the necessary access to sources to be the author. But his linguistic argument was inaccurate (McIntosh, 1968) and his own candidate, a Yorkshire Thomas Malory, was never a knight. The same problem faces the recently suggested East Anglian Malory (Griffith, 1981). The weight of the evidence still points to the Warwickshire man as the author (Field, 1979). Some of the material brought forward in this chapter about the historical context of the Arthuriad supports that view, since events connected with the Yorkist cause and the Earl of Warwick himself are prominent.

Matthews did show that the sources Malory used were rare in the period. But the knight whose authorship he doubted might have had access to them in two places. As Matthews himself mentions, one was in the south-west of France, where under the patronage of the Duc de Nemours a work in many ways like Malory's was produced, a shortened and unified French Arthuriad written by Michel Gonnot in the 1460s. Sir Thomas of Warwickshire, it has since been shown, had at least some connections with the area (Field, 1979, p. 225). But if, as seems most probable, he was Warwick's man, it is very likely that he was with the great earl in at least some of his many contacts with Burgundy in the late 1450s and early 1460s. Philip the Bold, Duke of Burgundy, was an Arthurian enthusiast and possessed many of the manuscripts Malory used (Kendall, 1957, p. 166; Matthews, 1966, p. 142). Translating, condensing and unifying earlier material was a major practice of the sophisticated Burgundian literary world, and there is a plain relation to Malory: he 'did for Arthur and Lancelot what the Burgundian translators and compilers were doing for Charlemagne and his paladins' (Pearsall, 1976, p. 79).

The Burgundian connection shows Malory's work was not unique but resembled cultural activities in the area most like England, another country whose economy was rapidly becoming mercantile and wealthy but which was still politically feudal in basis. Such a socio-economic structure was the basis for what has been called *The Indian Summer of English Chivalry* (Ferguson, 1960), a period in the mid to late fifteenth century when a great amount of material on the theory and practice of chivalry was produced, at a time when the mounted knight was no longer a force on the battlefield, when feudalism had been transmuted into the financial and contractual arrangements of bastard feudalism, and when the incomes of the great were increasingly derived from business, especially the sale of wool and cloth.

Malory's role was to offer chivalry as an ideology to those who could not understand French. It is not easy to say exactly who was Malory's audience but it is fair to assume they were the same as Caxton's. He learned his cultural trade in Burgundy, transplanted it with success to England and produced a very high ratio of chivalric works. As with other early booksellers, his audience was predominantly the urban rich, who might well be landed country gentlemen as well, and would inevitably include those wealthy merchants and powerful peers whose success and influence were interdependent. For them Malory defined in credible terms the tensions and shocks of the fifteenth century, as well as its ideas of how best to continue the powerful, wealthy, book-buying life.

Malory's Arthuriad is very long; it could hardly be dealt with exhaustively even in a book, let alone a chapter. Here I will try to give the essence of its character and its historical relevance. The first five 'Tales' as Vinaver calls them will be discussed as a group. They occupy some two-thirds of the whole Arthuriad and include the enormously long, under-read and under-rated Tristram tale; they have a reasonably coherent socio-historical character. Tale VI, the story of the Quest for the Holy Grail, will be treated briefly – it has a limited contemporary value for Malory but leads him to crucial features of both the approach and resolution to the last tales, VII and VIII.

These are Malory's most clearly original work, and the ones to which modern readers respond most strongly. In them contemporary concerns are both most evident in the text and most disturbing. The final catastrophe both realises and resolves the dramas of the later 1460s, when the Yorkists fell out among themselves, when the great Warwick came to oppose the king he had largely created and had powerfully supported, when international and domestic politics rose to a tragic climax in civil war again. And when somewhere, excluded from pardon, Sir Thomas Malory was earning posterity's forgiveness by completing the most famous of all the Arthurian stories in English.

II

The social and historical relevance of Tales I to V falls into two major areas. The first deals with royal and national matters – establishing the kingship, defending it at home and extending its dominion overseas. These topics occur in the first part of Tale I and throughout Tale II. The second area, dealt with in the rest of the first five tales, is the problem of keeping order in the community. Those two concerns were also central to Malory's period: 'the functions of English government in the later middle ages were distinctly limited – limited externally to defence and internally to ensuring that public order did not fall below a certain, but somewhat indefinite, standard, which most people regarded as tolerable' (Lander, 1980, p. 65).

Malory details these two functions of government, shows both under pressure, and outlines, especially in the case of domestic order, the values needed and the rewards gained by those who bear the burden of government. The process is partly created by Malory's own additions, but more often it comes from an intelligent exploitation of his sources.

In Tale I Malory's basis is the French prose *Suite de Merlin* (the 'continuation' of the *Merlin*: for source-details see the notes on each tale in Vinaver's third volume). The *Suite* tells an altered and expanded version of Geoffrey of Monmouth's account of the establishing of Arthur. The enemy are no longer Anglo-Saxons but troublesome petty kings, especially of north Britain, who do not accept the right of the young king Arthur to rule all of England. Rivalry for the kingship and the threat of anarchy when the throne was uncertain were common when the prose Arthurian stories were formed and they remained major threats in fifteenth-century England. Malory puts it with characteristic crispness: 'Thenne stood the reame in grete jeopardy long whyle, for every lord that was myghty of men maade hym stronge, and many wende to have ben kynge' (12.11–13).

Several early events are especially relevant to Malory's England, see Vinaver's notes to 12.5–7, 16.12–17, 16.21–37 (1967: this edition will be quoted). He sums up: 'Malory obviously thinks of Arthur's household in terms of the fifteenth-century royal court' (note on 99.2–3). The problems Arthur faces after becoming king are also historically familiar. ' "Alas," seyde Arthure, "yet had I never reste one monethe syne I was kynge crowned of this londe" ' (127.1–2). Rebellion in Wales and the north was a common medieval experience, but Henry IV, Henry VI and Edward IV were notably harassed in and from those areas. Not by kings, it is true; but the fighting, the tactics, the use of overseas allies and reasonably appropriate military strategy are all events familiar from fifteenth-century civil disturbances.

Vinaver has argued that Malory refers to real battles in what has come to be called the Wars of The Roses and that he has a consistently Lancastrian viewpoint. This has been disputed by Griffith (1974). Malory describes a set of battles in the north and Arthur's domination of the area south of the Trent (see Vinaver's note on 16.35–7). This sounds less like a picture of Yorkist aggression against Henry VI than the problems Edward IV had in the north – first against Margaret of Anjou, Henry VI's queen, in 1462, against the French and the Scots in 1463 and then with the Lancastrians in Wales and the North in 1464.

But though the figure of Arthur has contemporary credibility and an ideological function, there remains the core of a hero king. The sword in the stone, the magical swords, the helpful wizard all point to that special, timeless, value by which Arthur can resolve as well as realise the contemporary tensions. Here for the first time in this study can be seen the clear lineaments of a mythic hero, and this topic needs a little attention, because it will explain events at the very end of the Arthuriad.

The events of the typical hero's life were separated by Raglan (1936) into twenty-two different 'functions' as structural study would later call them. The hero's reputed father is a king, but may actually be a god, because the circumstances of his conception are unusual. He is spirited away after birth and raised in obscurity by foster parents, returning to seize his kingship in early manhood. At the other end of his career, he is betrayed when in triumph and driven from his throne to meet a mysterious death. He is not succeeded by his children, if he has any. His body is not buried and the myth of his return is widespread; places are made sacred to him throughout his former territories. Raglan scored heroes out of twenty-two. He gave Arthur a rather generous nineteen (more cautiously, it would be seventeen); Christ himself scored heavily, as is obvious from the list above. Hercules, Jason, Siegfried and Asian heroes all did well. Julius Caesar and Napoleon, real heroes who lived in times of accurate history, did poorly: Alexander, a real hero who underwent legendary development had a high score – perhaps Arthur should be in the same category.

This fascinatingly consistent pattern across many cultures has naturally been interpreted by a Jungian through the collective unconscious (Campbell, 1949). The point here is that having had this development from the beginning of the Arthuriad, there is a special quality to the figure of Arthur; not only king, he is also hero, and the hero-pattern gives his figure a weight greater than all the other knights however noble, however much stronger than Arthur himself. The problems Arthur faces, the solutions he attempts, are set within the archetype of true heroism. For centuries the force of that pattern has made readers see this as the story of Arthur, not of Launcelot, Gawain, Galahad or even of the Round Table.

After establishing his kingship, the hero usually extends his rule. The rest of Tale I deals with this in terms of ordering the community, to be discussed shortly. But Malory emphasised military and imperialist royalty by inserting into the structure of the French prose Arthuriad his Tale II, a story taken from the English alliterative poem *Morte Arthure*. Probably written about 1400, this tells how the Emperor of Rome sent envoys demanding from Arthur the tribute formerly paid by Britain and how Arthur punished them in war. It is Geoffrey of Monmouth's story, that came early into English in Layamon's *Brut*, a long and often spirited alliterative poem of the late thirteenth century.

Arthur's imperialist grandeur was English wish-fulfilment: in Peter of Langtoft's *Chronicle* he has conquered thirty countries outside England, from Iceland to Babylon, (Plate 11). For Malory the emotive context of this grandeur is contemporary defeat – as it had been in Geoffrey's version with Arthur's manoeuvres against Lucius. By the middle of the fifteenth century the English had lost all of their continental possessions except the mercantile port of Calais. Normandy passed into French control in 1450 and Gascony was lost in 1453. The glories of Henry V's day were gone, bitterly regretted by many: Ferguson has a chapter on the connection, as he puts it, of 'Chivalry and Chauvinism' (1960, ch. 5).

Aurner saw Arthur here as a plain model of Henry V (1933, p. 367) and Vinaver has argued that some detailed changes to the source suggest the hero of Agincourt (1967, pp. 1366–8) especially that Arthur's military journey is a magnified version of Henry V's march from Fécamp to Calais via Agincourt (1967, pp. 1396–7).

A twelfth-century reason for the roundabout route Arthur takes was suggested in chapter 2. This could have been retouched for relevance to fifteenth-century events, but the specific references do not seem as strong in this case as they are in Geoffrey of Monmouth's. There is, rather, a general picture of English heroic glory as a consolation for recent losses.

Two other features of this tale are exposed by a comparison with its source. Malory clearly has plans already for Launcelot, because he has emphasised his role at the expense of Gawain in particular, as Vinaver points out briefly (1967, note on 185.1–7) and as Mary Dichmann has argued at greater length (1964).

It is all the easier to single out a favourite hero like Launcelot because where the alliterative poem has major battle scenes, Malory's version is a curiously personalised, even trivialised, war. Great emphasis is given to Gawain's embassy to the Romans which turns into a fight, and to the prisoner escort to Paris, which is ambushed. After the major battle there is a skirmish in which Gawain also stars, and this is treated at more length than the great battle. Such small scale war might perhaps relate to fifteenth-century experience – many of the so-called battles in the period were little more than skirmishes (Lander, 1977, p. 158): only Towton, the decisive battle in 1461, was a really big affair with perhaps 50,000 men involved.

But there is also a strongly ideological impact to this curious limitation of battle. The war seems to take place between a small number of men. Arthur, Launcelot, Gawain, Kay and Bedivere do have supporting knights, and they intervene to avenge them, but the presentation of the war is unrealistically narrow, privileging the aristocracy almost to the point of ignoring all others.

The same concern for a united, orderly and powerful nation – and one thoroughly controlled by the aristocracy – is equally plain in Malory's wide-ranging presentation of the defence of order throughout Arthur's realm, the essential topic of the bulk of Tale I and the next three tales after Tale II.

III

Ordering the kingdom is essentially a sort of chivalric policing, as one critic has seen, identifying Malory's 'notion of the knight as a sort of policeman enforcing a Christian peace' (Field, 1978, pp. 14–15). The pattern is present in the sources, and Malory is clearly aware of this as a major aspect of his work. Late in the story he sums it up, making Launcelot's knights say in a symbolic unison: ' "by the noble felyshyp of the Rounde Table was kynge Arthur upborne, and by their nobeles the kynge and all the realme was ever in quyet and reste" ' (1203.32–1204.1).

This process of defending the peace is by no means a whimsical chivalric dream. It has great structural similarity to the actual peace-keeping systems of the fifteenth century. For various complex reasons, including the loosening of feudal and manorial ties, the increasing pressure on the legal system, and the related development of a money economy and social and geographic mobility, the period was notorious for civil disorder. John Bellamy says: 'In the England of the later middle ages the preservation of public order was very often the biggest problem the king had to face. Neither before that time nor since has the issue of public order bulked so large in English history' (1973, p. 1).

To keep this tenuous peace, the king could only turn to the upper class. Lander puts it concisely: 'With institutions in practice so defective, with direct power at the government's command so limited, the maintenance of order depended upon the tolerance and cooperation of the well-to-do, through the combination of patronage and discipline which they could exercise upon their dependants and their neighbours' (1977, p. 167).

Knights like Launcelot or, in Tale I, Pellinore and Ywayne, awe people by their connections and Round Table authority as well as by their force, and the rewards of Round Table fellowship are often extended to offenders who reform, or who have had good reason for disturbing the peace. Those are versions of 'patronage' and the many occasions when a knight defeats a wrong-doer and imposes punishment are direct and by no means unrealistic versions of contemporary 'discipline'.

The quite specific relevance of knightly activities in the story to contemporary disorder has not been properly recognised. Many commentators have talked vaguely about the 'moral' character of the knights and their actions, and have seen the events as definitions of chivalry. But the meaning of the text is much less ideal, much more urgently real than that. Yet it is not a simple reflection of reality: ideological distortion is at work. Neither patronage nor discipline have their malign contemporary meanings. The armed 'affinities' which depended on a lord's patronage and which made his discipline entirely convergent with his self-interest are quite absent from the text even though – perhaps because – Malory's career is a classic of such activities. The knights act alone, act well, and act for the communal good: the aristocrat is honoured, applauded by contemporaries and modern critics alike, and so given solid cultural support by the ideological work of the story.

Yet Malory is not writing a story of naïve wish-fulfilment. He recognises the problems inherent in a world where the king could not 'even imagine a substitute for a system of law maintenance based very largely on the unpaid assistance of gentlemen and noble amateurs, yet there was a great need to do so since much of the crime originated in the misdeeds of those same classes' (Bellamy, 1973, p. 2).

From the very beginning of Malory's series of chivalric adventures Arthur's own knights contribute to or even initiate disorder. Contemporary conflict is vividly realised, from within the very system that offers order. The forces that bring the collapse of the Round Table in the last two tales are only larger versions of a tension which is present but contained in the earlier tales, and which grows steadily worse, especially in the second part of the long Tristram tale.

In looking now at the details of the structure that has just been described, it is necessary to be highly selective – or this chapter would grow as large as Malory's massive book. I have tried to give the most vivid cases, ones which clarify the pattern found in the many other instances where a knight meets an evil doer, fights him, makes him surrender and administers suitable punishment. These myriad events should properly be seen as a huge set of cases that establish the common law of chivalric peacekeeping. They establish, for example, when a villain should be beheaded, when he should be given mercy and told to sin no more, when he should be invited to Camelot and hope in time for Round Table membership.

There is a general theoretical basis to the case-law structure of chivalric policing. References are often made to the values of 'the Order of Knighthood', and these are set out at the end of the chapter which describes, and should be called 'The Weddyng of King Arthur' as the manuscript names it (Vinaver, in one of his weak moments, calls it 'Torre and Pellinore'). When Arthur has a queen and a Round Table, he can operate as a heroic king and 'give laws' – one of the constant functions in the archetype of the mythic hero:

> than the kynge stablysshed all the knyghtes and gaff them rychesse and londys; and charged them never to do outerage nothir morthir, and allwayes to fle treson, and to gyff mercy unto hym that askith mercy, uppon payne of forfiture of their worship and lordship of kynge Arthure for evirmore; and allwayes to do ladyes, damesels, and jantilwomen and wydowes socour: strengthe hem in hir ryghtes, and never to enforce them, uppon payne of dethe. Also, that no man take no batayles in a wrongefull quarell for no love ne for no worldis goodis. So unto thys were all knyghtis sworne of the Table Rounde, both olde and younge, and every yere so were they sworne at the hyghe feste of Pentecoste.   (120.15–27)

This is Malory's own work and it shows his grasp of the policing theme. The king gives the knights lands, and can take them away again. The generally feudal nature of the oath is not its only contemporary relevance. Both Henry IV and Edward IV held, soon after taking the crown, a public swearing-in of knights to the Order of the Bath. The secular orders of knighthood were still a reality, if no longer militarily very effective (Barber, 1970, ch. 20): they all had oaths, and defending the peace was a constant feature of them. Malory's particular oath also resembles the contemporary ordinances for war, the standing orders for armies on campaign which Malory and many of his audience must have known (Field, 1978, p. 46).

Within this formalised but vague structure, the knights roam off on their peace-keeping adventures. By the actions of their enemies the elements of disorder, seen from an aristocratic viewpoint, are defined. On Arthur's wedding day, before the oath is administered, Gawain, Pellinore and Torre confront abduction, murder and bullying violence. In the 'Arthur and Accolon' chapter Arthur deals with an inheritance dispute and Morgan le Fay, sister to Arthur and ever-present troublemaker, urges Accolon into treason and attempted regicide. She also tries to kill Urien her husband, pressures Uwayne their son towards parricide, and then tries to kill Arthur herself. As a result Uwayne faces unjustified charges of treason, and goes into exile: his friend Gawain goes with him. On their adventures they encounter Marhalt, who has been slandered by women, and then the three knights ride off on the adventures of the fountain. Gawain meets Pelleas, who will not fight because of his unrequited love; Marhalt faces severe odds and then deals with a giant who has imprisoned knights and ladies; Uwayne fights for a lady whose inheritance has been seized by two 'perelous knyghtes'.

These breaches of order were, with the probable exception of unrequited love, widely known in the fifteenth century as real disturbances of the aristocratic peace, though many of them stem from Malory's thirteenth-century source. The disturbances occur suddenly, and are dealt with briskly. But these easily righted wrongs are by no means the sum of disorder in this first tale, and by no means the most serious aspect of it. A consistent set of problems occurs from within the body of knights themselves. This will eventually be the force which brings the Round Table world to collapse, and it is evident here at the beginning of that hopeful institution.

Before the order of Arthurian chivalry comes into being the 'Tale of Balin le Sauvage' sets out the stark story of a knight who was instinctively ferocious; he started by beheading a maiden and eventually he and his brother Balan killed each other. Balin is the figure of a knight of unrestrained prowess. He is known as 'The Knight with Two Swords'; he is over-phallic, over-ferocious. In a period of serious disorder and often random violence, Balin's story is credible enough and a dramatic warning about sheer physical force.

Within the Round Table world, Gawain represents a similarly disturbing force, but one protected by royal kinship. He refuses mercy to a fallen knight and kills a lady as a result (106.15–21); later he betrays his colleague Pelleas by seducing Ettare (168–70). Being Arthur's nephew saves him from worse than shame: a royal prince's malignity was familiar in the fifteenth century, and for all its existence in the sources, the Gawain material strongly resembles the way Edward IV had to accept the outrageous behaviour of his younger brother George, Duke of Clarence.

Treason was a constant fear in the period. Accolon is accused of it justly, Uwayne unjustly. In both cases the prime mover is Morgan le Fay. She is a witch, of course – that figure who protects male characters from final guilt – but she also partly represents the power of a royal female who plots fiercely for her own family, just like Margaret of Anjou, Henry VI's queen and a major enemy of the new Yorkist king.

Minor problems also occur – Pellinore's lack of flexibility, Damas's rejection of a brother's property rights, Marhalt's problem with false accusers. The vision of Tale I is not an aristocratic world confidently facing external threats, but of a divided and uncertain social group confronting its own weakness and divisiveness as much as the threat of others. That is a remarkably realistic portrayal of the land-owning class in the fifteenth century, but an ideological text cannot speak with such frankness without also offering some consolations.

Pellinore learns from his error, Torre shows that others have learned from Gawain's error, Damas yields to his brother, Marhalt's name is cleared; Arthur forgives Accolon, Uwayne is reinstated and Gawain at least promises to do better in future. The forces of error and aggression from within the Round Table are to some degree contained. But not eradicated: dissension will return in a severely exaggerated form.

There is a cause of this internal strife much more far-reaching than the sheer weakness or mere ill-will that erring knights have openly shown in Tale I. As the story progresses, grave conflict will arise increasingly from the essentially competitive nature of honour, and it is already a disturbing force. When Arthur fills up the Round Table, he leaves out Bagdemagus, preferring (in a credibly nepotistic way) his own nephew Gawain and Pellinore's son Torre. Bagdemagus is angry and leaves in a tantrum to fight

Round Table knights. He will eventually do well, but the competitive edge of honourable action is realised.

Malory is already conscious of the issue he will later develop, that there is a private dynamic within the public world of honour. That is not his perception alone as the previous discussion of Chrétien showed, but it was a perception very much in key with Malory's time. A recent study has traced the honour system itself as the basis of so much disorder in the period:

> the root of the matter lies in the mentality defined by the concept of honour. This, emerging out of a long-established military and chivalric tradition, is characterised above all by competitive assertiveness; it assumes a state of affairs in which resort to violence is natural and justifiable; the recurrence of personal and political situations in which conflict cannot be otherwise resolved than violently. Honour could both legitimise and provide moral reinforcement for a politics of violence.
>
> (James, 1979, p. 1)

That pattern is in Malory's mind in Tale I and it remains there. If 'competitive assertiveness' is not to become the politics of violence, a great effort of chivalric control must be exerted. Malory does show the attempt being made, especially by the knightly teachers. Pre-eminent among them is Sir Launcelot, whose adventures are set out compactly in Tale III. Yet, just like the fifteenth-century magnates he represents, he gains and defends his portion by physical power. And like so many of them, the honour so powerfully established will eventually lead him to fight against his king.

IV

The opening sequence of Tale III is Malory's own preface and sums up much that is important in his Arthurian ideology. First, it shows how ordinary knights can fight their way to honour which is publicly 'proved' (253.7), then that 'competitive assertiveness' is given a supreme model in Launcelot. He is so powerful that he is the best knight: and more than that, he cannot be beaten by normal processes of honourable war. Only treason, behaviour outside the aristocratic self-defence of honourable behaviour, and enchantment, a super-rational force, can threaten the greatest of

Arthurian magnates. That is consoling, a way of making 'unnatural' the threats to a great lord, but the story that follows outlines the disturbingly aggressive inner core of honour.

The knight is strangely isolated. He rides alone, without even a squire to help him. Between each of the four sets of adventures, Malory's own links show Launcelot wandering through the wild forests, symbolising (like Yvain in success and Calogrenant in failure) the knight making his way in a difficult world by arms.

A very common motif creating a sense of individualist aggression is the incognito battle. Like many other Arthurian heroes Launcelot rides in borrowed armour, fights other Round Table knights and they soon discover he is not an unknown nobody, or the weak somebody his shield proclaims – very often Sir Kay. Then there is recognition and his name is accorded its earned honour: he has recreated himself. If the knight were not incognito he could not fight those battles against his Round Table brothers in arms. The motif demonstrates the limits of public honour, the essential core of private aggression working within that imposed structure of control.

The last of these self-assertive motifs is when a knight fights to save somebody, usually in trial by battle, but for various complicated reasons he only arrives at the last minute. This pattern is dominant later in the Arthuriad, but a minor version of it occurs in Tale III when Launcelot rides to help King Bagdemagus in a tournament and waits until he is doing badly before intervening. There is no doubt a suspense element involved, but that emphasises the basic effect, to make the hero all the more individually heroic.

Dignified by these recurrent devices as well as his sheer power, Launcelot moves through the tale righting wrongs, and as in Tale I there is a remarkable degree of credibility in his policing. Many of Launcelot's actions against crime realise, in their displaced way, fears held by any medieval aristocrat, especially in the disorderly fifteenth century: being suddenly imprisoned (by Morgan or Tarquin), caught when out of armour (by Belleus and Phelot), opposed by overwhelming odds or power (at the Chapel Perilous, by multiple knights and Tarquin), confronting uncouth violence (of Piers and the giants), suffering shame through trickery (that of Pedyvere). Within the conventions of romance, the dangers Launcelot faces with courage and almost complete success are far from unreal.

Disorderly men are not the only danger: women bring their own brand of threat to the hero. Launcelot survives enchantment and sexual temptation from Morgan le Fay and Hallewes the Sorceress, just as he defeats the treachery of Phelot's wife. There is also talk about his relationship with Guinevere. In the opening of the tale Malory says 'quene Gwenyvere had hym in grete favoure aboven all other knyghtis, and so he loved the quene agayne aboven all other ladyes dayes of his lyff' (253.15–18).

Morgan and Hallewes both interpret this relationship as sinful and a maiden Launcelot has just helped says 'it is noysed' he loves Guinevere and she has enchanted him to love her alone. He makes no answer to the assertion about Guinevere, but defines his own position. He will not marry 'for than I muste couche with hir and leve armys and turnamentis, batellys and adventures' (270.30–2 – the Gauvain position from Le Chevalier au Lion). But he goes on to say – with more relevance to his own role, in the future at least – that he will not take a paramour 'in prencipall for drede of God, for knyghtes that bene adventures sholde nat be advoutrers nothir lecherous, for than they be nat happy nother fortunate unto the werrys' (270.33–6). Adventurous knights who are adulterers or fornicators will be unfortunate in war – 'unhappy' and 'unhap' mean unlucky and bad luck in Malory.

This is an important statement of the principle that bad luck follows bad behaviour, and it will have telling relevance in the last tales, when the narrative has made it quite clear that, however noble they may be, Guinevere and Launcelot are adulterous lovers. For the present, though, it seems that Malory does not mean that. The young Launcelot avoids all debilitating female entanglements. This chief of Arthur's chivalric police force is chief of masculine ideology as well as an ideal figure of chivalry who personifies both noble honour and its aggressive real basis.

There is little interest here in Launcelot's origin, though Merlin saw him as a child (125.32–126.14). In Malory's version this hero lacks the beginning – and indeed will lack the ending – of the heroic archetype. But in other texts, such as Le Chevalier au Lion, the problem of where the new warriors come from and how they can fit into the existing pattern is a matter of some concern. That is one of the major ideological issues dealt with in Malory's most original single tale, Tale IV, 'The Tale of Sir Gareth of Orkney'.

V

In spite of the refusal of many scholars to believe Malory capable of creating the tale of Gareth, there is no need to imagine a lost 'Gaheret' romance with Vinaver (1967, pp. 1427–36). However, the labour of innovation is unusual for Malory and must have had a cause. The effect and apparently the purpose of creating the Gareth story was to introduce the ideological issues inherent to the 'Fair Unknown' type of story, some of which have already been seen in the shape of *Le Chevalier au Lion*.

Gareth first appears as an example of a disturbance coming to court. He is a model of the *arriviste* whose strength is a threat that must somehow be absorbed, acculturated into the aristocratic society. The nature of the threat is specified by Kay's suggestion that Gareth may be no higher in birth than a mere kitchen knave.

When he is given knighthood and a quest, his physical power at first only amplifies the threat. This is now uttered by Lyonet, the maiden who has come to court for a knight to save her lady and sister, Lyonesse. She abuses Gareth as a low-born knave assuming knighthood, but to save the audience too much anxiety he privately reveals to Launcelot that he is in fact a king's son. An evident nobility of manner and physique, itself legitimised by noble birth: this is in Gareth, just as in Yvain, the mechanism which defuses ideologically the threat of virile vulgarity.

The new hero proves himself a knight – 'proving' motifs are thick on the ground in the Gareth story, especially in the motifs which seem without parallel in the other English 'fair unknown' romances (Benson, 1976, pp. 99–101). And Gareth also wins a great property through the love of a lady; Malory obviously grasps the connection of love and land, for he gives his lady the name of a mythical kingdom; Lyonesse lies off the coast of Cornwall.

Gareth wins her in war, defeating the Red Knight who has besieged her property for years. But the triumph of physical power, so pointedly relevant in the period, is euphemised. Like Yvain, Gareth also wins his lady by love. After they have made a post-battle agreement to marry in a year he goes off adventuring, and is immediately led to her brother's castle, where he falls in love with her, wishing that his own lady 'were so fayre as she is' (331.20). This bizarre event often puzzles modern readers: is Gareth a feckless womaniser; is Malory hopelessly muddled; has Gareth never seen Lyonesse close up? These questions are not appropriate and only show the ideological strain of the moment as the text attempts to prove that the hero wins his lady by love as well as war. Malory presses the euphemisation of sheer prowess a stage further, for Gareth then wins a stylised tournament where the prize is the hand of Lyonesse.

The fair unknown proves himself, reveals his name, becomes a lord, and Arthur travels to meet him. The myth of reproduction without disturbance is forcefully enacted, the strength of the Round Table is increased without having to fear new men and new values. It is obvious that in a period of dramatically increased social mobility like the fifteenth century the audience would find this myth of value.

But the impact of 'The Tale of Gareth' is a good deal more specific than that. R. S. Loomis suggested (1939) a number of contemporary references in this tale. He linked the nickname 'Beaumains', given ironically by Kay to his dirty-handed new scullion, with Beauchamp, the family name of the early fifteenth-century Earl of Warwick (not the later kingmaker, who was a Neville). Loomis also connected Gareth's colour-changing armour at the tournament with this Warwick's famous appearance in different colours on different days at a grand tournament, and he thought the Duke de la Rouse, Gareth's last opponent, took his name from John Rous, a priest working for the Beauchamp family.

None of these points is strong and this Warwick died in 1439, when Malory was only about twenty-three according to the latest view (Field, 1979/80). If there is any force in Loomis's arguments it would be to connect the fair unknown myth with the house of Warwick, and so help legitimise the status of Richard Neville himself, who succeeded to Warwick's title when his eldest son Henry Beauchamp died in 1449.

Neville had married Richard Beauchamp's daughter – but a fortunate marriage had also helped his father. A minor son of a minor son of the Earl of Westmorland, he first inherited Yorkshire castles through his mother and then married the Countess of Salisbury in her own right: 'but for his father's marriage to an Earl's daughter and his own to Anne Beauchamp, he would only have been Sir Richard Neville, a North country knight' (Kendall, 1957, p. 58).

What Gareth and Neville did, many other men continued to do. Between 1439 and 1504 twenty-one peerages were continued by men marrying the heiress (Lander, 1977, p. 170). Apart from his good marriage, Gareth's military build-up takes him from a nobody to a magnate. The enemies he defeats on his path to rescue and appropriate Lyonesse and her lands all become his men, bringing with them large numbers of knights. By the end of the tale Gareth has a personal following of some two hundred knights, as great an affinity as mid-century magnates like Warwick, Somerset or York. His revealed nobility, like the rapidly assumed gentility of some contemporaries, casts a validating veil over the actual processes by which he becomes powerful.

Apart from the special ideological application of the fair unknown story, 'The Tale of Gareth' does share major features of the other tales. The private core of assertiveness by prowess in Gareth has already been mentioned. That tension between hero and chivalric collectivity is also realised, firstly in the incognito fight with Gawain (one of the many elements shared with *Le Chevalier au Lion*), and then in a more strained form when Gareth leaves the tournament where he has once again won Lyonesse, to go off on a final and entirely private self-proving against the Duke de la Rouse. There is also a movement from the heart of the fair unknown story in the direction of chivalric policing for aristocratic ends. The Red Knight, the personal enemy of Lyonesse and the personal victim of Gareth in his ascent, is generalised into an enemy of the Arthurian aristocracy (325.7–8).

The specific ideology of the tale of Gareth is that the Round Table world has a new magnate, just as in the 1450s the remarkably young Warwick (born in 1428, succeeded to the title in 1449) became a force in the country. Both Gareth and Warwick went on to engage in complex and increasingly threatening activities: one in the world of Arthur as revealed in 'The Tale of Tristram', one in the developing disorder of the 1450s, which had not yet settled into the two-sided conflict of York and Lancaster.

VI

In Tale V, 'The Book of Sir Tristram de Lyones', the hero's love for La Beal Isode, as Malory always calls her, and the feud with King Mark, her husband and Tristram's uncle, are important elements but they are by no means dominant. Tale V is also the major development in the whole Arthuriad, of the theme of chivalric policing and its problems. Here are the comings and goings, the encounters, the fights, the punishments and the pardons that chart very fully the case-law of the Arthurian world. The major impact of the Tristram story is that all the themes and motifs of chivalric policing are recreated here in a stream of Arthurian activity which strongly resembles the disorder and peacekeeping of the fifteenth century itself.

The internal disorder that confronts the chivalric police force throughout the tale has various sources. King Mark is the major figure of autonomous evil. He is especially violent towards Tristram, but also to King Arthur and Round Table knights in general. In Chapter 7 he manages to fail at all the classic events of a knight's proving pattern and is correspondingly dishonoured in public, first by Launcelot before the Round Table and then by Tristram at his own court in Cornwall.

A very large number of the disturbers of the peace in the Tristram story act not out of random malice but because they are hostile to the Round Table, against the establishment. There are 'dangerous knyghtes' about, and two are named at one point (638.27–8). Only one of them appears much, the villain known variously as Sir Breunys or Sir Breuse but always given the shameful cognomen, Saunze Pité. He commits three murders and fails in five attempts at murder; an assaulter of women with a special penchant for riding down unhorsed knights, he is described on his first appearance as 'a grete foo unto many good knyghtes of kyng Arthur's court' (406.6–7).

Morgan le Fay is another recurring threat. She is a determined enemy of Arthur and his knights, specifically making war 'to dystroy all thos knyghtes that kynge Arthure lovyth' (597.18–19), but her appearances are intermittent.

These elements of disorder are unconnected and easily dealt with. For the first time in the Arthuriad the most serious conflicts are caused by dissension among Round Table knights themselves or between them and other knights who are in no way out-and-out villains. There is a whole series of jealousies, feuds, misunderstandings in this tale: many blows and quite a few deaths are the result.

Much of this surrounds Tristram. His sheer nobility and honour is enough for some to be envious, especially Mark and Palomides. His love for Isode causes wider problems: Lamerak admires her for a while, Bleoberys and Palomides are determined rivals for her love. A whole series of hostile encounters arise from love: it is seen as a private, socially disruptive force and in one telling episode, which Malory has carefully reshaped, this even extends to Launcelot himself. He comes upon Lamerak and Mellyagaunce arguing about female beauty and turns on Lamerak for supporting Morgause against Guinevere. A serious fight is only avoided when Bleoberys, a spectator to all this, asserts that all lovers think well of their ladies, referring to the fact that Morgause is Lamerak's mistress. This distinctly private reasoning calms the great warrior (486–7). But if even he can be so aroused, the peace is tenuous indeed. Lamerak himself falls out with Gawain and his brothers partly because Morgause is their mother, but also because their father, King Lot, died at the hands of Pellinore, Lamerak's father. Eventually they ambush and kill Lamerak.

Feuds between families were more common and more severe in the fifteenth century than previously. Bellamy describes the general situation (1973, pp. 25–8) and Lander describes how a 'dangerous development of armed private feuds preceded the "Wars of the Roses" ', and as a result 'between 1448 and 1455 at least one-sixth of the peerage were, at some time or another, imprisoned for violent conduct' (1977, p. 66).

An even more common source of contemporary disorder was the misuse of power for personal gain. Through Palomides Malory expresses in a particularly clear form the 'competitive assertiveness' basic to the honourable man. So often he just cannot control the envy, the violence, the willingness to forget the rules, that were in reality the dynamic forces behind so much contemporary behaviour – but forces that chivalric ideology strives to conceal. In Palomides' case there is another useful euphemistic explanation for his behaviour: because he does not have Christianity, that ultimate cultural sanction of knighthood, he is suitable as a model of the knight divided between private desires and public sanctions.

Malory has developed out of some suggestions in the source a very striking example of 'competitive assertiveness'. Throughout Chapter 6 in which Tristram joins the court – and which Benson feels is the happy ending to the first part of the tale (1976, p. 116 and pp. 119–24) – there is a recurrent disturbance. A very powerful mysterious knight keeps riding through the scene, defeating knights with contemptuous ease and disappearing. He has beaten Tristram, Palomides, Gawain, Bleoberys – all excellent fighters. There is considerable suspense before the mystery is solved.

It is Launcelot, of course, in violently playful mood. The sequence realises the innate fury that is within his great power. That hostile potential by which the nobleman achieves and protects his honour is brought out in this most disturbing of incognito passages. Yet all the time Arthur knows who he is. This intriguing motif, which will recur, ensures that the great warrior at his most dangerous is never quite beyond control of society, though that possibility is raised. The position is the same as that of the fifteenth-century magnates, apparently serving the state but in the last instance serving their own interests, with only a personal link to the king to keep the fiction of corporate entity in being. The classic example is Warwick: Lander says of him: 'For the earl high morality was a stick with which to beat opponents rather than a guiding light for his own conduct. . . . Brought up in a background of family feuds where, to say the least, rampant acquisitiveness and ambitious injustice had, with royal acquiescence, long prevailed, he had spent his earlier active years in the atmosphere of political disintegration peculiar to the 1450s' (1980, p. 253).

This world of violence and aristocratic dignity is richly dramatised in the conflict and the honour of the Tristram tale, and while the essence of the matter is in the source, Malory has often sharpened or created its contemporary point. Without Tale V, Malory's Arthuriad would no doubt still be famous. But with it, with this heavy keel of jumbled reality and awkward, unmanageable confusions and dissensions, the whole work is given, in contemporary terms especially, much greater credibility and a much stronger function.

These are the problems that the Arthuriad has dealt with so far. But an ideological text does not only raise threats; it must offer solutions of a kind. Those given in Tale V and in the previous tales as well, are no more than the hopeful continuance of the existing, and crumbling, power structure. The positives that are offered are aristocratic, military and masculine, and their ideological character rises not only from their doubtful power to equate the disorder of the text, but also, and primarily, from their distorted presentation of the contemporary world.

The ideology is aristocratic because the middle or lower orders hardly have any presence in the work. Servants, townspeople, farm labourers or even farm owners are hardly ever seen, let alone heard. Nor are there very many aristocrats involved: the Round Table is said to have one hundred and fifty knights but many fewer than that appear and operate to keep order. These elements are all historically unrealistic, interpretations of fifteenth-century reality which favour the viewpoint of the upper aristocracy.

That is to some extent also true of the presentation of war, limited as it is to mounted combat, usually between individuals, a pattern far from the mundane realities of contemporary fighting where the archer, the pikeman, the professional soldier and the tactically trained officer were crucial and where gunpowder was emerging as a force. It was certainly not realistic in the period to think of peace-keeping being conducted by single men on horses – but it was an acceptable ideological view. By its insistence that this was true warfare and true peace-keeping, the text obscures unpleasant realities of historical process such as armour-piercing arrows, castle-destroying guns and cash-heavy townspeople. The omission of insoluble, unmentionable questions is a basic part of the process of ideological consolation.

The pattern of Tales I and V sustains the male sex as firmly as the aristocratic clan. There are many female characters in Malory, but they do not act for themselves. They either assist or hinder the male characters in their career towards honour and self-definition; they vary enormously in their exact function, from Morgan the hostile witch-queen, through noble beauties who disturb male poise like Guinevere and Isode, to the crowd of humble helpful maidens who pop up to assist a wandering knight without needing any reward. A structure showing women as having entirely secondary roles must in itself have been historically inaccurate, in a period when many noblewomen inherited extensive properties in their own right and by no means always succumbed to marriage with some opportunist title-seeker. But ideology, in this case massively strengthened by the Catholic church's historical abasement of real women, was able to cope with those facts as well as with the obvious reliance in everyday life on the skills and fortitude of women, not only in the home.

The first five tales are unified in more than their aristocratic and masculine ideologies. Right through that long sequence no categories for bad behaviour have been used other than shame and 'disworship'. Concordantly, no concepts of behaviour and the person have been used other than an external representation of people following or breaking public codes – in spite of the consistent sense, brought out clearly by Malory at times, that it is the private desires that cause conflict at a public level. But through the quest for the grail, new types of value will be imposed on Arthurian chivalry: sin and innocence will be brought into play as evaluative terms. As a result, people will emerge as entities who hold power over their own lives, and by extension those of the others for whom they are responsible. That is the major effect of the quest on Malory's Arthuriad, and one which itself relates to new socio-economic forces and new structures of feeling in fifteenth-century England.

VII

The story of the quest for the grail, like so much else in medieval Arthurian literature, can be traced to Chrétien de Troyes. His *Perceval*, or *Le Conte del Graal*, was completed by other writers, but he established the notion of the grail as a symbol of Christian perfection in a human world. The idea of a grail and a quest was attractive and within fifty years the more broad-based *History of the Grail* appeared in French, and in German Wolfram von Eschenbach wrote the richly complex *Parzival*.

Helen Adolf has argued (1960) that this enthusiasm for grail stories was based on the loss of the real sacred places in Jerusalem in 1181. That created a vacuum of sanctity which was filled by the grail myth and the contemporary drive for the intensification of feeling towards the mass. The grail was represented as either the dish or cup used at the last supper, or as the cup in which Christ's blood was caught as he hung on the cross.

In the version Malory used, the grail story has a more specific basis. The *Queste del Saint Graal* was composed in the 1230s, produced by 'white' Cistercian monks who were not only aiming at secular sinners. As a new and expanding order, founded to reform monasticism, their special hostility was reserved for the Benedictines, the long established 'black' monks, deeply involved in urban and worldly affairs. The grail story plays on black/white symbolism to create traditional notions of bad and good, but also to advance the spiritual imperialism of the Cistercians.

These historical meanings are in the past for Malory, but the grail story does relate to the remarkable boom in personalised faith and private devotion that was an important part of fifteenth-century cultural activities. Called *devotio moderna*, it was practised by very notable people such as the Duchess of York and Lady Margaret Beaufort, Henry VII's mother. However, Malory seems to tell the grail story simply because it was there: it turned up in the French prose Tristan, and it was a well-known part of the whole saga, as the forward references in Tale I indicate.

At first the quest seems like another adventure. The grail appears at court, and Arthur can eat as a result of the wonder. But here the amazing disturbance has a much more powerful impact than usual. Through Galahad and the grail, the scales of value change from secular and chivalric to Christian and heavenly. Some good knights like Ector and some doubtful ones like Gawain fail utterly. Launcelot is a qualified failure: he tries to atone for his sin with Guinevere, yet cannot 'achieve' the grail. Bors and Perceval come to live in its aura, Galahad is assumed into heaven with it. Finally Bors, armed with the sword that Galahad drew from the stone – the new sword of Christian chivalry – advises Launcelot to remember at least the new insight he has achieved in the quest.

That final scene between Bors and Launcelot is Malory's own work. It meshes with the fact that Malory has not criticised Launcelot with the gleeful, even vicious relish of the source. Detailed comparisons of the text with a surviving version of Malory's source indicate he has moderated the criticism of Launcelot and inserted passages and phrases which make him more a noble striver for perfection than an abject failure (Simes, 1977).

From the new moralisation of action comes the other important step made in the grail story. The narrative goes inside the character for an explanation of events. Neither the source nor Malory turns their characters into the feeling, judging individuals of the novel. But the fundamental shift from external secular values of honour and shame to an internalised scale of guilt and innocence is evident here; in the later tales it will trigger a remarkable change in the way in which Malory presents people.

A new concept of people and a much sharper sense of contemporary relevance are visible as soon as Malory turns back to his story of action at and around the court. The beginning of

1. Maen Huail, 'Huail's Stone', on which Arthur allegedly beheaded his rival.

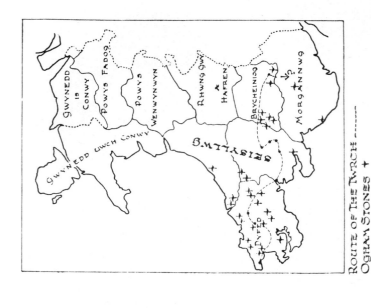

2. References to Arthur in the 'Cambrian Annals'. 'Bellum badonis' and 'Gueith camlann' are first and last in the right-hand column.

3. Hywel Dda's Wales, with the route of the Twrch Trwyth and Ogham – inscribed standing stones.

VBI HAROLD:SACRAMENTVM:FECIT:
VVILLELMO DVCI:
HIC HAROLD:D

4. Bayeux Tapestry: Harold swears a great oath of allegiance to William.

6. Bayeux Tapestry: the mysterious scene titled 'Where a certain clerk and Aelgyfa', apparently a private and risqué joke — see the lower margin.

5. Bayeux Tapestry: war-horses in trouble at the Battle of Hastings.

7. Launcelot crossing the sword-bridge with Guinevere waiting in the castle, defended by a lion.

8. Cernunnos, 'the horned one', lord of the animals, on the silver Gundestrup cauldron.

9. Prowess: a knight is about to kill a disarmed and bloodstained enemy, to public disapproval.

10. Courtesy: two armed knights fighting a tournament. The audience is only concerned whether the queen will stop the fight now blood has been shed.

12.

13.

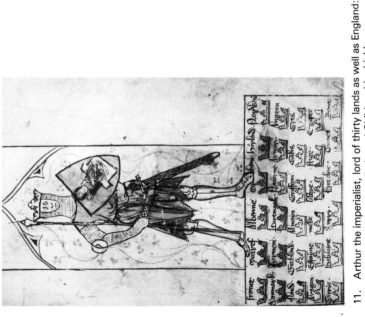

11.

11. Arthur the imperialist, lord of thirty lands as well as England: note the legitimising Virgin and Child on his shield.

12. Wynkyn de Worde's edition of Malory: Launcelot divided in loyalty between Arthur and Guinevere.

13. Copland's edition of Malory: single combat at a tournament.

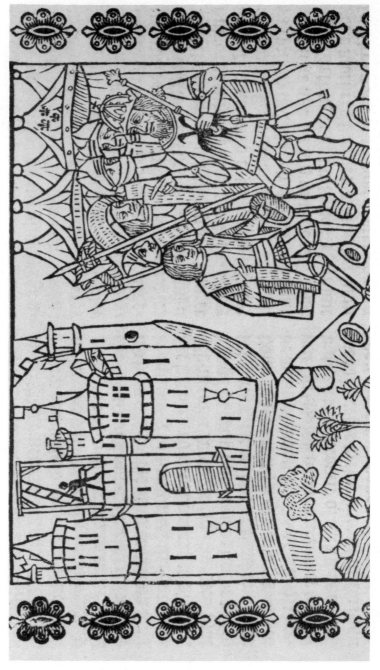

14. Wynkyn de Worde's edition of Malory: Mordred, in the role of king, attacks the Tower of London with artillery.

ENID AND NIMUË:

THE TRUE AND THE FALSE.

BY

ALFRED TENNYSON, D.C.L.,

POET LAUREATE.

LONDON:
EDWARD MOXON, DOVER STREET.
1857.

15. The Unique copy of the 1857 trial edition of Tennyson's earliest Arthurian idylls.

16. Francis Palgrave's note on the fly-leaf of *Enid and Nimue*: 'owing to a remark upon *Nimue* which reached him, he at once recalled the copies out'.

17. Burne-Jones's 'The Beguiling of Merlin': note the snakes in her hair and how she is advancing on the audience.

19. Detail from Burne-Jones's 'The Sleep of Arthur in Avalon': this enormous painting stresses the palatial and sensual comfort of Arthur's last moments on earth.

18. Doré's illustration of the last scene in 'Guinevere': she is now distinctly fair-haired.

20. Archer's 'La Mort D'Arthur': alfresco comfort for the passing king.

21. *A Connecticut Yankee:* Sandy cooling Hank the knight errant.

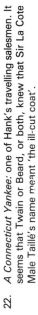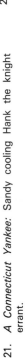

22. *A Connecticut Yankee:* one of Hank's travelling salesmen. It seems that Twain or Beard, or both, knew that Sir La Cote Male Taillé's name meant 'the ill-cut coat'.

24. *A Connecticut Yankee:* Merlin is a very recognisable version of Tennyson.

23. *A Connecticut Yankee:* Hank's modernised cavalry.

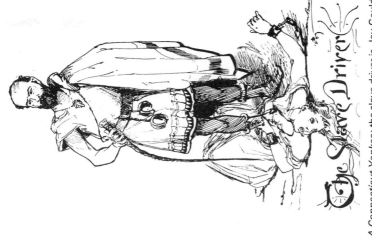

26. *A Connecticut Yankee*: the slave driver is Jay Gould.

25. *A Connecticut Yankee*: the top and bottom 'Chuckleheads' are clearly the Prince of Wales and the Kaiser.

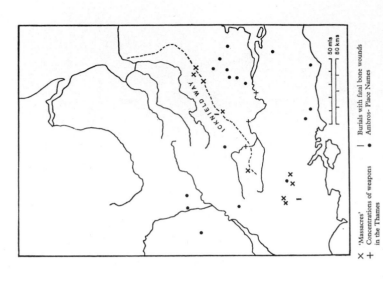

'HELLO-CENTRAL!'

27. *A Connecticut Yankee*: the heart of the lost land — Hank in 'sixth century' domestic bliss.

X 'Massacres'
+ Concentrations of weapons in the Thames
| Burials with fatal bone wounds
• Ambros- Place Names

ICKNIELD WAY

50 mls
80 kms

28. The historical Arthur industry at work: a confidence-inducing map from John Morris's *The Age of Arthur*.

Tale VII is the start of the increasingly connected and increasingly compelling final sequence of Malory's Arthurian story, which brings to a head his imaginative account of his own period and its problems.

VIII

The dominant theme of 'The Tale of Launcelot and Guinevere' is how the private love between those two great characters increasingly disturbs the public life of the Round Table. At the same time Malory insists, as he did in the grail story, that Launcelot remains noble. His original chapters, 'The Great Tournament' and 'The Healing of Sir Urry', ameliorate the doubtful position of Launcelot, expressed in the other three chapters which have been assembled from various sources, French and English.

There is growing tension between Launcelot and Arthur because of Guinevere, a theme well portrayed in one of the illustrations from Wynkyn de Worde's edition of 1529 (Plate 12). This is fully traditional in the legend, yet Malory exploits its patterns to find a remarkable contemporary reality. It curiously resembles the growing hostility between Warwick and Edward IV which flared up after Edward married Elizabeth Wydeville instead of making the great political marriage that Warwick was trying to arrange (Kennedy, 1970). Not only was he put out by the king's independence and insulting lack of consultation: the queen's family closed around the king and made Warwick much less powerful at court than he had been previously. This process steadily separated Warwick from the king and in the late 1460s brought him to turn his support to Lancaster again. Finally he invaded England with a combination of French support, his own troops and revived Lancastrian forces. They actually forced Edward from the throne in 1470, but he came back from defeat and exile, and Warwick was killed in the crucial battle of Barnet in 1471. As a long-term Warwick man Malory must have been party to these tensions, and the shift of the Warwick party was no doubt why Malory was excluded from a general royal pardon of other Lancastrians in 1468, reissued several times by 1470.

Malory arranges his story to suit these circumstances. In the sources Arthur knows of the queen's adultery earlier than in Malory and is much more hostile to Launcelot as a result. But Malory makes Launcelot's enemies expose his love, and then after his accidental killing of Gareth, the king's close kin urge the reluctant king to oppose the nobleman who was formerly his greatest friend and supporter. This is a new pattern in the Arthurian story, reducing Launcelot's guilt and increasing his honour. It is an interpretation of current events very gratifying to Warwick, legitimising his steady drift into opposition to the king and into the Lancastrian camp.

The opening chapter of Tale VII, 'The Poisoned Apple' as Vinaver calls it, is essentially a chivalric police action. Guinevere is wrongly accused of poisoning a knight; trial by battle is arranged; Launcelot arrives at the last minute to save the queen. That seems simple and familiar. But there are complexities. Launcelot is absent because he and the queen have argued. At the very start of the chapter and the tale, in an original and arresting dialogue, Malory makes Launcelot remember 'the promyse and the perfeccion' of the grail story (1045.11–12), but he is drawn back to Guinevere, 'in his prevy thoughtes' and they have many 'prevy draughtis togydir' (1045.13 and 19).

The chapter creates the tension between the private love of Launcelot and Guinevere and the public world of honour and authority. But that drama is not merely literary: it takes place in a remarkably contemporary structure. Charges of poisoning were well known in the fifteenth century – Humphrey, Duke of Gloucester, was widely thought to have died of poison in 1447, and five years previously his wife was convicted of trying to kill Henry VI by poison and sorcery.

If the disturbance is contemporary, the means of resolving it are not. Trials by battle were still known in the fifteenth century, but they were notable for the humiliating conditions which were forced on the fighters: in one famous case they were dressed in skins and fought with clubs, teeth and nails (Bellamy, 1973, p. 131). But Launcelot's battle here is noble, not awkwardly modern: as usual, Malory's law is not unreal, just a conservative use of ancient practices (York, 1969). Later, when the disturbance is more serious, the resolution of a trial by battle will be less old-world and less consoling.

The chapter which follows illustrates more serious tensions rising from the love of Launcelot and Guinevere. First, he decides not to go to a tournament but to stay with her. Another argument between the lovers about the threat of 'noise', that is public accusation, makes Launcelot go late to the tournament. He also goes to fight against Arthur. This seems somehow associated with his love of Guinevere, though he later calls it sheer 'pryde' (1084.1–2) – another recognition of the individualistic core of knightly honour.

In the tournament Launcelot fights against the Round Table knights and has especially bitter encounters with his own kin; he is severely wounded and hovers on the edge of death. This conflict has arisen not simply from love, but from behaving by private standards rather than public normality, breaching one's duty to king and – apparently the more serious disloyalty – to the kin group. Launcelot is healed, of course, and he apologises to Arthur and his kin, but the threat has been chillingly manifested.

Another type of disturbance is also described here which Vinaver has unduly emphasised by calling the chapter 'The Fair Maid of Astolat'. Elaine is the 'maid' and she loves Launcelot at sight, tends him when he is hurt and offers herself to him, as wife or paramour. He refuses, and she dies in composed grief. The sequence is an extended development of the scene in Tale III where a maiden deplores the abnormal fact that Launcelot will love no one (see section IV above). There he stood on chivalric dignity in his defence; here, with his adulterous love for Guinevere and their tense private conversations so forceful, his position is less easily defended. A sense of wastage and things beginning to go publicly wrong is conveyed in the final memorable scene as Elaine's body floats, by her own last wish, down the Thames to the court at a realistically located Westminster.

The following chapter, 'The Great Tournament', is created by Malory. He obviously enjoyed a good tournament, like his early illustrators (Plate 13), but the chapter has further purposes. It is written to lighten the developing gloom, but the light itself casts a shadow later on. At 'The Great Tournament' Launcelot once more fights against his kin, but this time they know it and avoid him. The robust honourable fighting obscures, temporarily at least, the grim events of the previous tournament. Seeing Launcelot hard-pressed, Gareth leaves his own kin to side with the great man.

Changing sides was common enough in the period, but rarely as ethical or admirable as Gareth's actions here. In the previous chapter the danger and enormity of side-changing was contemplated; here it is given a noble aspect. Both sequences seem relevant to the growing split between Warwick and the king; as the great earl came to face the real possibility of changing sides himself, he and his party saw its dangers and needed the act to be made acceptable. At the same time, Gareth's side-changing will deeply emphasise the later tragedy. Malory is preparing for the battle where Launcelot rescues Guinevere and kills Gareth by accident.

One other incident in the chapter has ideological weight. On his way to the tournament Launcelot is resting by a spring, and is suddenly shot in the buttock by a female hunter: she has missed the hind she was aiming at. This makes it harder for him to fight well, but he manages to triumph, heroically avoiding comic shame. Malory has something in mind here: in the French source the hunter is a man. The point is apparently to rework symbolically part of the previous chapter. Elaine was a troublesome woman who fired the arrow of love (a very common medieval motif) at Launcelot when he was least expecting it, and made things awkward for him, both privately and in public. The passage is a reminder that the Arthuriad weaves its ideological web on behalf of men as well as aristocrats.

But love is still a real force and the fourth chapter, entitled 'The Knight of the Cart', begins by stressing the social connections of love. It is a matter of loyalty – at its best to God, next to your lady. Guinevere's fidelity to Launcelot is so firm that although it is not faith to Arthur or God, it still has value. The contemporary point of this stress on order and loyalty is clear through one of Malory's rare direct criticisms of his period. He says modern people are fickle in love – but implicitly in many other ways as well. A concern with political stability comes through the love theme here and that pattern will recur in the following story and as the whole Arthuriad moves towards its end.

'The Knight of the Cart' chapter tells of the abduction of Guinevere and her rescue by Launcelot, but Malory alters his source to show Launcelot in a dubious light. Guinevere is abducted by Mellyagaunce when she is out celebrating May day with knights who are especially loyal to her. Such a 'queen's party' was a common feature of court organisation but the story has a more searching and ideological relation to the fifteenth century. Mellyagaunce attacks the unarmed knights with forty of his own men, twenty 'men-at-arms' and a hundred archers. The men-at-arms would be mounted sergeants, professional soldiers. They and the archers are mercenaries, 'purveyde' for the purpose (1121.34). This is an entirely credible contemporary force, the first in the whole Arthuriad. The military realities which the text has steadily ignored suddenly strike into the most vulnerable part of the court, the queen herself and young future knights.

Launcelot suffers a related fate, when he is galloping to Guinevere's rescue. Mellyagaunce has left an ungentlemanly ambush of archers: they do not challenge him to joust, but shoot down his horse – just like the British archers at Crécy, Poitiers and Agincourt. However much those lower-class professionals provided security and plunder for the English lords, their military supremacy over heavy cavalry brought anxiety to the aristocratic class. Love may be the overt medium of Mellyagaunce's threat, but the abduction bears a coded version of the political message that was evident on every battlefield in Malory's day.

Launcelot continues to meet peasant reality, but the way he deals with it is a consoling reassertion of chivalric dominance. Without a horse, he walks after the queen, but a cart passes by. It belongs to Mellyagaunce and the carter refuses Launcelot's demand to ride. So Launcelot simply kills him with a 'reremayne', a 'backhand blow' of his gauntleted fist – a comfortingly casual dismissal of a churl. He seizes the cart, forces Mellyagaunce's castle gate and kills his porter with a punch under the ear. Chivalric honour is re-established against lower-class upstarts.

This important chapter goes on to indicate that Launcelot is perhaps not the ideal defender of his class and its values that this scene has suggested. He forces open the bar on Guinevere's window, cuts his hand, and sleeps with her. In the morning Mellyagaunce finds blood on the sheets, and accuses Guinevere of sleeping with one of her wounded knights. So Launcelot will once again fight for her in trial by battle.

In strict terms he can do so truthfully. The queen did *not* sleep with any of the wounded knights, and he is careful only to swear to that fact, avoiding Mellyagaunce's second point, that she is untrue to Arthur (1133.29–33). But Launcelot's rectitude rests on a legalism, not on the firm right he and Guinevere had in the poisoned apple affair. The outcome of the battle shows the difference.

After another heroically late arrival Launcelot knocks Mellyagaunce down and he demands mercy 'as ye be a knyght and felow of the Table Rounde' (1138.23–4). Launcelot's response is startling: 'Than sir Launcelot wyst nat what to do, for he had lever than all the good in the worlde that he myght be revenged uppon hym' (1138.27–8). Revenge, a private urge rising from his private relationship with Guinevere, cuts across his sworn public duty to give mercy when it is asked – and he wants to kill a fellow Round Table knight, which is unjustifiable whatever his villainy.

Launcelot's wishes and actions are now running quite counter to his leadership of the chivalric police force. The private nature of this problem is etched by Malory as Launcelot looks at the queen and she 'wagged hir hede uppon sir Launcelot, as ho seyth "sle hym" ' (1138.31–1139.1). In the heart of this public scene they communicate privately, wordlessly, and against the honour of Launcelot and the Arthurian world.

So Launcelot offers Mellyagaunce odds: he will let him up to fight, and will himself unarm his left side and fight with one hand literally tied behind his back – a physical emblem of his moral, dubious position. Mellyagaunce, foolish as ever, accepts the odds and is killed with Launcelot's first blow.

When private wishes cut across public order the result is grotesque and disturbing. It is the awkward, conniving and half-unarmed figure of Launcelot which is finally prominent. Mellyagaunce's motives are not important, nor is the whole problem he raises: as Lambert observes, nobody worries how the blood *did* get into the bed (1975, pp. 187–8). The contemporary military detail seen as a threat, the anxious insistence on fidelity in love and loyalty, the growing tension because of private desires: these matters are brought to a head in a powerful image of a great lord finding it embarrassingly difficult to combine public order and his private interests.

The inevitable reflex of disturbingly real material in an ideological text is consolation. The last chapter of this tale ennobles Launcelot again, though also making him and the reader aware of the conflicts about him and within him. 'The Healing of Sir Urry' is Malory's own work (though there are some vaguely similar incidents in French). It tells how a knight from distant Hungary has a wound which, through sorcery, will heal when 'the beste knyght of the worlde' examines it and removes the poison by the force of his virtue. Launcelot is absent from court, but Arthur makes all the knights of the Round Table search the wound. They all fail. A complete list of them is given, with occasional comments on their fame and relationships. It is oddly like the roll-call in *Culhwch ac Olwen*, though less fantastic, and is the only list of its kind in the whole Arthuriad. It functions as a public demonstration of the Round Table community, surveyed as a collectivity before its collapse.

Finally all but Launcelot have tried, and he arrives just in time: here the late arrival motif is used overtly in the 'best knight' context, showing Malory's comprehension of its meaning in the other cases. Launcelot demurs out of modesty; Arthur commands him to act. He does so, but not with any idea of surpassing the others (1151.28–9) and with a devout prayer that 'Thou mayste yeff me power to hele thys syke knyght by the grete vertu and grace of The, but, Good Lorde, never of myselff' (1152.23–5).

Urry is healed at once. All but one give thanks to God: 'ever sir Launcelote wepte, as he had bene a chylde that had bene beatyn' (1152.35–6). Launcelot's action has intrigued critics and provoked many interpretations (see Benson, 1976, p. 229). The basic image is that of a child, weeping when beaten: the sense is one of near-innocence and penance. It takes the reader back to the Launcelot of the grail quest and of the opening of this tale, the earthly hero who went so close to heavenly achievement, who was surpassed by his son but is still 'the best knyghte of the world'.

Malory appears to have created this chapter partly to present the whole Round Table before its debacle, but especially to indicate that Launcelot is not only a capering murderous adulterer; he is also a great knight capable of at least recognising the spiritual virtues. In Tale VII Malory realises, and even intensifies, the disruptive course of events centering on the love of Launcelot and Guinevere. But he also, especially, in 'The Great Tournament' and 'The Healing of Sir Urry', insists that his hero still has great nobility. The relevance to the warring lords of the mid-fifteenth century is obvious. The contemporary meaning is even clearer in the last tale of all, as Malory chronicles social collapse in the world of Arthurian fiction and contemplates it in the world of fifteenth-century reality.

IX

Malory ends the Arthurian story with such impact that his version has become classical in English. The links between the story and contemporary reality are now so extensive that they need to be outlined before discussing how Malory uses his fictional narrative to process that reality in a suitably ideological manner.

Fierce accusations of treason are directed at Launcelot several times. That was a familiar occurrence, a striking example being in 1459 when the 'Parliament of Devils' (a Yorkist term) attainted York and Warwick of treason and prescribed the most severe and cruel penalties. After the open breach with the king, Launcelot gathers his kin and they form a powerful party. That is especially relevant to Warwick: 'through his numerous Neville relatives he had kinship with half the English aristocracy' (Green, 1955, p. 343). Like any great magnate Launcelot also gathers in those personally indebted to him, and, as they so often did in reality, the forces of Wales and the south-west side with the rebellion – in this case for the memory of Launcelot's friendship with Lamerak and Tristram.

Powerful though his party is, Launcelot is still outnumbered because the king can summon his feudal host, and so he retires to Joyous Garde, identified later as either Alnwick or Bamborough (1257.27–8). They were two great castles of the north-east, often held against the crown in the period and regained for it by Warwick in 1462 (Malory was on the campaign). The king's use of Carlisle as a base confirms that Launcelot has gone north, as so many did. Warwick was a prominent case. In 1464 and again in 1467 he withdrew 'to regain assurance by standing upon the bedrock of his power, his lordship of the north' (Kendall, 1957, p. 212).

In this disturbed situation the Pope makes an initiative, telling Arthur to accept his queen again and be at peace with Launcelot under threat of interdict, the excommunication of the kingdom. This too is rather more than fantasy. As the Yorkists gathered their somewhat tattered forces after the defeat and death of York at Wakefield in 1460, Warwick used every lever he could find. The papal legate was in his control and Warwick intended him to 'give his benediction to all soldiers fighting for the Yorkists, and publicly excommunicate, in the name of the Holy See, all who took arms for Lancaster' (Kendall, 1957, p. 78). It did not happen; Coppini wavered at the last and the Yorkists managed to seize power without the church, but Malory's papal intervention is perfectly credible in the mid-fifteenth century.

So is the highly formal scene where Launcelot returns the queen. Warwick was well known for the extraordinary formality of his public actions and, to historians at least, for his shrewd grasp of the impact of grand display. After Wakefield he buried his own father with more pomp than even the future king buried the Duke of York. When he met the King of France in 1467 he took an enormous retinue and moved with the ultimate in ceremonial. And if the form of this scene is familiar, so is its content. A reconciliation scene took place with high ceremony in 1458 when the leaders of the opposing factions of Lancaster and York walked hand in hand to St Pauls in a 'great formal procession '(Lander, 1980, p. 200).

Aurner argued some time ago that Launcelot's speech of self-exculpation is like that given by Suffolk when he was being attainted by Parliament in 1450 (1933, p. 376), and there may well be something in this, because Suffolk was also exiled – though caught and murdered as he left England. But the tenor of Launcelot's words also sounds much like the confident arrogance of Warwick himself, who, in exile in 1469 'told Margaret of Anjou – to whose misfortunes, after all, he and his family had contributed to no small extent – that he had done nothing except what "a nobleman outraged and dispersed ought to have done" ', (Lander, 1980, p. 253). More specifically, Launcelot's offer of atonement for Gareth's death is just like the proposed arrange-ments for prayer-houses discussed in the York-Lancaster negotiations in 1458 (Field, 1978, note to ll. 1102–2). It was with France that Warwick's alliance lay in the final years, and there was much talk of an independent princedom for him there. Launcelot and his forces withdrew to France. He occupies the far south-west, much as the English had done until forced out by the mid-century, and the detailed account of the lands that Launcelot distributes (1205) implies that the area is still well enough known for its alienation from the English crown to be painful.

In this way the rift between Arthur and Launcelot is filled with reminiscences of recent hostilities. It is not a direct allegory of one particular series of events; rather, the major scenes all relate to well-known occurrences in the disturbed years of the mid-century. Through these similarities Malory makes the steady fall of a society into chaos very much a story for his own time. This continues to be true as the narrative turns to the rift between Mordred and Arthur.

Mordred has been made regent 'bycause Sir Mordred was kynge Arthurs son' (1211.10), a reference which quite ignores the violence Arthur did at Mordred's birth, and merely makes the regency a normal fifteenth-century practice. But it was also normal for regents to be troublesome – hence the refusal to give York full powers of regency when Henry VI was insane. The fear was that regents would soon become kings, and Mordred fulfils the threat. He forges letters announcing Arthur's death (as York and Warwick had done about Henry VI at Ludlow). He assembles the peerage to elect him king in parliament. In 1460 York walked into parliament, put his hand on the throne and turned for an acclamation, but none came. When after York's death his son Edward seized the throne, he judiciously gathered a pre-selected and non-representative collection of lords to acclaim him.

Mordred also seizes the queen but fails to hold her – as the Yorkists never did manage to pin down Henry VI's queen, Margaret of Anjou. Aurner feels Guinevere here represents Margaret (1933, p. 375) and she is the only queen from the period who was capable of this sort of vigorous defence. Because Guinevere is in the tower Mordred attacks it with guns – an unchivalric and modern practice vividly depicted in Wynkyn de Worde's edition (Plate 14). The Yorkists did use artillery against the Lancastrian stronghold of the tower in 1460. Queen Margaret was not there, unlike Guinevere in Malory's story. But Malory himself was present, as a Lancastrian prisoner, released when the Yorkists won in 1461.

The contemporary references in this Mordred sequence all point in the same direction. Mordred is clearly fulfilling a Yorkist role, and when he raises the south-eastern counties (1233.5–10) he relies on areas which were a well-known Yorkist base (Field, 1978, note to l. 1807). Many critics have thought the whole Arthuriad has a Lancastrian bias, but this is the only sequence that justifies that opinion; as Griffith has shown (1974) the general tendency, like that of Malory's own career, is Yorkist if anything.

This last stage shows a swing to a Lancastrian position just like that made by Warwick in the late 1460s and, to judge from his exclusion from the 1468 pardon, by Malory himself. By associating the Yorkist activities of about 1460 with Mordred's rebellion against a noble and rightful king, Malory is exorcising the role Warwick played in those events and legitimising his new position as a loyal Lancastrian. The point is reinforced when Arthur and Mordred make peace based on Mordred's agreed succession to the throne after Arthur's death. Henry VI and York made the same agreement in 1460.

A more general contemporary credibility occurs after the battles, as Launcelot and Guinevere withdraw to a religious life. It was quite familiar for a noble figure, even a war leader, to shelter in the cloister in his declining years. Sir Stephen Scrope recommended it to those who 'could no longer do the active work of a knight' and was himself a famous example of such a retreat (Ferguson, 1960, p. 56). For noble women to be in a nunnery was even more common; it was a place of refuge for those who did not want to marry or marry again, and those who had other reasons to seek religious protection. With specific relevance to Guinevere's actions, after Warwick's death at Barnet his Countess went straight to Beaulieu Abbey, and after Tewkesbury, where Edward IV finished off the Lancastrians, Queen Margaret and Warwick's daughter Anne also took refuge in a convent.

If monastic seclusion was one recognised form of turning to religion from a secular life, the other path was to combine war and worship and go on crusade. After the fall of Constantinople in 1453 crusades were often discussed. Arthur may return, Malory suggests, to win back the Holy Cross – St Helena's version of it was at Constantinople. Edward IV himself long planned to go on a crusade against the 'Turks', the Saracen enemies against whom the last members of Launcelot's great affinity die fighting in the final lines of the Arthuriad.

Throughout Tale VIII the contemporary credibility of the action and Launcelot's resemblance to an idealised Warwick seem inescapable. But the text is not a covert chronicle or a simple reflection of the period. Resemblance and distortion work together to ideologise the turbulent reality of the mid-fifteenth century. Malory was able to realise some major problems, offer some explanations of their origin, and, in the face of the tragic collapse inherent in the Arthurian story and widely feared in the fifteenth century, provide a series of attractive consolations.

Vinaver's title for the first chapter, 'Slander and Strife', points to two elements which are new in this Tale. There is now to be quasi-political strife between parties. Previously Launcelot fought against his kin, or people like Elaine of Ascolat were crushed in the face of great forces. Malory explains this development through the fact that private feelings are no longer contained by and within the public structure. But he does not see private forces as a power: they now find public means by which to express their disruptive power. Once Mordred and Aggravayne turn their 'prevy hate' into open 'slander' the machine of justice has to go into action. Arthur's own private feelings, his affection for Launcelot and his wish for peace, are powerless: ' "And now hit is fallen so," seyde the kynge, "that I may nat with my worshyp but my quene muste suffir dethe" ' (1174.16–18). His honour leaves only one course open, no matter what he feels: as a result he 'was sore amoved'.

Similarly, it becomes entirely a matter of Launcelot's honour that the queen should not suffer for his sake, a public reaction affirmed by Launcelot's affinity in solemn and symbolic unison: 'therfore us semyth hit ys more youre worshyp that ye rescow the quene from thys quarell, insomuch that she hath hit for your sake' (1172.19–21). Private love may be the cause of the crisis, but like the speeches between the lovers in the queen's chamber, it is expressed in fully honourable, even ceremonial terms. Launcelot never says that he must rescue the queen because he loves her: it is his own self-concept, his own public image that guides his action in this crisis. The contemporary character of that position and the broad relationship between Launcelot and Warwick is clear from the startling relevance to this sequence found in Kendall's summary of Warwick's reaction to the breach between him and Edward IV:

> Edward's blow had opened a gap between the shape of the facts and the shape of the Warwick legend and had forced an unbearable cleft in Warwick himself between the public and the private man. His personality had been organized around his sense of himself as a figure of state. He had identified his *self* with his position in the world, and that self could only reach avidly to regain its identity. (1957, p. 211)

So the queen is to go to the stake for the third time but now when Launcelot rescues Guinevere he is in direct breach of the law. In the 'Poisoned Apple' case he was a thoroughly respectable defendant; in the Mellyagaunce affair he was still just about on the side of law. But Arthur has refused the right of trial by battle a

third time because he judges the case already proved
(1174.20–29). So the rescue is an act of anarchy and its extreme
and military nature brings its own result: bad luck follows error
once more, and catastrophically. Gareth and Gaheris are both
killed by Launcelot in the skirmish.

This gives rise to the most striking and carefully realised
transposition of private feeling into public action in the whole
Tale. When he knows his brothers are dead at Launcelot's hands,
Gawain is overcome and responds emotively: 'And forthwith he
ran unto the kynge, criyng and wepyng, and seyde, "A, myne
uncle kynge Arthur: My good brother sir Gareth is slayne, and so
ys my brothir sir Gaherys, whych were two noble knyghtis" '
(1185.13–17). Running, weeping, and the hasty, almost gabbled
speech mark this as a moment of private feeling, far from the
stately speech and manner of a great lord.

After Arthur and Gawain have exchanged grief and explanation about the event, Gawain formalises his grief and projects it
into public action: ' "My kynge, my lorde and myne uncle," seyde
sir Gawayne, "wyte you well, now I shall make you a promyse
whych I shall holde, be my knyghthode, that frome thys day
forewarde I shall never fayle sir Launcelot untyll that one of us
have slayne that othir. And therefore I requyre you, my lorde and
kynge, dresse you unto the warres, . . ." ' (1186.1–6). This is a
firm demand by a liege for help from his lord when in distress. The
balance of 'My kynge, my lorde, and myne uncle', the poise of the
whole speech, the technical language – 'requyre', 'dresse you' 'be
my knyghthode' 'from thys day forewarde' – all these things
express the crucial moment which sets Launcelot's honourable, if
unlucky, actions against Gawain's own family honour and the
public duties of his king, lord and uncle.

The lengthy scene between Arthur and Gawain is entirely
Malory's; it not only shows his mastery of tense action and terse
dialogue, but his perception that such transitions of private
feeling into public and honoured action are central to the
development of crisis. The conviction he puts into the scene also
makes credible the great weight to be laid on Gawain as the
aggressive continuer of hostilities – a very important part of the
pro-Warwick theme, and one that creates some potential strain on
credibility. Malory obscures this problem by making Gawain's
reactions so convincing.

In spite of Launcelot's private feelings that he does not want to fight Arthur or Gawain, in spite of Arthur's private feelings that he would like to be at peace with Launcelot (two elements that Malory amplifies from both his sources), Gawain's fierce determination to have his revenge keeps the civil war going. At the end of the great formal reconciliation scene, Gawain demands Launcelot's exile, and Malory stresses his aggressiveness in doing so. Gawain's behaviour is very extreme. The whole Launcelot-Arthur conflict is now over, Guinevere has been returned, the Pope has reconciled king and baron. Launcelot's public pageant and formal speech are the means of healing the rift with honour on both sides, however much his remarks are based on a lie. Gawain also recognises that this source of conflict is now forgotten (1200.25–29).

The matter between Gawain and Launcelot is the death of Gareth. Here Launcelot does not lie. He admits the act, bitterly regrets it, and makes a handsome offer of public and elaborate penance, a practice familiar in the period as part of peace negotiations. Gawain, who previously felt that Launcelot was right to rescue the queen (1184.18–24) can have no sound reasons to refuse, other than the fury that Malory has stressed. In order to provide an indirect legitimisation of Warwick's separation from the king in the later 1460s, Malory has made Gawain the prime creator of the continued hostility, which enables Mordred to rebel – as Launcelot predicts after a passage original to Malory which states firmly and clearly the 'policing' theme and identifies Launcelot as the chief in that process (1203.29–1204.11).

In his dying speech Gawain admits his error, saying it is 'thorow me and my pryde ye have all thys shame and disease' (1230.24–5). In the same way Guinevere confesses that 'Thorow thys same man and me hath all thys warre be wrought, and the deth of the moste nobelest knyghtes of the worlde' (1252.8–10). Launcelot himself finally says 'how by my defaute and myn orgule and my pryde that they were bothe layed ful lowe, that were pereles that ever was lyvyng of Christen people' (1256.33–5).

Each of the three confesses, not to sin, but to having personally caused a public tragedy. The private sphere has intruded on the public, and that is a perception in many ways relevant to fifteenth-century life and culture, as will be discussed shortly. But the fact that each of those three major figures confesses does not mean that they alone are responsible. There are a number of ways in which Malory makes the causes super-individual: a process which also leaves the erring characters room to be more noble. The selfish urges behind contemporary crisis are both recognised and obscured.

Some readers have thought that Arthur is at least partly responsible for the collapse. Brewer feels he is concerned so entirely with community, with public virtues and necessities, that he neglects private virtues and necessities; that is, 'he fails to cherish his wife as an individual' (1968, p. 28). Feeling that the later Arthur represented the feeble Henry VI, Aurner also deprecated his behaviour (1933, p. 367). But private action is not an option for Arthur: his many speeches about the value of the Round Table assert his concern as primarily public, and the text fully supports him when he says 'And much more I am soryar for my good knyghtes losse than for the losse of my fayre quene; for quenys I myght have inow, but such a felyship of good knyghts shall never be togydirs in no company' (1184.1–5).

Arthur does one personally motivated thing: he insists on killing Mordred for vengeance, against Lucan's advice. But it is after his public world has been destroyed. Lucan's idea that they have won the battle because three survive against one is grotesque, a deformation of public judgement to match Bedivere's private refusal to throw away the sword. Arthur is right to say that there is nothing left to trust in (1240.32).

Throughout the last tales the apparent weakness of Arthur is no more than a realisation of the position of the fifteenth-century king, dependent for authority on the forces of his great lords and very limited in his own power and income. Expected, even forced, to 'live of his own' and needing to operate through his commanders and favourites, when strife broke out between them and himself he was in a very weak position, as the series of threats to the crown and actual depositions throughout the period indicated. The reasons for which the king had been presented as weak in Chrétien were no longer specifically relevant, but for new reasons the model of the passive king was still appropriate.

Mordred and Aggravayne certainly bear some of the blame. Tale VII ends, and the second paragraph of Tale VIII begins, with a direct statement to that effect – 'And all was longe uppon two unhappy knyghtis' (1161.9). Arthur himself blames them

(1184.8–11). They are direct instruments of the catastrophe in that they actively project the private into the public sphere. But there are other forces too, especially bad fortune. In the very first paragraph of the Tale Malory talks of 'a grete angur and unhappe' and he adds the adjective 'unhappy' to Mordred and Aggravayne: they are not only themselves unlucky but bear ill-luck with them. Similarly in the fight to rescue Guinevere 'hit mysfortuned' Launcelot to kill Gaheris and Gareth. When the adder bites the knight and the final battle is joined, Arthur says 'Alas thys unhappy day' (1235.28) and he does at least briefly dream of the Wheel of Fortune, which only raises kings in order to bring them down (1233.11–21).

A good deal depends on fortune and a knight's response to it as Mann has recently argued (1981). This does not mean that chance is responsible for everything: Launcelot's self-exculpating opinion to that effect in his farewell speech before exile (1201.14–22) is to a large degree invalidated by his lies about Guinevere and himself then, and by his later confession. The key was given by Launcelot in Tale III; that ill-luck follows wrong behaviour.

Gawain, Guinevere and Launcelot all come to recognise their errors, yet they are not left in guilt and moral disarray. Their confessions are as honourable as their other actions, and throughout the last tale there are clear signs that Malory deliberately makes Launcelot and Guinevere particularly noble even as they are shown to be prime causes of disaster.

Malory goes out of his way in the prologue to 'The Knight of the Cart' chapter of Tale VII to make Guinevere, and by implication Launcelot, a 'trew lover'. Later in that story Launcelot is faithful to Guinevere even at the cost of staying in Mellyagaunce's dungeon (1136.1–12). In the bed-chamber scene in Tale VIII Malory even refuses to tell his audience what the lovers were doing (1165.11–13). That embarrassing place is the scene for very noble speeches, and even when they repent they remain very much *grande dame* and great lord, still with authority and a following. The most striking example of this, and the most patent assertion of the continuing validity of chivalry, even among its ruins, is that after Launcelot's potent confession of sin and his holy death, he is taken to a grand secular burial in his own fortress and his brother arrives to speak the famous eulogy. Ector talks of Launcelot in entirely secular terms as the best knight of all, the perfect mixture of prowess and courtesy: 'thou was the mekest man and the jentyllest that ever ete in halle emonge ladyes, and thou were the sternest knyght to thy mortal foo that ever put spere in the reeste' (1259.18–21).

The Christian resolution is, though, pursued beyond Ector's resumé of chivalric values. Launcelot's kin and knights go on crusade as he commanded them and the whole Arthuriad ends with the words 'And there they dyed upon a Good Friday for Goddes sake' (1260.14–15). The effect of the Christian ending is to provide a convenient resolution. It does apportion blame, does recognise human error; but Malory does not let it obliterate knighthood and the values of chivalry, just as his treatment of the grail and his invention of the Sir Urry story absorbed Christian values into the world of chivalry.

The real institution of withdrawing to a monastery after a military and sinful life resolved the moral problems of such a life. This ending is a satisfying ideological resolution to the stresses and strains of the Arthuriad. It is especially satisfying in that the Christian resolution is private, in that Gawain, Guinevere and Launcelot in turn all speak of themselves alone; but it is also public in that they speak in the formal language of Christian confession. Dissent from the chivalric collectivity finds expression through the collective voice of the church, as it did in the grail story, as it does in that other late medieval Arthurian text that is uneasy about public and chivalric values, *Sir Gawain and the Green Knight*.

Only Arthur does not receive so simple a resolution. He, rather, recedes into the collective reality of myth, as the motifs of magic and history cluster about him. Malory writes of his end in a deliberately cool, even dry style 'Now more of the deth of kynge Arthur coude I never fynde' (1242.15–16) and hedges carefully to find a valid form of words, summing up the possibilities of his survival as 'rather I wolde sey: here in thys worlde he chaunged hys lyff' (1242.26–7). Arthur, like the other noble characters whose private feelings have so conflicted with public forces (and unlike Mordred and Aggravayne), is finally brought to publicly honoured rest. Gawain lies at Dover Castle; Launcelot in his own fortress, perhaps Alnwick, perhaps Bamborough; Arthur with Guinevere at Glastonbury. It is important to recognise that Malory's audience, especially those who read Caxton's preface, would see those not only as dignified and publicly honoured shrines, but *real* ones, capable of being visited, credible and contemporary like so much in the story. The legend of Arthur's survival itself is added by Malory to his source because of its currency and credibility in British oral tradition (Benson, 1976, p. 240).

In the context of a recognisable world in crisis Malory has made the forces of private desire urgently pressing, especially in his last tales, but they are also present in earlier tales to a degree not recognisable in the sources. Such forces are themselves a dominant feature of the fifteenth-century world. The increasing recognition of the power of the individual is a feature of the period in many spheres. Financially, a market economy has developed to the point of capitalist take-off and as a result personal mobility, both social and geographic, has become a reality that cannot be ignored as it was in previous centuries. The same patterns exist in religion; the Lollard movement had been in essence an individualist struggle for the collective property, both economic and spiritual, of the church, but that quasi-heresy had largely been suppressed. In the fifteenth century those same forces were channelled into the cult of *devotio moderna* which focuses on the private Christian. In literature and art there is a marked development of concern with the individual, in the 'dance of death' motif especially, but also in the development of realism, a mode which bases itself on the validity of the individual sensual response.

Malory's own literary form shows this development, as he moves away from a fully medieval Gothic structure in the early tales, especially I and III, to a much more modern-seeming climax-oriented structure (Knight, 1969, chs 3 and 4). In the same way his style and his presentation of character changes from the formulaic treatment of the early tales to a much more individualist presentation in the last books, where feeling is heard in the voice and types of personality are visibly evolved, as in Gawain's radical change from friend to hater of Launcelot, and the distinctly naturalistic tension between Launcelot and Guinevere that is developed through Tale VII.

In these respects Malory is at the deepest level responding to a fifteenth-century development. It is ultimately a level of meaning in the text's own form which makes all the more forceful the destructive private tendencies at work, just as they were in the period among the class that provided Malory's audience. That powerful artistic veracity makes seem all the more ideological and merely optimistic Malory's resolution of the destructive private forces of the story into consolingly public forces – Christian confession and forgiveness, mythic grandeur in the case of Arthur, and an honourable chivalric afterglow for the destructive magnates of the Round Table.

In many ways Malory's work is a last statement of medieval chivalry: already defunct in practice it was soon to be uprooted as an ideology in favour of the model of the humanist gentleman, so that in 1570 Roger Ascham's *The Scholemaster*, which was itself teaching the new ideology, could dismiss the Arthuriad as containing no more than 'bold bawdry and open manslaughter'. With that radical change of world-view among the powerful, responding to the emergence of the modern state and its social and economic practices, the legend of Arthur itself was to be greatly weakened as a story to believe in and a framework within which to analyse the nature of authority and disorder. Only when the social and economic forces of bourgeois capitalism had developed sufficiently to impel a wholesale critique of that new formation would the Arthurian legend revive as a major cultural force. In the hands of nineteenth-century artists such as Tennyson the legend of Arthur was once again, as it had been for Malory and his predecessors, a story which could be brought from an old world both to confront and obscure the fears of the present.

REFERENCES

Primary Source
Malory, Sir T. (1967) *The Works of Sir Thomas Malory* ed. E. Vinaver, 2nd edn (London: Oxford University Press).

Secondary Sources
Adolf, H. (1960) *Visio Pacis, Holy City and Grail* (Philadelphia: Pennsylvania State University Press).
Aurner, N. S. (1933) 'Sir Thomas Malory – Historian?' *Proceedings of the Modern Language Association of America* 48, 362–91.
Barber, R. W. (1970) *The Knight and Chivalry* (London: Longman).
Bellamy, J. (1973) *Crime and Public Order in England in the Later Middle Ages* (London: Routledge).
Benson, L. D. (1976) *Malory's Morte d'Arthur* (Cambridge, Mass.: Harvard University Press).
Brewer, D. S. (1968) Introduction to *The Morte Darthur* (London: Arnold).

Campbell, J. B. (1949) *The Hero with a Thousand Faces* (New York: Pantheon).

Dichmann, M. (1964) ' "The Tale of King Arthur and the Emperor Lucius": The Rise of Lancelot' in *Malory's Originality*, ed. R. M. Lumiansky (Baltimore: Johns Hopkins University Press).

Ferguson, A. B. (1960) *The Indian Summer of English Chivalry* (Durham: Duke University Press).

Field, P. J. C. (1978) Introduction to *Le Morte Darthur* (London: Hodder and Stoughton).

—— (1979–80) 'Thomas Malory and the Warwick Retinue Roll', *Midland History*, 2, 20–9.

—— (1979) 'Thomas Malory, the Hutton Documents', *Medium Aevum*, 47, 213–39.

Griffith, R. R. (1974) 'The Political Bias of Malory's *Morte Darthur*', *Viator* 5, 365–86.

—— (1981) 'The Authorship Question Reconsidered' in *Aspects of Malory*, ed. T. Takamiya and D. S. Brewer (Woodbridge: Brewer).

Green, V. H. (1955) *The Later Plantagenets* (London: Arnold).

James, M. (1979) *English Politics and the Concept of Honour 1485–1642* (Oxford: Past and Present Monographs).

Kendall, P. M. (1957) *Warwick the Kingmaker* (London: Allen and Unwin).

Kennedy, E. D. (1970) 'Malory and the Marriage of Edward IV', *Texas Studies in Literature and Language* 12, 153–62.

Knight, S. (1969) *The Structure of Sir Thomas Malory's Arthuriad* (University of Sydney Press).

Lambert, M. (1975) *Style and Vision in Malory's Morte Darthur* (New Haven: Yale University Press).

Lander, J. R. (1977) *Conflict and Stability in Fifteenth Century England* 3rd edn (London: Hutchinson).

—— (1980) *Government and Community in England 1450–1509* (Arnold: London).

Loomis, R. S. (1939) 'Malory's Beaumains', *Proceedings of the Modern Language Association of America* 54, 656–68.

Mann, J. (1981) 'Taking the Adventure' in *Aspects of Malory*, see under Griffith (1981).

Matthews, W. (1966) *The Ill-Framed Knight* (Berkeley and Los Angeles: University of California Press).

McIntosh, A. I. (1968) Review of Matthews, W. (1966) *Medium Aevum* 37, 346–8.

Oakeshott, W. F. (1963) 'The Finding of the Manuscript' in *Essays on Malory* ed. J. A. W. Bennett (Oxford: Clarendon).

Pearsall, D. (1976) 'The English Romance in the Fifteenth Century', *Essays and Studies* 29, 56–83.

Raglan, Lord (1936) *The Hero* (London: Methuen).

Simes, G. R. (1977) 'Chivalry and Malory's Quest of the Holy Grail', *Parergon* 17, 37–45.

York, E. C. (1969) 'The Duel of Chivalry in Malory's Book XIX', *Philological Quarterly* 48, 186–91.

5 'The phantom king': Tennyson's Arthurian *Idylls*

I

In the sixteenth and seventeenth centuries the Arthurian legend diminished in status. It was too Catholic for many Protestants, especially with its grail connections, and its propaganda use by the Tudor monarchs had made it much too royalist for many parliamentarians (Hill, 1958, pp. 60–1). One major writer was neither aggressively protestant nor republican: Edmund Spenser contributed strongly to the Tudor royal myth in his long but unfinished epic poem *The Faerie Queene*. 'Prince Arthur' is the model of the 'magnanimous man': he embodies all the virtues that are allegorically demonstrated through particular knights in separate books. In the end Arthur will marry Gloriana; she is the 'Faerie Queene' herself and an apotheosis of Elizabeth I.

This poem is rich in social and ideological material, but it will not be discussed at length here, for two main reasons. The Arthurian material in it is not slight (Millican, 1932) but it is an overlay, not an integral element. The essence of the poem is its moral allegory. Secondly, it had no wide impact in the period or afterwards: Spenser's unofficial title as 'the poet's poet' indicates his narrow range of audience. The poem cannot have major interest for a study concerned with the inter-relations of Arthurian story and broad social forces.

Most historians of the Arthurian legend after Malory state simply that, apart from the questionable case of Spenser, the legend went underground, to re-emerge in the nineteenth century. This is not true: it merely recreates the interests and attitudes of the literary élite in that period. The legend did not disappear at all; but it no longer fitted the ideology of that sub-class. When James Merriman undertook a book on the post-Malory legend he

149

had to stop before Tennyson, because there was so much material to cover (1973, p. viii).

Some commentators admit the existence of the Arthurian material from this period but deplore its literary quality. That 'fact' is itself based on the distance between these texts and the attitudes and modes of writing of the literary élite, but the possibility of such a judgement indicates that those who still believe in 'serious' Arthurian poetry like Blackmore and Heber (Merriman, 1973, pp. 64–71 and 167–73) are speaking with a conservative complacency that causes a lack of tension in form and content alike. But their work does exist and does expound widespread attitudes which are silenced by conventional literary history in making total the loss of interest in Arthur at the high cultural level: that level itself is more divided than its self-appointed controllers like to recognise.

A widespread rejection of Arthur remains a fact; the legend that was medieval, monarchic and Catholic was passed over by some of the most powerful writers in British literature. Shakespeare only recognised the legend by using its greatest hero's name for his most stupid clown, Launcelot Gobbo in *The Merchant of Venice*. Milton long planned to write *the* English epic on Arthur, but changed his mind, almost certainly on historical as well as religious-political grounds (Hill, 1977, p. 361). Dryden did write an Arthurian text, the masque of *King Arthur* (1691), but what weight the piece has comes from Purcell's sparkling music; Dryden's source was Geoffrey of Monmouth, whose Latinity lent classical authority to the now distant legend. Arthur's nadir was Fielding's inversion of the tradition in his satirical *Tragedy of Tragedies, or The Life and Death of Tom Thumb the Great* (1731).

That use of a popular story to degrade the status of Arthur is partly authentic and points to another range of culture which kept the legend alive. Broadsheets, romances and ballads indicate that Arthur remained well-known outside the metropolitan élite culture during the period. Six examples appear in Percy's *Reliques of Ancient Poetry* (1765) and Child prints three more (1882–98, see Vol. I, nos. 30, 33–4). But the continuing popularity of Arthur is clearer in two areas which are still almost beyond the control of those who own or administer the means of publication, namely the little-regarded cultural genres of place-names and children's stories.

Michael Drayton's *Poly-Olbion* (1622) is a national (and

nationalist) survey of Britain, but it includes many Arthurian stories and fragments associated with places. Many of them still bear the old names and associations (Ashe, 1980). The popular respect for Arthur which was embodied in such traditions was the groundswell of the surviving Arthurian legend in Britain, out of which high cultural formations could again develop.

If the countryside provided a local habitation for the legend, many people heard the name of Arthur first as children. Under the influence of bourgeois literary culture folk-lore has become restricted to the non-literate nursery, but once it permeated the whole house (Zipes, 1979, chs 1 and 2). Heroes like Jack the Giant Killer and Tom Thumb were not originally restricted to children, and so it was quite normal for them to become attached to Arthur's court just as previous heroes like Launcelot and Tristram had been recruited at the aristocratic level. Fielding made that popular connection the medium of his urbane and Augustan contempt for the culturally debased Arthurian legend, but in reality it was a widespread and continuous element of the legend. The actual survival of the Arthurian legend in the seventeenth and eighteenth centuries at an oral and popular level has been well described by MacCallum, a learned and lively analyst of the legend:

> Thus King Arthur was laid up in the humble Avilion of juvenile fiction, the best he could find, till he should be healed of the grievous wound that the rationalism of the period had dealt him, and return once more to gladden the hearts of his Britons.
>
> (1894, p. 167)

The reasons for the return to high culture popularity of the legend of Arthur are as multiple and complex as the reasons for the major changes of taste among the controllers of high culture between the mid-eighteenth and the nineteenth century. There is a great deal of literary criticism on the period, but not very much work that traces the cultural changes to social and historical roots. However, some important causes can be identified.

There were specific attractions in medieval material. J. W. Burrow (1978, p. 126) draws attention to A. W. N. Pugin's influential *Contrasts* (1836) 'with its juxtaposition of a gentle, harmonious, beautiful medieval world and an abhorred, callous, hideous, modern commercial one'. Carlyle's *Past and Present*

(1843) gave the same message in more strident and more influential terms. The value of medievalism for the anti-progressive forces was recognised by George III himself, an early gothiciser (Girouard, 1981, pp. 22–6). The interest of the Tory 'Young England' movement in feudalism as a model of a combination of aristocracy and peasant at the expense of Whiggish intermediaries is another conservative application of the medieval revival. This force was both recognised and countered in the 'Norman Yoke' theory, widespread among radicals, which argued with at least some basis that Anglo-Saxon freedoms were quenched by the Norman imperialists (Hill, 1958).

While medievalism could be an attractively conservative resource, it could also be a pleasing alternative to aristocratic and classical eighteenth-century culture. The romantic poets were as dissatisfied by the Augustan literary style as they were separated (in different ways) from the tightly knit world of the contemporary power élite. Augustan writers, whatever their party, had no sense of alienation from the owners and rulers of the country with whom they shared a faith in rational approaches, classical restraint and moderate religion. The medieval world of naïve romance was one of the non-establishment modes, one of the alternative channels of feeling that attracted the romantics (Chandler, 1970, ch. 3).

In the works of Scott medievalism was a crucial resource in the formation of an autonomous bourgeois culture. His impact on the resurgence of the Arthurian legend was indirect because several editions of Malory came out while he was thinking of producing one, including Southey's (1817), the version Tennyson used. But Scott's influence was nevertheless powerful. Almost single-handedly he created among his English audience a taste for gothic and medieval material in novels like *Ivanhoe*. His Scottish material was historically more recent and dealt often quite directly with the formation of a new urban and bourgeois self-consciousness – made into a gratifyingly false consciousness through the romance of origins, rural, highland or medieval. Rejecting the culture of legal Edinburgh for the dreams of 'clannit' Scotland and medieval England, Scott both typified and greatly facilitated the bourgeois use of history to create an ideological shelter for the isolated individual; it provided the dual comforts of a wish-fulfilling non-commercial sentimentalism and a broader aggressive nationalism. Lukács has exposed this structure in *The Historical Novel* (1962, ch. 1 pt. 2) and the pattern is also strongly present in Scott's poetry, both the new romantic poems like 'The Lay of the Last Minstrel' and the ballads he collected and carefully reworked.

For Tennyson, as for Scott, literary and scholarly culture provided a world in which to live, as well as a retreat from the disturbances of both family life and the social world. Somersby rectory had a fine library and Tennyson read very widely – again like Scott, his sheer intellectualism has been much under-rated. Tennyson knew a great deal about the Arthurian legend before he started shaping his *Idylls* in earnest. Kathleen Tillotson has shown the originality of his Arthurian interest and how he personally wakened a wide public to the Arthurian legend (1965). The *Idylls* are the work of a very well-read and thoughtful poet who is using a deliberately accessible style in order to address a massive audience (Gray, 1980, pp. 129–31). Tennyson achieved that audience with remarkable success and the reasons for his urge to speak to so many, and also for his success in that attempt, lie largely in the ideological patterns he worked into his Arthuriad, and the way in which they corresponded with the anxieties of his audience.

II

Tennyson's earliest Arthurian poems are merely part of a wide literary experience and experimentation, fragments recreated with the emphasis on sentiment. 'The Lady of Shalott', a rather gothic piece, was published in 1832. Two other early Arthurian poems exist, 'Sir Lancelot and Queen Guinevere' and 'Sir Galahad'. The former was written 'partly if not wholly' in 1830 (H. Tennyson, 1897, II.122), the latter by 1834 (Ricks, 1969, p. 610: all quotations will be from this edition). Both celebrate the characters at their most admirable; Lancelot and Guinevere are relished in a highly sensual spring setting and Galahad is praised for his interwoven purity and strength. The idylls of 'Guinevere' and 'The Holy Grail' see these matters in a much more complex and negative light.

A weightier use of the legend as a medium to fix feeling is the 'Morte d'Arthur', written in 1833–4 and published in the 1842 collection of poems. Later it became the bulk of 'The Passing of Arthur', the last of the idylls. Tennyson had been thinking about a major Arthurian work: the allegorical plan of a long narrative survives, as does a preliminary sketch for part of it, and a synopsis of a five act masque (H. Tennyson, 1897, ii.122–5). These are hard to date precisely, but it seems likely that some at least precede the death of Arthur Hallam in October 1833. That event, a tragedy which remained with Tennyson all his life, focused the poet's interest and gave a specific role for part of the legend: by the following year he had completed his 'Morte', reworking in epic blank verse Malory's account of Arthur's last battle into a sonorous and powerful poem.

This monument to Hallam was not the end of Tennyson's interest in the legend. He was still toying, as he knew Milton had, with the idea of an Arthurian epic, a British Aeneid, and these thoughts appear in the frame he wrote for the 'Morte d'Arthur' in about 1837–8. It gave a setting for a performance by Everard Hall of his 'Morte d'Arthur', described as the eleventh book of his own Arthuriad epic – all the rest now destroyed because of his dissatisfaction. Hall says his genre and style were too old and '. . . nature brings not back the Mastodon (36)'. The metaphor indicates Tennyson's up-to-date learning in geology and evolution. The framework in general indicates his dissatisfaction with the idea of a merely literary and emotive use of the Arthurian legend, his growing sense that a poet should, while still mastering emotion and lyricism, be socially responsible, take notice of the conflicted world about him.

Tennyson's own politics rose from his family's traditionally Whig position, were radicalised to some degree by his personal sympathy for the oppressed, but were always controlled, as in so many liberals, by a hostile reaction to any real or threatened change in the power-structure. Charles Tennyson, the poet's grandson, presents a laudatory version of that position in his essay on 'Tennyson's Politics' (1954). The attitudes are clear enough in Tennyson's life. He rang the bells at Somersby to welcome the 1832 Reform Act but turned out with other undergraduates at Cambridge as vigilantes against rick-burning and the direct action forces of Captain Swing.

At Cambridge he came into contact with the Apostles, a self-selected undergraduate society with 'strongly liberal views' (C. Tennyson, 1954, p. 39). They conducted quite weighty discussions on matters of public policy and 'serious philosophical subjects' (Martin, 1980, p. 86). F. D. Maurice, later a prominent Christian Socialist, was a kind of 'second father' to the Apostles

(Maurice, 1884, I, 56). They supported Tennyson's rejection of the merely literary life. Chenevix Trench asserted 'Tennyson, we cannot live in art' (Ricks, 1969, p. 400). Tennyson himself wrote 'The Palace of Art' (1832) in response to the challenge, to show that contemporary material can be united with art itself. The more serious-minded Apostles remained on guard. When Tennyson published the 'Morte d'Arthur' in 1842 it was one of them, John Sterling, who wrote in the influential *Quarterly Review* (September 1842) that in spite of its literary fineness it did not 'come very near us' (quoted in Jump, 1967, p. 119–20): three other Apostles reviewed the volume and kept up the same pressure (Martin, 1980, p. 265).

Many critics have argued in recent years that there are two Tennysons, one (the one they value) is the quintessential lyric poet, creator of exquisite images and sound-patterns. But this sensitive creature, they feel, was muffled by the weight of Victorian dutifulness, the dulling sense that art must be socially responsible. That interpretation of his essence as a poet was not Tennyson's nor that of near contemporaries like Stopford Brooke (1894) and W. C. Gordon (1906): they wrote knowledgeably and approvingly on the inter-relation of Victorian society and Tennyson's poetry. Nor did the first of the anti-Tennyson critics separate the art and its world: they blamed both together. Fausset found in the blind certainties of the poetry and the society the cause of the war that had shattered his own generation (1923). Nicholson, in a less serious-minded book (1923), merely found the Victorian poet and his age both equally limited.

For all his interest in the aesthetic and for all his inherent individualism, there was no gap between art and society for Tennyson: he held the traditional view that the artist was the voice of a particular group and expressed contemporary problems with traditional craft and wisdom. He was very comfortable with the idea of group patronage of the artist, as is shown by his fondness for reading aloud to a social meeting of influential people. He had a corresponding distaste, even hatred, for the mass buying public – on whom in fact his economic access to the influential world depended.

Tennyson's own admiration went, until late in his life, to those with strongly social and worldly interests, especially men of power like Charles Kingsley and F. D. Maurice, Christian Socialists, and Gladstone and Jowett, both quite radical in their policies. He knew them all well in the period when the *Idylls* were being slowly developed, and talked with them long and hard. From a modern standpoint these men may well seem to be rather limited in their reformism. There were genuine radicals like Robert Owen and the Chartist leaders about, even before the emergence of self-consciously socialist forces. But all the same, in their time Tennyson's friends were radical and often too much so for his own distinctly cautious and nervous feelings. His descendant says he agreed with Kingsley and Maurice about the bad effects of 'the commercial spirit of the age and the liberal doctrine of laissez-faire', but went on to sidetrack their radical thrust into nationalism and idealism, much more comfortable positions for him: 'the same causes seemed to him responsible for the country's reluctance to face the duty of national defence and for the new spirit of materialism' (C. Tennyson, 1954, p. 52).

Tennyson's own analysis of contemporary problems is important and revealing. Hallam Tennyson records that in 1847 his father 'said that the two great social questions impending in England were "the housing and education of the poor man before making him our master, and the higher education of women"' (1897, I.249). The first point recognises the social reforms that men like Maurice and Kingsley argued for, but takes a defensive, even churlish tone. The second matter, distinctly controversial for the time (Killham, 1958), is the one Tennyson thought most deeply about – though the remark does not indicate whether he is for or against 'the higher education of women'. His major statement on the topic, *The Princess* (finished and published in 1847) both proposes and rejects the notion of a separate and highly skilled role for women in society. The poem finally argues that women should find fulfilment through men, helping them and accepting a patriarchal structure, with the Prince saying to Princess Ida:

> Accomplish thou my manhood and thyself;
> Lay thy sweet hands in mine and trust to me.

(VII.344–5)

Kate Millett has effectively exposed the masculine anxiety and ideology created in the poem (1970), but there is a brief glimpse of another type of tension in *The Princess*. It opens and closes with a narrative frame set at a squire's fête for his villagers. They have an

educational institute and are all apparently happy. In the
end-frame, 'the Tory member's eldest son' (50) talks of modern
revolutionaries as being 'Like our wild Princess with as wise a
dream' (69) but the narrator is more tentative, more sympathetic
with dissent:

> Ourselves are full
> Of social wrong; and maybe wildest dreams
> Are but the needful preludes of the truth.   (72–4)

However, he soon slips back into a full and consoling confidence
that the people *will* be patient, that the genial squire (himself a
model of masculinity – 'No little lily-handed Baronet he' 84) will
through fêtes and sympathy guide the future . . . and remain in
power.

The first of Tennyson's stated concerns, the education of our
future masters, is both hinted at and obscured in 'The Princess', a
poem directly about the second concern, the higher education of
women. There are two other poems where Tennyson deals with
the poor and their problems and in both of them he approaches
the topic through the medium of a woman. In 'Locksley Hall'
(written 1837–8) the speaker has been rejected by his cousin Amy
and his political remarks are the excited hopes and the jaded fears
of the unnaturally lonely man who hurries off into foreign parts.
The poem and its politics are much more like the frenzied
excitement of 'Maud' than the judicious social commentary
suggested by the usual brief quotations from it in the context of
'Tennyson's politics'. The feeling for woman, the need for a
suitable mate, is the drive of the poem and social and political
comment is restricted by that problem.

Later on when Tennyson considers the values (and value) of
the ordinary working man in 'Enoch Arden' (written 1861–2), the
whole action is focused on a broken family, a wife abandoned by
Enoch. There is economic reality in the cause of the abandon-
ment, it is true, but Tennyson can only realise the pressure of
trade and the selflessness of a working man in the context of the
family. The evidence is quite clear that although Tennyson
identified two problems as dominant, in his poetry both in that
period and afterwards the whole role (not just the education) of
women was the primary issue.

This pattern is plain in the *Idylls of the King* once they are read in order of composition and publication, that is, in the order of their social relations, both in terms of their creation and impact. Tennyson first works through the problem of women and provides resolutions to the threats posed by women. Later he widens his scope to consider the weakness of social authority. But having partially faced the socio-economic forces that actually threatened the power-holding classes in the period, he turns eagerly back to the troublesome women. They provide a convenient explanation of what has gone wrong with the authority of the king . . . or, more exactly, with the authority of a male sex who felt born to own and to rule a country as they did their own families.

III

Although Sterling's review of 'Morte d'Arthur' confirmed Tennyson's doubts about an epic and medievalising Arthuriad, and although the 1840s were much occupied with his restless and sometimes distinctly neurotic personal feelings (both chronicled and partly laid to rest in *In Memoriam*) he did not forget the Arthurian topic. In 1848 he was in Cornwall to work on his Arthur project. He met R. J. Hawker, the scholarly and eccentric Cornish clergyman; they examined Tintagel together. In 1849 the *Pre-Raphaelite Journal* reported that Tennyson was 'maturing the conception' of a major Arthurian work (Richardson, 1962, p. 110).

But what Tennyson actually first produced was not really Arthurian. Apparently, when he first seriously turned back to writing about King Arthur in about 1854 (Ricks, 1969, p. 1593) he thought about the story of Merlin and Vivien – a very strange choice of topic for a man allegedly mesmerised by Malory. Vivien (or 'Nimue' as Malory sometimes calls her and as Tennyson did up to the publication of the poem as 'Vivien' in 1859) has a small part early in Malory; the story of her enchantment of Merlin is told on about a single page of a very long book. Much of the detail came from Southey's summary of the French *Merlin* in the Introduction to his Malory (1817). The idyll was actually written early in 1856 and Tennyson went straight on to another, which he called 'Enid'. (This was divided in 1873 into two idylls, 'The Marriage of Geraint' and 'Geraint and Enid'. 'Vivien' was later called 'Merlin and Vivien'. Here the early titles will be used, but references will employ abbreviations of the later titles, since

Ricks' edition naturally depends on the revised text. Lines 6–146 of 'Merlin and Vivien' were not included until the 1875 edition.)

The story of Geraint and Enid tells of a strained though finally successful marriage. It comes from the Welsh *Mabinogion* – a complete translation had been published in 1849. So at the beginning of the long sequence of idylls, Tennyson was not guided by a deep love of Malory nor a burning commitment to remodel the stories of Arthur. Rather, he started to write in a medieval (and consequently distanced) mode to deal with the problems that he saw arising from women and through their relations with men both inside and outside marriage.

Tennyson intended to publish the two completed idylls together. A few copies of a trial edition were printed in 1857, entitled 'Enid and Nimue: The True and the False' – only one copy survives (Plate 15). This edition never came out, and according to a note by Francis Palgrave on the fly-leaf of the single survivor Tennyson withheld it 'owing to a remark on "Nimue" which reached him' (Plate 16).

That is highly credible: there were many remarks about the idyll when it did appear. Bagehot found it more suitable to 'the court of Louis Quinze' than Arthur (quoted in Jump, 1967, p. 278) and Jowett wrote to Tennyson calling that idyll 'the naughty one' (H. Tennyson, 1897, I.449). It is a strongly erotic piece and Tennyson encodes sexuality through natural imagery. The defeat of Merlin takes place after he and Vivien enjoy sex – the meaning is especially clear when the passage is read aloud, Tennyson's normal practice:

> she called him lord and liege,
> Her seer, her bard, her silver star of eve,
> Her God, her Merlin, the one passionate love
> Of her whole life; and ever overhead
> Bellowed the tempest, and the rotten branch
> Snapt in the rushing of the river-rain
> Above them; and in change of glare and gloom
> Her eyes and neck glittering went and came;
> Till now the storm, its burst of passion spent,
> Moaning and calling out of other lands,
> Had left the ravaged woodland yet once more
> To peace; and what should not have been had been,

> For Merlin, overtalked and overworn,
> Had yielded, told her all the charm, and slept.
>
> (MV.951–64)

Vivien's gasping, the double entendres of 'passion', 'came', 'spent', 'ravaged', 'woodland' as well as the final postcoital exhaustion – all this makes her triumph and Merlin's defeat a fully sexual encounter.

The Victorian male's fear of female sexuality is well enough recorded. Johnson discusses many details (1975, ch. 3), and Tennyson clearly shared it. A fine instance occurred when Mrs Caroline Norton, a fully-fledged society beauty, sat beside him at a party: he rushed away and later said he thought she was snake-like (Martin, 1980, pp. 283–4). Vivien 'clung like a snake' to Merlin (MV.240) and in 'The Beguiling of Merlin' Burne-Jones turned the 'snake of gold' in her hair (MV.886) into a Medusa-head of real snakes which, at first glance, seems like a sinuously enticing headdress (Plate 17). He also portrays with brilliance the dress 'that more exprest Than hid her' (MV.220–1).

But Vivien is not only, and not ultimately, a sexual threat. The inner dread is that Vivien through her sexual force will make men trust her and then she can betray them. She first asks for Merlin's faith (MV.332) and then when he calls her 'harlot' (MV.841) she combines her frailty and love with his lack of trust to position herself for the sexual conquest of him, his confidence and so his confidences.

Vivien represents more than a fear of loose women. She is a grotesque version of sexuality within the house, a woman requiring, demanding a husband's trust in return for her sexual favours. Vivien is not only a sexually active woman, she is also one who demands to share her man's knowledge. She challenges not only masculine potency but patriarchal wisdom as well – a link back to *The Princess* and Tennyson's worry about education of women.

The contemporary threat of the intimate women rose from historical changes to the family. It had become increasingly inward-directed and feeling was increasingly located within the nuclear unit, as Stone has argued in his description of 'The Closed Domesticated Nuclear Family' (1977, Section IV). In the newly restricted family unit the wife was powerful in reality because she ran the house and tended the family; she mediated all physical needs ranging from health through food to sex. It was now all the more necessary to ideologise away that power in order to preserve the patriarchal role. Although the weight of his position was intensified by the narrowing of the family unit, with now only one senior male in it, the continual absence of the father at work or in compensatory male company meant he was represented in the household only by his authority – supported by his financial power. In that situation any encounters where men and women were equal, or she potentially superior, were distinctly threatening whether they were physical or intellectual. Having realised both through Vivien, Tennyson sets to work in Enid to create a mechanism for their control.

After a long flashback to their meeting and marriage, in which Geraint is thoroughly dominant in status, will and energy, the story of Enid and Geraint is that he comes to suspect her of infidelity. In fact she is only trying to tell him that his underlings feel he is weakened by being uxorious towards her. So to prove himself masterful he imposes great dangers on both of them and puts constraints on her behaviour. Finally through her submissive obedience and dutiful help, they return to court and are happy again; she is forgiven for the disturbance she (according to the poem) caused.

The idyll opens with an interesting contrast to the sexual activity which concluded 'Vivien'. Geraint and Enid are in bed, and he:

> bared the knotted column of his throat
> The massive square of his heroic breast,
> And arms on which the standing muscle sloped,
> As slopes a wild brook o'er a little stone,
> Running too vehemently to break upon it.   (MG.74–8)

The scene is richly sensual, that is, sexual. But the essence is male narcissism, not a mutual sexuality – that has just been found perilous from the male viewpoint. The columnar throat and heroic chest have not deflated through sexual involvement, the muscle runs smoothly as a stream over a pebble – or an autocratic husband over a submissive and immobile wife. And there she is in the next line. Enid woke and:

> sat beside the couch,
> Admiring him, and thought within herself,
> Was ever man so grandly made as he?   (MG.79–81)

But not all is so simple, or not yet. He is accused of being too
attentive to his wife and this too is encoded as postcoital
exhaustion; he is seen as:

> a prince whose manhood was all gone,
> And molten down in mere uxoriousness. (MG.59–60)

The action of the story will exorcise the threatening power of
women. Geraint first refuses Enid her enticing finery and makes
her ride in her plainest dress (GE.130). He tries to make her
the submissive audience of his spontaneous virility – she must be
silent as he encounters sudden foes. But she cannot resist helping
him, however angry this makes him; service is natural to her and
attractive to him. This is acceptable to Geraint finally, because it
is clear she has no separate identity. Just as Ida was told to
'Accomplish thou my manhood', so Enid's complaisance has in
some way sustained, even created that masculinity that was, in so
beefcake a fashion, the starting point of the poem.

Geraint is finally renowned as 'the great Prince and man of
men' (GE.960). Previously he was less sure of this position,
shouting:

> 'Effeminate as I am
> I will not fight my way with gilded arms,
> All shall be iron;'   (GE.20–2)

And when enemies approach he orders Enid to be silent, 'Seeing
that ye are wedded to a man' (GE.425). This theme will recur
through the early idylls, a sense that only in complete dominance,
especially of women, can a man be secure in his possession of
masculinity. Male narcissism, fear of effeminacy, a resulting
control of women: the elements are central to the nervous
sustenance of a patriarchal position and they dominate 'Vivien'
and 'Enid', the idylls Tennyson first completed.

It is clear that Tennyson was himself a typical Victorian man in
his concept of marriage. He long hesitated over it, breaking off his
two-year engagement to Emily Selwood by 1840 and then
marrying her in 1850. The overt reasons, that he was short of

money and that her father disapproved, seem no more than rationalisations. Tennyson's family was sure enough that his uncertainty was to blame. When they did marry eventually, Emily very plainly took up Enid's role as a 'household Spirit' (GE.403) and did indeed accomplish herself through Tennyson's own being and success: his acquaintances often remarked on the difference she made to him (there was room for improvement in manners) and to the organisation of his career. Ideologies do enact themselves, especially to please the powerful.

The emphasis on the dangerousness of Vivien and Enid acts out Tennyson's ideas of what is false and true in women – as the projected title of the pair of idylls makes clear – from a firmly and even neurotically male viewpoint. The Arthurian world and especially Malory's works are no more than a frame for those telling and powerful ideological idylls. But having decided not to publish them alone as a pair (perhaps because of their naked urgency, perhaps because of the negative power of 'Vivien'), Tennyson went on to develop the topic of the role of women in a less strident if no less polemical way, and in order to do this he used stories which were fully Arthurian and did come from Malory himself.

Tennyson began work on the 'Guinevere' idyll in July 1857, and completed it by April 1858. He almost immediately went on to write 'Elaine'. Finishing that early in 1859, he published the four in that year as *Idylls of the King*. They all bore as their titles the name of a woman. A male name was later added in all but the case of 'Guinevere' when these idylls were republished with new idylls in 1869.

The two new 1859 idylls were both from Malory, but to different degrees. 'Guinevere' is very much a work of Tennyson's imagination, reworking Malory's final sequence quite radically to emphasise Guinevere's humiliation in sin: first a novice nun and then the wronged husband wring repentance from her. The point driven home so strongly by Arthur and the poet is that, in seeing Arthur as inhuman because he was non-sensual, Guinevere was using a very restricted, sensually-based system of evaluation. She may complain that he was 'cold High, self-contained, and passionless' (G.402–3) but she comes to agree, under the weight of his attack, that 'Thou art the highest and most human too' (G.644) and that 'We needs must love the highest when we see it, Not Lancelot, nor another' (G.655–6).

If we read the idylls as they were composed, Guinevere is clearly a composite of Vivien and Enid, a sexually erring wife who is disciplined and brought to recognise her sin and the correctness of male authority. This is implied, like so much in Tennyson, by a dramatic visual image, when Guinevere lies before Arthur's feet. Her position is like that of the serpentine Vivien creeping seductively up Merlin's legs (MV.217–8 and 236–7), but her attitude is supplication like the all-humble Enid (G.524–5). Doré's engravings of the idyll in the de luxe edition (1867) make the point very clear. In all the earlier plates Guinevere's hair is dark, but this scene shows it distinctly light (Plate 18). That is a visual realisation of Tennyson's consistent equivalence of dark and light with the presence or absence of sin.

As an amalgam of the two women, Guinevere's sexuality is not nearly as potent as Vivien's: in fact Tennyson alters his source so that when she meets Lancelot in her chamber it is only to say a last farewell (G.95–7) and Vivien herself is brought into the idyll to symbolise sexual vice: she betrays the lovers to Mordred. Like Enid Guinevere acknowledges guilt, but being part-Vivien she has in fact sinned (Enid believes she has because Geraint insists she has, GE.46–8 and 743–6). So Guinevere's repentance is greater than Enid's, even grotesquely so. She dreams that her own shadow extends and, 'blackening, swallowed all the land, and in it Far cities burnt' (G.81–2).

That image does suggest the political, socially destructive impact of her sin. The point that Guinevere caused the fall of the Round Table is made by the novice among others (G.217–8) but its full ideological impact and possibilities will be developed later when Tennyson is tackling – or rather not tackling – the wider political implications of the fall of the Round Table.

The bulk of the feeling about Guinevere in her idyll concerns the disruption caused to a marriage. Her major crime in terms of the drama and the dialogue is the betrayal of Arthur. The final exchange between Arthur and Guinevere is more that of a wronged husband and an erring wife than a king and a national traitor. Tennyson has exploited Malory's story to bring together the threads of sexual anxiety and patriarchal self-defence that were so forcefully but separately developed in the two previous idylls.

The response was enormous. Prince Albert admired these 'beautiful poems' (H. Tennyson, 1897, I.455) and Gladstone wrote in his review of the 1859 Idylls, 'We know not where to look in history or in letters for a nobler and more over-powering conception of man as he might be than in the Arthur of this volume'. He admired especially the 'aweful severity' of Arthur's speeches (Jump, 1967, pp. 257–8). So spoke two powerful and liberal men, and others agreed – Macaulay, the Duke of Argyll, the editor of *The Times* (H. Tennyson, 1897, I.445–7). They are the voice of that élite to whom Tennyson deferred, which led the opinions and attitudes of the much larger audience his poetry won, and for whom the containment in moral and patriarchal bounds of powerful and sensual women was an absolute necessity.

Not everybody would agree. People with advanced opinions, especially writers like Swinburne and Meredith found Arthur's ethical self-righteousness quite unacceptable and made fun of it (Jump, 1967, pp. 318–21; Martin, 1980, pp. 423–4). William Morris, more positively, produced his 'Defence of Guinevere' (1858) at almost exactly the same time. He rewrites Malory's scene as Guinevere is brought to the stake, giving her most of the dialogue and presenting both her sensual beauty and, without condescension or sentiment, her own statement of guiltlessness.

But Tennyson and his audience were quite satisfied with his work, and the idyll stands strongly with the two previous ones, an ideal resolution of the woman problem as Tennyson felt about it. In spite of the coherent balance achieved in 'Guinevere' Tennyson went on to write another idyll, perhaps in order to make two pairs and fill a volume – he always had a strong sense of format and the merchandising of poetry. Yet although 'Elaine', later to become 'Launcelot and Elaine', does not relate to the other three as strongly as they do to each other, it does have certain links with them, and its own peculiar power.

In 'Elaine' Tennyson stresses the destructiveness of the lovers' relationship, continuing the theme of 'Guinevere'. The general hostility to women is also directed at Elaine to some degree as Tennyson suggests that she is less innocent than Malory lets her be. When she examined Launcelot's shield she barred her door, 'Stript off the case, and read the naked shield' (LE.16). Then 'in fantasy' (LE.27) she imagined the power of his 'stroke', his 'thrust' (LE.24–5). If she is innocent, it is an excitable, easily aroused innocence, related to the 'wilful' quality her father sees in her (LE.745) and in her urgent pressing of herself on Launcelot: 'I have gone mad. I love you: let me die' (LE.925).

Apart from this sexual trace in Elaine's importunacy, the 'Elaine' idyll presents other ideological features of the recently completed idylls. Like Enid, Elaine offers to be Lancelot's squire (LE.382) and she too plans to be 'sweet and serviceable' (LE.762, cf. MG.393). By contrast, Guinevere is an uncontrollable force, described as 'wild' (LE.609, 737, 1236). Tennyson gives Lancelot a central position and sympathy far beyond Malory's treatment of him. At the end Lancelot goes off alone, in a scene newly created by Tennyson, to reflect ruefully that Elaine's love was 'Far tenderer than my queen's' (LE.1384). He suffers further and Tennyson sympathises: the last two lines of the idyll favour the hero and promise him peace:

> So groaned sir Lancelot in remorseful pain
> Not knowing he should die a holy man.
>
> (LE.1417–18)

So Tennyson uses Malory's story of 'The Fair Maid of Ascolat' to rework the themes of masculine anxiety and feminine containment that were the driving force and the source of much of the innovation in the three earlier idylls. That makes the 'Elaine' idyll sound repetitious and dull. Yet it is a coherent and sharply imagined piece of work, with a tenseness and introspection that is absent among the more confident certainties of 'Guinevere'.

That quality and the fact that this story was selected to complete what seemed a reasonably complete group may derive from its plot. Launcelot's oppressive entanglement with Guinevere destroys the possibility of union with a suitable and submissive young woman: that suggests readily the shadow of Tennyson's own long-lasting feelings about Arthur Hallam and his own refusal to marry Emily Selwood.

The most famous and tensely imagined lines in the idyll described Lancelot's position:

> His honour rooted in dishonour stood
> And faith unfaithful kept him falsely true
>
> (LE.871–2)

This could refer to the love of Hallam, regarded as impure by contemporaries and doubted even by Tennyson now. His poetic honour largely derived from *In Memoriam*, itself based on that love. These lines are introduced by the phrase that Lancelot is tied by the 'shackles of an old love' (LE.870). Equally applicable to Tennyson and Hallam as to Lancelot and Guinevere is the oddly specific statement 'Our bond is not the bond of man and wife' (LE.1199), an almost complete repetition of line 1184.

Perhaps the idyll gains its force simply because Tennyson was excited by exploring the results of adultery. But only the 'Morte d'Arthur' was as faithful as this idyll to Malory, and that was certainly a displaced realisation of Hallam. Another detailed reworking of Malory may well be the bearer of another Hallam-based anxiety. His ghostly presence continued to control Tennyson's life through the disturbed 1830s and 40s: this was the residual Hallam problem for Tennyson, rather than any fear of homosexual charges like those raised by 'Christopher North' and Bulwer Lytton (Martin, 1980, pp. 168–73). That force would certainly explain the rather surprising impact of 'Elaine'. In terms of Tennyson's contemporary 'woman problem' the idyll seems a confident and unadventurous resumé rather than a bearer of the innovative and disturbing power suggested by its tense and strongly imagined quality.

As a whole the 1859 *Idylls* were a great financial and critical success. They sold ten thousand copies within six weeks (not the one week that Hallam Tennyson claimed in the *Memoir*, 1897, I.443) and at seven shillings a copy had an audience among the reasonably well-off. The critics enjoyed and admired the poems, though they found 'Vivien' strong meat – even Gladstone felt he had to say it was the least popular of the idylls.

Tennyson seemed to have made a decisive statement on women, and that achievement was clearly remembered after his death when *The Times* asked 'Who has better pictured at all events for our race, woman, pure, self-forgetful, consoling; or man, valiant, upright and courteous, marriage with its serene trust?' (quoted in Richardson, 1962, p. 269). Nobody had. Tennyson was the master ideologist of the relations between the sexes, and that is the social meaning of the 1859 *Idylls*. Some were later to be altered both in title and in text, and their dispersal through the structure of the final *Idylls* would give them implications and emphases absent in the original quartet. But they were effectively the conclusion of Tennyson's engagement with the threats that he and other men felt were posed by women. When he returned to the Arthurian world, other things were on his mind. Nevertheless, his early attitude to women had not changed, and in itself it would offer a way out of the impasse he came to, a means of explaining in a comforting and confidence-building way the new problem he was facing, namely the fact that traditional social authority seemed to be threatened with collapse.

IV

Tennyson did not return to the Arthurian topic for some time. His admirers were keen for more but he seems to have had no urge to continue. He later said that he always had the whole *Idylls* in his mind and could have written it out, with enough confidence and inclination (H. Tennyson, 1897, II.125) but this is a rationalisation of the piecemeal and changing nature of the entire poem. The self-contained character of the 1859 *Idylls* is clear from his remark in a letter of 1862 that 'Guinevere' would make a fine ending to his Arthuriad (Gray, 1969, note 5).

This separateness is also suggested by a change in topic when he started to write a new group of idylls: they are concerned with the politics of the state, not those of the family. There had been traces of social material in the 1859 idylls (MG.33, 39; GE.796, 894, 906, 934), enough to show that Tennyson knew the tradition of social reformers as chivalrous knights. Houghton describes practical chivalry and its specific setting:

> In his speech on sanitary reform, Kingsley called on every one of his hearers to be a knight-errant or lady-errant 'even now in the nineteenth century, for the alleviation of misery among the poor is a noble work, a chivalrous work – just as chivalrous as if you lived in any old fairy land. . . .'   (1957, p. 319)

But it was not till he wrote his grail idyll that Tennyson gave any serious attention to the idea of a progressive, reformist chivalry in Kingsley's terms. He indicates that for anyone but a true saint like Galahad the grail is a delusive and destructive force. He has the highly spiritual Oxford Movement in mind, sharing the views of men like Kingsley, Maurice and Shaftesbury, who felt that the church should act in the forefront of social reform, not withdraw into an intellectualised and ritualised hermitage.

The anti-social force of the grail is stressed. Percivale, who narrates the whole idyll, sees in a dream the destruction of family life – a wife and baby crumble to ashes (HG.379–400). Then he meets again his first love, now widowed, but he cannot marry her as his vow urges him onwards (HG.572–611): Tennyson also replays an old strain by making her a little forward, like Elaine (HG.593–6). There is no doubt of Galahad's priority and fitness for this mystical experience, but for others it is an error. As such it parallels that other individualist indiscipline, sexuality. Percivale's sister, who makes him believe in the grail, has been disappointed in love and so is willing to accept the faith in the grail pressed on her by the old priest (HG.83–97). The grail itself is associated with red light and is sometimes 'blood-red' (HG.473–6); elsewhere it has 'rosy quiverings' (HG.123). In Tennyson's moralised palette, these colours have distinctly sexual connotations. He also suggests the grail has no real existence, is no more than a delusion. Malory's account of its appearance at Camelot is retained in essentials, but Tennyson's version *could* be no more than mass hysteria during an electric storm. He commented later that the appearance of the grail to Bors 'might have been a meteor' (HG.691–2 note): there is a consistent rational undertone in the idyll (Culler, 1977, pp. 228–9).

In spite of Galahad's status as a true mystic, the strange final scene stresses his escape from the world that needs hard social work. Percivale sees him move easily over:

> A great black swamp and of an evil smell
> Part black, part whitened with the bones of men
>
> (HG.499–500)

He crosses it on ancient bridges from which run piers opening into 'the great Sea'. They then burst into flame and prevent Percivale following. Galahad disappears out to sea, where 'the spiritual city' lit by the 'rose-red sparkle' of the grail welcomes him (HG.501–32). From the muddy, groined low-tide flats of his beloved east coast Tennyson has developed a powerful scene, suggesting rather than Malory's journey to Sarras the contemporary flight by Newman, leader of the Oxford Movement, to Rome – that spiritual city, seen as red to scarlet by Protestants, set in what Chaucer called 'the grete see', the Mediterranean (a usage Tennyson would certainly have known). Like Newman Galahad leaves behind the bridges burned, a filthy shore 'rotten with a hundred years of death' (HG.495). That swampy plague spot symbolises for Tennyson the insanitary and disease-ridden world begging for urban and social reform, the true work of a dedicated church. Percivale, himself tainted by the grail, turns from it, and goes to his monastery 'leaving human wrongs to right themselves' (HG.894).

But Arthur takes a different course. When the grail appeared at Camelot he was away putting down 'a bandit hold' (HG.214). As Arthur returns there is a unique image of hard-working knights: 'their arms Hacked, and the foreheads grimed with smoke, and seared' (HG.264–5). The king is angry to hear the quest has been sworn, and tells his knights they are not Galahads, nor even Percivales, but simply 'men With strength and will to right the wronged, of power To lay the sudden heads of violence flat' (HG.308–10).

Just as he idealised and generalised the opinions of Maurice and Kingsley, so Tennyson blurs the specific social awareness of this idyll. Its final lines, and for him the most centrally important passage of the whole *Idylls* (H. Tennyson, 1897, II.90) make Arthur minimise the importance of dutiful social work, subdue it to a mystical and religious sense of transcendence, a sublimation of both the world and the individual.

Arthur says that he would not have sworn the quest if he had seen the grail, because a king 'must guard That which he rules' (HG.901–2) and cannot go wandering. His property rights impose duties to tend his own – something less than radical wrong-righting. But when those concerns are laid aside, when duty is fulfilled, the powerful person can tend to himself. Then:

> Let visions of the night or of the day
> Come, as they will; and many a time they come,
> Until this earth he walks on seems not earth,
> This light that strikes his eyeball is not light,
> This air that smites his forehead is not air
> But vision – yea his very hand and foot –
> In moments when he feels he cannot die
> And knows himself no vision to himself,

Nor the high God a vision, nor that One
Who rose again: ye have seen what ye have seen.

                                        (HG.906–15)

A sense of transcendence can arise after – and by implication
through – dutiful work (which is also the defence of property). As
a result a sense of immortality and unity with God is generated.
This is not only a piece of very powerful poetry: it is fully central,
as Tennyson said, to the ideology of the whole *Idylls*. Up to this
point the idyll has offered social collective action as its major
positive, with mysticism as a rare and fugitive possibility for some.
Now though, social action is seen only as a stage, not a goal, and
a type of mysticism is suddenly offered: the individual fills the
stage again and fear of death, that reflexive bogey of individualism, is consoled as richly as by Percivale's monasticism –
but arrived at by an apparently less selfish path.

'The Holy Grail' is certainly the most socially aware of the
idylls so far written, but that creates its own ideological riposte
within the idyll. Tennyson solves the problem not only of how to
handle the grail story as a topic (a problem he pondered for some
time, H. Tennyson, 1897, I.456–7 and II.126), but also of how to
absorb the demand for social progress and still speak in a way
which was essentially individualist and authoritarian.

Tennyson pressed on immediately to write an opening idyll for
what he could now see as a total poem. Much in 'The Coming of
Arthur' connects with earlier themes. The role of the woman in
the family is recognised in the opening emphasis on Arthur's need
for marriage. He could not achieve happiness as 'a lonely king'
(CA.80) and his need of a woman seems partly physical, as
without her he would be 'Vext with waste dreams' (CA.84).
Consistent with the 'Guinevere' idyll, physicality is her central
force: within decorous limits she is a sexual being, 'fairest of all
flesh on earth' (CA.3). A trace of the related worry about
'manliness' also surfaces: Arthur's enemies 'since his ways are
sweet, And theirs are bestial, hold him less than man'
(CA.179–80).

The theme of dutiful social action is euphemised through
nature, more like its treatment in 'Enid' than in 'The Holy Grail',
but is still present. Leodegran's kingdom is surrounded by 'great
tracts of wilderness Wherein the beast was ever more and more
But man was less and less' (CA.10–12). This reverse evolution (a

possibility by no means excluded by Darwin and other scientists)
takes place in a suitably gloomy and wild context: 'the land of
Cameliard was waste, Thick with wet woods, and many a beast
therein' (CA.21–2). Here there grew up 'wolf-like men Worse
than the wolves' (CA.32–3). Arthur deals with these problems in
ways that obviously suggest contemporary urban reforms, especially the provision of peace-keeping, light, drainage and new
roads driven through the slums that bred crime and disease. He:

> slew the beast, and felled
> The forest, letting in the sun, and made
> Broad pathways for the hunter and the knight.
>
> (CA.59–61)

So necessary marriage and proper social action are the opening
motifs of the idyll, compact and confident recapitulations of
earlier material. But as 'The Coming of Arthur' proceeds it raises
social concerns of a quite new sort that bear on the anxieties of the
ruling class, not the problems of the nation. These emerge from
the lengthy discussion about Arthur's birth: is he a royal heir, a
pretender, or a wonderful child left by supernatural forces to rule
Britain?

The discussion is not simply an Arthurian version of the 'higher
criticism' which was then investigating the bible and which is
satirised in Merlin's riddling response (CA.401–10). It has
important ideological effects: it insists that Arthur's right to rule is
entirely a matter of birth, not of performance. Like the many
inheritance puzzles in Victorian literature, the text is insisting on
lineage, inherited power, not self-made authority in a period when
that was an increasingly real threat to the classes who inherited
property and power. Right action, including right social action,
are part of a king's role, but they do not give him authority.

The context of this uncertainty is social disorder and chaos. If
the status quo is threatened, if inherited right to rule is challenged,
if a ruler without true lineage is authorised, then disaster will
follow. The core of the matter – with its consoling resolution – is
presented in the dream where Leodegran ponders whether his
daughter should marry Arthur.

He saw a sloping set of fields leading up to a misty peak, where
Arthur was visible only as a 'phantom king, Now looming, and
now lost' (CA.429–30). On the hillside, raiders murdered

cowherds, drove off the cattle, burned the buildings. The king merely *spoke* against the chaos and the raiders denied his authority. Then:

> with a wink his dream was changed, the haze
> Descended, and the solid earth became
> As nothing, but the King stood out in heaven,
> Crowned. (CA.440–3)

Leodegran at once agrees to the marriage and Arthur becomes king, a divinely empowered despot. The birth problem is side-stepped with divine aid. Arthur is one 'In whom High God hath breathed a secret thing' (CA.500) and his knights 'Fulfil the boundless purpose of their king' (CA.474). Unity and certainty are contrived out of conflict and doubt. It is a distinctly strained resolution and after publication Tennyson must have felt Arthur's grandeur needed more emphasis to be credible. In the 1873 edition he added a song 'Blow trumpet' in which the refrain line couples military violence and the king's continued rule: 'Fall battleaxe and flash brand. Let the king reign' (CA.486).

Tennyson's need to find a sure and strong authority is prominent in 'The Coming of Arthur' and the feared failure of that authority was to be the main topic of 'The Passing of Arthur', which he started next. Authority within the family had been ideologically engineered in the 1859 *Idylls*, but now he was concerned on a wider front. In the 1860s, with the pressure for a new reform bill showing that the repressive tolerance of the 1832 act was not enough, with business interests steadily increasing their powerful demands for power, with continued radical movements overseas and at home, Tennyson was growing increasingly alarmed about the stability of the country.

When he worried about authority he meant the authority of the power élite, among whom he was increasingly accepted. And though his term 'authority' is abstract and now seems vague and idealistic, it was in fact no more vague than was the contemporary theorisation about how and why the powerful retained their position. It is Tennyson's word for the structure usually called 'deference'.

Bagehot described Britain as 'the very type of a deferential country' in so thoughtful and influential – and so contemporary – a book as *The English Constitution* (quoted in Harrison, 1971, p. 90).

Altick has described the situation well: 'The belief that the hierarchical structure based on hereditary privilege had something sacred about it survived into an age of increasing social fluidity, and not alone in stuffily conservative minds.' (1974, p. 18). That description of the deference system fits extraordinarily well with Leodegran's dream. The hierarchical pattern is implied by the hill; correct birth is what Leodegran is trying to establish; the sacred element is found in the divine selection of a king. And all the time the threatening forces are climbing the hill, making off with the basis of the prosperity of those who feel sanctified and protected by a system of deference to authority which may now be weakening.

'The Coming of Arthur' imagines finally a divinely ordained world of unquestioning authority and mass obedience. That world was a dream. There could be little hope of creating, or re-creating, a totalitarian authority for the propertied classes, and Arthurian tradition itself did not promise success even for such a highly supported royalty. The best Tennyson can say is that 'Arthur and his knighthood for a space Were all one will' (CA.514–5).

He had already written a poem which came after that 'space', telling the end of the Arthurian enterprise, and he now decided to amplify it, partly to build it up to idyll length, but also, and much more importantly, to begin the task of finding consolations for the failure of such an attractively authoritarian kingdom and patriarchy – and by extension for the contemporary loss of confidence and power among the propertied élite.

Tennyson turned the original 'Morte d'Arthur' into 'The Passing of Arthur' with two passages. His new opening (PA.1–169) gave some action from Malory, especially Gawain's death and ghostly visit and the manoeuvres with Mordred before the 'last weird battle in the west' (PA.29). As the end of 'The Coming of Arthur' implied, the fame of the king and his knights – now only a memory – had nothing to do with 'righting wrongs', it rose from the appealingly nationalistic conflict with the Saxons (PA.67–70). Leodegran's dream is also remembered in reverse. There Arthur was authorised by God; here he is baffled by divine dispensation: 'in His ways with men I find Him not. I waged His wars, and now I pass and die' (PA.11–12). As a result Arthur has experienced the reverse evolution that was feared in the dream – 'all my realm Reels back into the beast' (PA.25–6), and a 'deathwhite mist' (PA.95) descends before the final battle, like that which swamped the king on the hillside.

Arthur has become again the unauthorised 'phantom king' of Leodegran's dream, supervising no more than chaos. Bedivere's failure to throw away Excalibur is the last act of infidelity, done when 'clouded with his own conceit' (PA.278) and against the knight's knowledge that it is 'Deep harm to disobey, Seeing obedience is the bond of rule' (PA.261–2). Authority, Arthur says, 'forgets a dying king' (PA.289): royal and personal power are lost together. But such despair in the face of death is itself contained by Tennyson's new ending to the poem.

The 'Morte d'Arthur' ended with Bedivere 'revolving many memories' (like Tennyson thinking of Hallam) as the barge carried Arthur to Avalon (Hallam's body had been brought back to England by sea). It disappeared 'against the verge of dawn' and 'on the mere the wailing died away' (PA.439–40). In 1869 Tennyson added some more lines which amplified the tenuous hope of that conclusion. Instead of simply sailing off inland up the 'mere', the barge turns through a formerly unseen gap in the 'dark strait of barren land' (PA.178) and so gains access to the open sea, from which, in the most mysterious and most authoritative version of his origin, Arthur originally came. That strange birth had heavenly supervision and here too a faint shout is heard 'as if some fair city were one voice Around a king returning from his wars' (PA.461–2). The city is the transmarine heaven where Galahad and the grail arrived, stripped of its Roman associations. Here, as in the last words of 'The Holy Grail', the final consolation is both individual and Christian. Like the authority that was divinely imposed and separated from social work and social chaos alike, Arthur's end is another divine gift and again it is an escape from disorder, not a reward for resolving it.

The journey across lake and sea, themselves female archetypes, is supervised by unobtrusive women: the resolution of anxiety, individualist and patriarchal, is complete. Contemporary paintings of Arthur's end develop the ideological elements that Tennyson created. Both Burne-Jones and Archer show a bulky, dignified Arthur, a patriarch if there ever was one, lying in luxury surrounded by 'serviceable' women (Plates 19 and 20). For his long rest the phantom king is given all contemporary comforts, physical and ideological.

That new conclusion to 'The Passing of Arthur' is a strong

consolation for those who felt that their power had ebbed, that disorder and ineffectiveness were convergent threats to their peace of mind and their property. But consolation is not enough for fully effective ideology: the text must lay blame as well as offer escape. So far, only God's mysterious movements and a general lack of fidelity in men like Modred and even Bedivere have been identified as causes of the Arthurian debacle.

In the last of this second quartet of idylls, Tennyson made a dramatic ideological movement to provide the crucial explanation of disaster. In 'Pelleas and Ettarre' he returned to the anti-woman attitudes established in the 1859 *Idylls*. This idyll is usually treated as a minor supporting piece, but in terms of the chronological and ideological development of the *Idylls of the King* it has great importance, making women bear the blame not only for disturbances to the family and the male psyche but also for the widespread weakening of royal authority and social order, as the propertied classes saw it.

The date of 'Pelleas and Ettare' is not quite clear. It appears to have been finished before 'The Passing of Arthur'; Tennyson apparently suspended the fairly straightforward operation of building up the 'Morte d'Arthur' into a final idyll for the more intriguing and original task of expanding a brief story from Book I of Malory (where he had also partly found 'Vivien') to create an idyll to explain just why and how the Arthurian authority was dissipated.

His first step was to move the Pelleas story from the uncertain start of the Round Table to the post-grail period when Arthur is trying to rebuild. At this delicate moment the old topic of sexuality as a disturbing force returns. Ettarre is suspect because she has sensual force on Pelleas: 'The beauty of her flesh abashed the boy' (PE.74). He knows little of women (PE.82–6) and after meeting Ettarre he cannot sleep 'for pleasure in his blood' (PE.131).

The idyll recreates in powerful terms the earlier pattern. Rather than the boyish Pelleas, Ettarre would prefer:

> Some rough old knight who knew the worldly way,
> Albeit grizzlier than a bear, to ride
> And jest with: (PE.185–7)

Tennyson's run-on from 'ride' to 'And jest with' conceals the *double entendre* in 'ride', but in oral performance the implication of her sexual experience is markedly frank. Covert sexuality is made dynamic by jealousy in the song that Pelleas cannot forget – 'A worm within the rose' (PE.390). This develops into a neurotically exaggerated fear and loathing of female sexuality (partly noted by Rosenberg, 1973, p. 71). The tiny figure of Pelleas makes his way into the gaping gates of Ettarre's castle, while 'the postern portal also wide Yawning' threatens the youth with another forbidding orifice. He scrambles up past a bramble patch and a rivulet to come to a place where 'red after revel' Ettarre's knights loll satiated (PE.405–22). After experiencing this negative sexual topography, Pelleas sees Gawain and Ettarre together. He explodes in rage and through his speech run both self-hatred and bitter contempt for women, emphasised in Tennyson's most emphatic type of play on sounds and words:

> Black as the harlot's heart – hollow as a skull!
> Let the fierce east scream through your eyelet-holes,
> And whirl the dust of harlots round and round
> In dung and nettles!   (PE.459–62)

However, Ettarre's role in the idyll is not only to focus an almost hysterical restatement of the earlier anxiety about woman. Her impact on Pelleas is used as both an actual and a symbolic explanation of trouble in the Round Table. Sexual sin, stemming from women, is made the basis of disorder in the Arthurian world. Pelleas has originally called Ettarre 'my queen, my Guinevere' (PE.44) and after his rage, when he laments that he held Ettarre 'pure as Guinevere' (PE.512), Percivale mentions the rumours about Launcelot and the queen. Pelleas responds:

> 'Is the Queen false?' and Percivale was mute.
> 'Have any of our Round Table held their vows?'
>   (PE.522–3)

It is an important moment. The queen's falsity, which is blackened by relating her to Ettarre, is prior, in syntax and by implication as a cause, to the knights' infidelity. That is both deliberate and tendentious: in this idyll Tennyson is shaping woman as the prime disturbance to Arthur's authority. Pelleas now even doubts the king and curses Camelot, ' "Black nest of rats," he groaned, "Ye build too high" ' (PE.544). He then links sexuality to disaster by confronting Lancelot with the threat of slander, a woman-motivated version of Aggravayne's hatred in Malory.

Guinevere meets Pelleas as he is raging, offers her help, but he 'lifted up an eye so fierce She quailed; and he hissing "I have no sword," Sprang from the door into the dark' (PE.589–91). The swordless Pelleas is the castrated man symbolised in his dream-like journey into Ettarre's castle. This idyll draws with crudely ideological lines, suggesting that authority has been stripped from, sucked out of men by these female demons who have surged back into the *Idylls*. It is convenient that they have done so, for they can explain the deeply disturbing loss of authority and power that is a final part of the Arthurian story and that the propertied élite in the nineteenth century were beginning to fear as inevitable.

The idyll ends by predicting the grim future; now it can be faced because blame is being apportioned. In the last lines the order of the action and the impact of the imagery sheet home the blame to loving and preying women:

> The Queen
> Looked hard upon her lover, he on her;
> And each foresaw the dolorous day to be:
> And all talk died, as in a grove all song
> Beneath the shadow of some bird of prey;
> Then a long silence came upon the hall,
> And Modred thought, 'The time is hard at hand.'
>
> (PE.591–7)

V

The new quartet of idylls came out in December 1869. They were very well received and Tennyson was already pressing on to complete what he now saw as a coherent sequence of episodes. It was obvious that the bulk of the existing idylls were late in Arthurian time and gloomy: the only 'happy' idyll after the first was 'Enid', still undivided and itself rather full of tension. The 'Vivien' came next and Tennyson recognised how this darkened the beginning, saying he wanted 'to make *Vivien* come later into the *Poem*' (Ricks, 1969, p. 1465).

As a result of this problem, 'Gareth and Lynette' was developed from Malory's 'Tale of Sir Gareth' to show the Arthurian world operating well. At the same time it recreated the main threads of ideology that Tennyson had by this time established. Arthur is briefly seen righting wrong, but it is a matter of the disposition of landed property, not any broad-based correction of evil practices (GL.326–75). Gareth's early desire to help 'cleanse' the realm (GL.23–4) is later concealed among a package of obediences when he says he must 'follow the Christ, the King, Live pure, speak true, right wrong, follow the King' (GL.116–7): obedience to authority is his first and last duty. Gareth's actions are even further desocialised. The knights he fights are not so much oppressors of a propertied woman as allegorised demons of time, and the fact that the last of them is no more than a boy in huge armour brings the message of hope, a reward for endurance like the recently written end of 'The Passing of Arthur'.

Though Tennyson reduces social action to a token, he sharpens the class-consciousness which is inherent to the source. Bellicent, Gareth's mother, thinks his class pride will make him abandon his lower-class incognito (GL.148–60) – Malory used Gareth's desire for fame in the same argument. After Gareth puts on lower-class clothes, Kay, whom Tennyson presents like a Tory squire (GL.45–6), emphasises the dirtiness of Gareth's new role. The poem stresses the bad teeth of the churls (GL.501), their general filth (GL.469–71) and even their 'grosser tasks', which presumably means handling excrement (GL.477). Tennyson only leaves Gareth in his servile role for a month (GL.515–20); he specifies Lynette's high lineage as soon as she appears (GL.574); he makes the thralls cheer for the king and his knights (GL.679–82). He alters Malory's story to sharpen the lines of class-consciousness, in a way that sees the lower classes as a threat needing to be bound in admiring deference to their historical superiors.

The other major motif that is raised is authority and the pervasive doubt of it. Bellicent restates the doubt of Arthur's origin (GL.119–29). Then as Gareth and his men arrive at Camelot both Arthur and the city itself are questioned as 'a city of Enchanters built By fairy Kings' (GL.196–7). Gareth has confidence, but on seeing the strange gateway and the city in the mist even he is puzzled, and asks Merlin for reassurance. Merlin dismisses the apparent illusions, which Tennyson's note explains, as 'Refraction by mirage' (GL.249 and note). Yet although

Merlin feels it is a city totally dominated by royalty (GL.260–1) he admits 'some there be that hold The King a shadow, and the city real' (GL.261–2). A royal figurehead set against a civic and commercial state – many felt that was the real and proper model developing in Britain, a view disturbing enough to be controlled at once, as Merlin mocks Gareth for pretending to be other than he is, like other upstart labourers. This seems enough: for the rest of the idyll Arthur is powerful and Gareth's nobility emerges inevitably from the chrysalis of the threatening fair unknown.

One intriguing innovation carries on the resolution of the 'woman problem' of the earlier idylls. Tennyson firmly rejects Malory's notion of a marriage between Gareth and the lady of the castle. Instead Gareth marries Lynette, the strong-minded damsel who comes to respect and help him (GL.1392–4). With no trace of sexuality about her person, she is the hero's suitable mate. That is the most original element in 'Gareth and Lynette', and it fits well with the 'Enid' idyll which follows it in the emerging order. In most other respects 'Gareth and Lynette' is a rather low-temperature reinforcement of the idylls written before.

'The Last Tournament', which Tennyson went on to write in 1870 and had finished by May 1871, also had a supportive role and filled in some narrative between 'Pelleas and Ettarre' and 'Guinevere', but it introduced new material of special contemporary relevance. One of Tennyson's most original idylls, it brings together the situation at Camelot with that in Cornwall, developing an idea he must have picked up while reading Malory's Tristram story. The idyll starts with 'The Tournament of Dead Innocence'. This symbolises the decline of the Round Table, which is linked to Guinevere – the title literally refers to a baby she cared for but could not keep alive. The title also refers back to the woman-caused derangement of Pelleas. He starred at the 'The Tournament of Youth' but in this idyll has become the Red Knight who has set up a second and violent anti-Round Table in the north. That may be a displacement of the culture of the fire-red industrial north which challenged the old order of the rural south, but it firmly links such disorder with sexuality and women.

This explanation of disorder is developed a great deal in 'The Last Tournament'. Tristram himself is the model of a cynical seducer with a rationale of his actions set out in his song 'Free love

– free field – we love but while we may' (LT.275–81). Tennyson uses Tristram to represent a growing attitude towards sexuality, politics and the world at large. Usually called 'naturalism' at the time, it was the projection of rationalism beyond the controls of faith and even of conventional morality and deference. Charles Masterman's book *Tennyson as a Religious Teacher* (1900, pp. 217–31) gives, despite its unpromising title, a careful account of how a 'new Epicureanism' developed in the later nineteenth century as a third stage of rationalism. Tennyson's own rational fideism and George Eliot's progressive humanism represented the two earlier stages. Fitzgerald's *Rubaiyat of Omar Khayam* was a good example of such 'naturalism' and this was no doubt why he and Tennyson fell out, in spite of their earlier friendship which extended to Fitzgerald's generous financial support.

Tristram's moral relativism is not only sexually licentious: it damages Arthur's authority, questioning whether he is 'king by courtesy or king by right' (LT.341–2). Tristram develops this at length later, finally seeing Arthur as being both without validity and unrealistic: 'a doubtful lord To bind them by inviolable vows Which flesh and blood would perforce violate' (LT.682–4). Launcelot himself is so sapped by his love of Guinevere that he does not care to enact the proper rules of the tournament (LT.160–3). Arthur senses that things are going badly wrong, for obedience is visibly failing (LT.1117–9) and he fears:

> . . . lest this my realm, upreared
> By noble deeds at one with noble vows,
> From flat confusion and brute violences,
> Reel back into the beast, and be no more.
>   (LT.122–5)

Such reverse evolution, already mentioned in 'The Passing of Arthur' as having happened, actually occurs in this idyll when Arthur's men, young post-grail knights like Pelleas (LT.99–100) lose control as they crush the Red Knight, Pelleas himself. They sack his castle, then kill, burn and rape. In summary they 'slimed themselves' (LT.470), getting filthy, going back to where men came from originally. What once would have been a good social action has become a police riot.

This gloomy vision of a falling, rotten, sex-crazed, filthy and above all disobedient land is buttressed by all of Tennyson's art with a richly negative, almost masochistic relish. The colours of this idyll are dark red, from Tristram's hand as he wins the diamonds (LT.192–3), through the dominant colour of his dream (LT.486), to the colouring of Isolt's hands as she grips the rubies that are the prize at the uninnocent tournament (LT.410–14). To stress the moral gloom, images of rain, damp and mud dominate the idyll, summed up in the bravura line that sets the final scene: 'All in a death-dumb, autumn-dripping gloom' (LT.570).

'The Last Tournament' is innovative in both narrative and ideological terms, with Tristram as a character and modern 'naturalism' as a force. But it does not in any way change the direction of the developed meaning of the *Idylls*. Nor does 'Balin and Balan', the idyll written last of all, which Tennyson produced in the years 1872–4 but did not publish until 1885. It acts, as he said, as 'some further introduction to "Merlin and Vivien" ' (H. Tennyson, 1897, II.121). In doing so, it makes some deliberate alterations to Malory in order to stress the destructive impact of sexuality on fraternal relations.

It is the sight of Lancelot and Guinevere apparently in love that leads Balin to leave Arthur's court, not the innate uncontrollability he has shown in Malory (BB.276–84). Guinevere has been the object of his special devotion, and her influence has led him to 'move In music with his Order and the King' (BB.207–8). Now, finding her false, his world is shattered and he rushes off, bemused, for 'strange adventure' (BB.284). Just as Pelleas' violence was Ettarre's fault, Guinevere bears the initial blame for Balin's return to his 'violences'. Tennyson alters the story further: Vivien appears, exaggerates the queen's sin to Balin and makes him even wilder. Guinevere and Vivien are brought in to Malory's story not to alter the plot but to explain away its violence through women and their allegedly disruptive force.

As a result of writing this idyll in this way and placing it early in the series, between 'Geraint and Enid' and 'Merlin and Vivien', the ideological shift performed in 'Pelleas and Ettarre' is anticipated. The arrangement of the idylls as Tennyson now has them binds together his two themes of women threatening men in the family and woman as the scapegoat for political and social disorder. In fact the two themes, separate in their production, now interweave through the whole poem. Only reading the idylls as they were composed can disentangle that development; the late creation and early location of 'Balin and Balan' is a crucial stage in Tennyson's successful concealment of the historical origins of his ideology.

In 'Balin and Balan' even more than in 'The Last Tournament' the argument is very powerfully supported by the persuasive weight of the imagery, especially that presenting the richness of nature. That is a consistent feature of all the idylls, of course, but here, as in the original 'Vivien', it is more than mere setting, more even than symbolic of a character's attitudes: nature is a force, and an enticingly dangerous one. Vivien clearly excited Tennyson's imagination at the end of the Idylls as she had twenty years before at their beginning. He wrote yet more about her, adding the present lines 6–146 of 'Merlin and Vivien' to the old 'Vivien', apparently after finishing 'Balin and Balan'. These lines involve her with Mark as 'The Last Tournament' had shaped him, and they make her trip to Arthur's court not merely the private and familial incursion of sexuality that it had been in the 1859 *Idylls*, but also a political threat from a rival and corrupt authority.

VI

In this way Tennyson finally wove together his two abiding anxieties, the threat of woman's power, especially her sexual power, within the family, and the threat of dissent and disorder within the state. Because the state was itself fully patriarchal and because the family was the basic social unit in the eyes of those who firmly resisted the emerging analysis of classes in conflict, it was not difficult for him to perform his supreme ideological act and avoid writing about the social and historical forces which really did disturb the poise of those who held power and property. That empty category was filled by the old enemy, the seductive woman. So the *Idylls* were made both partly realistic in terms of the fears they created and satisfyingly ideological for a male and powerful audience by blaming all trouble on the nearest and dearest source of disturbance for the adult male, his assembled womenfolk.

It is quite true, as Tennyson claims in his epilogue 'to the Queen', that in Arthur he has not evoked 'that gray king' of legend, though many misreaders and misquoters have thought he speaks of his own topic when he dismisses the Arthur of popular imagination:

> whose name, a ghost
> Streams like a cloud, man-shaped, from mountain peak
> And cleaves to cairn and cromlech still.   (TQ.39–41)

Tennyson was not interested in the popular and magical king of fairy tale and numinous place names. But his Arthur was another sort of ghost, a 'phantom king' in reality, because he was a figure of ideology created to grapple with issues without revealing their full nature. Tennyson, like Leodegran in his dream, lifts Arthur above the brawling world of power and profit in order to authorise him and to preserve authority.

The true concern of the Arthuriad was to defend the patriarchal family and the conservative state. The epilogue to the queen accordingly uses her own family and her kingdom as the locations for that concern. Tennyson states clearly his anxiety about social revolution. He actually says we should be optimistic, but, imaginative poet that he never ceases to be in spite of his opinions, his syntax allows his final words to speak with fear. The long earnest poem, the moral assurances, the blame of women – like all ideology they are only talk and the basic fear of historical process remains, the fear of, in the last lines:

> The darkness of that battle in the West
> Where all of high and holy dies away.   (TQ.65–6)

In the end Tennyson finally spoke, in a sideways and officially optimistic way, about the fear of social cataclysm without blaming it on women. But his text as a whole was less realistic; it made woman the essential threat, the intimate enemy who could because of that intimacy be mastered. For his audience the fear of democratisation in the family and in society remained strong, and the value of his work as a consolation in the face of those fears remained powerful.

After a time, when both the non-propertied classes and women were less easily brushed aside, though no less feared because of that, Tennyson's reactions came to seem unacceptable and simplistic in both form and content, and so the long poem lost its consoling force and sank rapidly in popularity and esteem. Now, though, the *Idylls of the King* can be read as a very revealing text about the response and lack of response by the Victorian male establishment to the forces generated in their society, about their attempt to realise in Arthur their sense of a fading authority.

However, that was not the only viewpoint from which the Arthuriad legend could be seen in the nineteenth century. A very different approach was offered by Mark Twain. He was the first of the distinctly modern writers who treat the Arthuriad in a quite new way. They see the world as drastically different from its recent past. In response to its modernity, they feel the need for radical answers and in order to shape them they produce radically new texts, among them startling modern versions of the Arthurian legend.

REFERENCES

Primary Sources
Child, F. J. (ed.) (1882–98) *The English and Scottish Popular Ballads* (Boston: Houghton Mifflin).
Doré, G. (1867) illustrations to *Idylls of the King* (London: Moxon).
Drayton, M. (1622) *The Poly-Olbion: A Chronological Description of Great Britain, Parts I and II* (facsimile edn New York: Franklin, 1970).
Dryden, J. (1691) *King Arthur* in *The Works of John Dryden* ed. W. Scott, corr. G. Saintsbury (Edinburgh: Paterson, 1882–9), vol. VIII.
Fielding, H. (1731) *The Tragedy of Tragedies; or The Life and Death of Tom Thumb the Great* (facsimile edn London: Scolar, 1973).
Morris, W. (1858) *The Defence of Guinevere and Other Poems* (London: Reeves).
Percy, T. (ed.) (1765) *Reliques of English Poetry* (London: Dent, 1906).
Tennyson, Alfred, Lord (1969) *The Poems* ed. C. B. Ricks (London: Routledge).

Secondary Sources
Altick, R. D. (1974) *People and Ideas in Victorian Britain* (London: Dent).
Ashe, G. (1980) *A Guidebook to Arthurian Britain* (London: Longman).
Brooke, S. A. (1894) *Tennyson: His Art and Relation to Modern Life* (London: Isbister).
Burrow, J. W. (1978) 'The Sense of the Past' in *The Victorians*, ed. L. Lerner (London: Methuen).
Carlyle, T. (1843) *Past and Present* (London: Chapman and Hall).
Chandler, A. (1970) *A Dream of Order* (London: Routledge).
Culler, A. D. (1977) *The Poetry of Tennyson* (New Haven: Yale University Press).
Fausset, H. I'A. (1923) *Tennyson* (London: Selwyn).
Girouard, M. (1981) *The Return to Camelot* (New Haven: Yale University Press).
Gordon, W. C. (1906) *The Social Ideals of Alfred Tennyson as Related to his Time* (University of Chicago Press).

Gray, J. M. (1969) *Man and Myth in Victorian England: Tennyson's The Coming of Arthur* (Lincoln, U.K.: Tennyson Research Centre).

—— (1980) *Thro' the Vision of the Night: a study of source, evolution and structure in Tennyson's Idylls of the King* (Edinburgh University Press).

Harrison, J. F. C. (1971) *Early Victorian Britain* (London: Weidenfeld and Nicolson).

Hill, C. (1958) 'The Norman Yoke' in *Puritanism and Revolution* (London: Secker and Warburg).

—— (1977) *Milton and the English Revolution* (London: Faber).

Houghton, W. E. (1957) *The Victorian Frame of Mind* (New Haven: Yale University Press).

Johnson, W. S. (1975) *Sex and Marriage in Victorian Poetry* (Ithaca: Cornell University Press).

Jump, J. D. (ed.) (1967) *Tennyson: The Critical Heritage* (London: Routledge).

Killham, J. (1958) *Tennyson and The Princess: Reflections of an Age (London: Athlone)*.

Lukács, G. (1962) *The Historical Novel* (London: Merlin).

MacCallum, M. W. (1894) *Tennyson's Idylls of the King and Arthurian Story from the XVIth Century* (Glasgow: Maclehose).

Martin, R. B. (1980) *Tennyson: The Unquiet Heart* (Oxford: Clarendon).

Masterman, C. F. G. (1900) *Tennyson as a Religious Teacher* (London: Methuen).

Maurice, F. (1884) *The Life of Frederick Denison Maurice* (London: Macmillan).

Merriman, J. D. (1973) *The Flower of Kings: A Study of the Arthurian Legend in England between 1485 and 1835* (Wichita: University of Kansas Press).

Millican, C. B. (1932) *Spenser and the Table Round* (Cambridge, Mass.: Harvard University Press).

Millett, K. (1970) *Sexual Politics* (New York: Doubleday).

Nicholson, H. (1923) *Tennyson: Aspects of his Life, Character and Poetry* (London: Constable).

Pugin, A. W. N. (1836) *Contrasts* (London: Dolman).

Richardson, J. (1962) *The Pre-Eminent Victorian* (London: Cape).

Ricks, C. B. (1969) notes to *The Poems*, see under Tennyson, Alfred Lord.

Rosenberg, J. D. (1973) *The Fall of Camelot: A Study of Tennyson's Idylls of the King* (Cambridge, Mass.: Harvard University Press).

Southey, R. (1817) Introduction to *The Byrth, Lyf and Actes of Kyng Arthur* by Sir Thomas Malory (London: Longman).

Stone, L. (1977) *The Family, Sex and Marriage in England 1500–1800* (London: Weidenfeld and Nicolson).

Tennyson, C. (1954) 'Tennyson's Politics' in *Six Tennyson Essays* (London: Cassell).

Tennyson, H. (1897) *Alfred, Lord Tennyson: A Memoir* (London: Macmillan).

Tillotson, K. (1965) 'Tennyson's Serial Poem' in *Mid-Victorian Poetry*, G. and K. Tillotson (London: Athlone).

Zipes, J. (1979) *Breaking the Magic Spell: Radical Theories of Folk and Fairy Tales* (London: Heinemann).

6 'A new deal': Mark Twain's *A Connecticut Yankee at King Arthur's Court* and the modern Arthurian legend

I

The earliest period of Arthurian writing, discussed in Chapter 1, produced minor texts with distinct social contexts and one major work rich with contemporary meaning, *Culhwch ac Olwen*. The modern period is remarkably similar. Many versions of the Arthurian legend have flourished, each with its special ideological interest, but only one fully realises the social and historical forces of its period. That is Mark Twain's *A Connecticut Yankee at King Arthur's Court* (published in 1889: the British edition dropped the place-name and then adjusted the rhythm to *A Yankee at the Court of King Arthur*).

Like *Huckleberry Finn*, Twain's other major work, *A Connecticut Yankee* has always been a success with the public. Irreverent wit and surging imagination have been very important factors – they have also made some literary critics find Twain not to their reverent and orderly taste. But the novels also deal with issues central to the self-consciousness and the anxieties of the recent developments of Western civilisation. In *Huckleberry Finn* Twain suggests that the structures of what Huck and he sceptically call 'sivilisation' oppress the freedom of the human being (Wilding, 1980, ch. 1). In *A Connecticut Yankee* Twain speaks in a more specific and more political way as he realises both the good and the bad that rise from the awkward partnership of democracy and industry. Where Tennyson urgently represses the social and economic forces of the nineteenth century, Twain makes them operate right through his Arthurian work.

He sets his story in the Arthurian sixth century, seen as a

187

generally medieval period. Into this world comes a time-traveller
– Twain is one of the first to use that potent device, a product of
the nineteenth-century consciousness of history. Hank Morgan is
a complex figure. In one way he criticises the past to show the
comfortable and democratic excellence of the American present.
Yet the traveller himself bears the central imprint of the
nineteenth century, he is 'a Yankee of the Yankees', a tradesman
and mechanic, with strong business instincts (Preface, p. 36.
Because there are so many differently-paged editions, chapter
numbers will also be given in references). By the end of the novel
his journey into history has also provided Twain with a means of
scrutinising those modern American values and predicting where
they will lead society. While the vices of the past, many of which
still survive in the European and even American present, are
revealed by the novel, modernisation itself is found to be
destructive in wholly new ways – a notion implied by the novel's
sub-title 'A Tale of the Lost Land' and finally left seething in the
reader's mind by its terrific, apocalyptic ending.

Twain was introduced to the Arthurian legend in detail when
George Washington Cable, his colleague on a lecture tour in 1884,
lent him a copy of Malory. In his notebook, he recorded his
immediate reaction, to mock the inconvenience of knighthood:

> No pockets in the armour. No way to manage certain require-
> ments of nature. Can't scratch. Cold in the head – can't blow –
> can't get at handkerchief, can't use iron sleeve. Iron gets red hot
> in the sun – leaks in the rain, gets white with frost and freezes
> me solid in winter. Suffer from lice and fleas. Make disagreeable
> clatter when I enter church. Can't dress or undress myself.
> Always getting struck by lightning. Fall down, can't get up.
>   (1975, p. 78)

This seems a typical piece of instant burlesque, Twain the
instinctive entertainer at work. But the novel will show that
modern society is in many ways as painful and constricting as
medieval practices, and there are indications that from the very
beginning Twain's response to the idea of the novel was not
simply comic. Notes made just after he started writing envisaged a
final desperate battle between the Yankee and the forces of
Arthurian chivalry and foresaw that he would lose his sixth
century girl-friend when he reverted to the present (Twain, 1980,

p. 216): already not all about him and his progress seems admirable or successful. The first three chapters were drafted by early 1885 and the hero, here named Sir Bob Smith, has distinctly 'Yankee' (that is, morally flexible) business methods, and his technical talents include gun-making, a skill which will lead to a climax synopsised as 'startlingly brutal' (Baetzhold, 1961, gives full details of the early notes and drafts).

The major elements of the complex mixture that was to be *A Connecticut Yankee* were in Twain's imagination very early in the development of the novel. He worked on a wide front that embraced burlesque, moralism, political comment, industrial history, business ethics and sheer nostalgia. These elements interweave dynamically in the novel, but before considering how that process operates it is necessary to follow each thread through and identify what Twain has to say about the past and the present, both in Europe and in America.

II

As Twain immediately saw, there were jokes to be made by juxtaposing modern practices with medieval institutions. The consistent effect is to make the world of chivalry seem ridiculous. He develops the uncomfortable armour idea when Hank, now known as Sir Boss, goes on an adventure with his lady Alisande – Sandy to him. The sun heats the armour, and she has to cool him down by the direct method: Dan Beard produced one of the liveliest of his two hundred and twenty illustrations from the incident (Plate 21). There are many other inventive moments. When Hank lights his pipe in armour, slaves and knights alike flee thinking he is a fire-breathing monster; he beats a whole group of knights at a tournament by using a lariat to pull each one to the ground; he employs knights errant as sandwich men for his various down-to-earth products like soap (Plate 22); knights are trained to ride penny-farthing bicycles for greater speed, even Sir Launcelot (Plate 23).

Highly entertaining sequences, these are also functional, and not only as light relief to offset the severer satire. They prick the balloon of medieval and Arthurian seriousness, they establish Twain's position as a new voice in the legend – in their colloquial way they operate much as did the stunning incident when Galahad defeated Launcelot, signalling that a new hero with new values had surged into the Arthurian world. The mockery of knights and Arthurian attitudes at all social levels is a tonally important part of the critique of medieval conservative practices. Twain was strongly aware of the value of 'irreverence'. While writing *A Connecticut Yankee* he remarked in his notebook that 'Irreverence is the champion of liberty and its only sure defence' (1980, p. 392).

The serious satire in the novel operates in a number of areas. The first to become a clear target is medieval society and its oppressions. Twain had carefully read Lecky's *History of the Morals of Europe* (Salomon, 1961, p. 98), and it gave him instances to dramatise an American's democratic scorn for the European past. In his role as a time-travelling observer the Yankee identifies a whole range of medieval viciousness. The lack of social and economic freedom is soon picked out:

> The most of King Arthur's British nation were slaves, pure and simple, and bore that namc, and wore the iron collars on their necks; and the rest were slaves in fact, but without the name they imagined themselves men and freemen, and called thcmselves so. The truth was, the nation as a body was in the world for one object, and one only: to grovel before King and Church and noble; to slave for them, sweat blood for them, starve that they might be happy, go naked that they might wear silks and jewels, pay taxes that they might be spared from paying them, be familiar all their lives with the degrading language and postures of adulation, that they might walk in pride and think themselves the gods of this world. And for all this, the thanks they got were cuffs and contempt; and so poor-spirited were they that they took even this sort of attention as an honour. (8.88)

This is further developed in Chapter 13, entitled 'Freemen', and in the sequence where the King and the Yankee are captured and sold as slaves (chs 34–8). Elsewhere incidents occur which bring specific cases of medieval aristocratic and church evil into focus, such as tithes (20.179), the forest laws (17.156–7), the seigneurial right to deflower a bride (18.165–6 and 25.227–8). There is one general discussion of the oppressive practices of the aristocracy and the church (13.126–7).

However, in a long book, this is not a great deal of anti-medieval material. Some of the most horrific details, such as burning a witch to warm the slaves (35.328) and executing a woman for stealing to feed her child (35.329–32), are non-medieval, features of more recent times. The weight placed on slavery is also foreign to medieval Europe: the source was the essays George Kennan was publishing currently about the plight of serfs in Czarist Russia (Baetzhold, 1961, p. 207). The medieval world is recognised in the novel and has its own criticism to bear, but it is inherently a fictional field in which Twain demonstrates types of oppression which are still going on. As his foreword says, 'The ungentle laws and customs touched upon in this tale are historical', but not necessarily in the sixth century: 'they existed in the English and other civilizations of far later times'.

It is hardly surprising, in the light of Twain's dislike of monarchy, aristocracy and an established church, that England of 'far later times', including the nineteenth century itself, should have been one of the targets of his criticism. He was well aware that his new Arthuriad would by its irreverence and criticism upset the traditional British. The illustrator caught the mood brilliantly. Merlin, the old-world magician of manipulative and incompetent superstition, whom Hank describes as 'that cheap old humbug, that maundering ass' (5.64), was drawn as a very recognisable version of Tennyson himself (Plate 24). The same mood is behind the 'Chuckleheads' illustration (Plate 25) where the Prince of Wales and the Kaiser are two of the aristocratic boobies who gain military commissions.

That is one of the issues where Twain clearly attacks a contemporary British problem, the inability to reform satisfactorily the notorious system of military commissions, so that merit, not birth, became the basis for choice and promotion. Hank has trained meritocratic 'West Pointers' but in Arthur's army they cannot gain a commission – the issue dominates Chapter 25, and was widely recognised in liberal circles in Britain as a serious problem, made obvious at the time of the Crimean War but difficult to resolve satisfactorily.

Morgan le Fay's outrageous misuse of her legal power in Chapters 16–18 is in itself a grotesque version of the abuses that nineteenth-century British liberals were trying to curtail by extending the powers of local government over the magistrates' benches (Budd, 1962, p. 121). Similarly they were disturbed by the expense and uselessness of royal pensions – Twain picks that issue up as part of the officer-commissioning problem (25.237). The material about savage laws of trespass and poaching is certainly applicable to the middle ages, but many people felt that the 1880 Game Laws had still not sufficiently liberalised the situation in Britain (Budd, 1962, p. 121).

In the same way, the attacks on the church's superstitious and exploitative grip on the people relate in many respects to the medieval and Catholic church. But by stressing it was an 'Established Church' and by rather rarely calling it Catholic, Twain extends the critique to the present, on one occasion quite explicitly. After explaining how this church was a basic element of the whole undemocratic world, he goes on:

> Even down to my birth-century that poison was still in the blood of Christendom and the best of English commoners was still content to see his inferiors impudently continuing to hold a number of positions. (8.88)

Apart from legitimising the acts of the aristocracy, the church has its own exploitations, ancient and modern. Tithing without mercy is referred to several times as a medieval sin, but in an especially bitter case the Yankee comments:

> How curious. The same thing had happened in the Wales of my day, under this same old Established Church, which was supposed by many to have changed its nature when it changed its disguise. (20.179)

It was in response to the continued power of church, crown and aristocracy that Twain developed his praise of the French Revolution. He described the long-lasting dominance of these forces as itself a 'reign of Terror', one of 'lifelong death from hunger, cold, insult, cruelty and heartbreak' (13.127). Against that, the terror of the revolution itself was a sharp purgative:

> a settlement of that hoary debt in the proportion of half a drop of blood for each hogshead of it that had been pressed by slow tortures out of that people in the weary stretch of ten centuries of wrong and shame and misery . . . that unspeakably bitter and awful Terror which none of us has been taught to see in its vastness or pity as it deserves. (13.127)

This is strongly radical talk, influenced by Carlyle's enthusiasm in *The French Revolution*, but it is also Twain's own response to the *ancien régime* he knew well through the recently translated *Memoirs of the Duc de St Simon* (Twain, 1975, p. 402). Some commentators feel that Twain's extreme anti-Europeanism was provoked by Matthew Arnold's widely reported criticism of America, published as 'Civilization in the United States' in 1888 (Budd, 1962, p. 119; Kaplan, 1967, p. 299). Twain's *Notebooks* certainly indicate that he rejected Arnold's views (1980, pp. 383–4 and 406) and they may have added sting to his remarks, but his attitude was much more than a personally motivated one. Nor was it a sheer distaste for Britain. He had enjoyed his visit in 1872 very much, and would later be deeply moved by an honorary doctorate from Oxford.

Twain's attitudes to nineteenth-century Britain were political ones, based on his deeply rooted sense of democracy. The novel contains a good deal with which British liberals would have agreed, as is clear from W. K. Stead's favourable response in *The Review of Reviews* (reprinted in Anderson, 1971, pp. 167–70). Such liberal views particularly needed stressing when the Liberals had just been shattered at the 1886 election, when the golden jubilee was re-establishing the monarchy as beyond reproach in 1887. *A Connecticut Yankee* sold very well in Britain and Stead put his finger on the cause and on the audience. There were many who dissented completely from the ideologies of Tennyson's Arthuriad, just as they were excluded from the privileges of its sponsoring class – and they were reading and buying books in increasing numbers. Stead summed up:

> the Education Act has turned out and is turning out millions of readers who are much more like the Americans in their tastes, their ideas and their sympathies than they are to the English of the cultured, pampered and privileged classes.
>
> (Anderson, 1971, p. 168)

III

If many of Twain's criticisms will not remain distantly medieval, but drift into the European nineteenth century, there are others which move often more uncomfortably close to the present in America. The slave issue, itself based on Russian and not British material, points irresistibly to the pre-Civil War south. That was Twain's own origin. Samuel Clemens, before he took his famous pen-name, was brought up in Hannibal, Missouri, a slave-holding area, and he briefly joined the southern forces in the Civil War before deserting (like Huck Finn) to the freer western territories. In his biography of Twain, Kaplan has argued that in many ways Arthur's sixth-century kingdom resembles the pre-war south (1967, p. 297), and not only in terms of slavery. Both have an agrarian economy and an elaborate chivalric tradition: both are opposed by the industry and democracy of the north. That old order was destroyed by civil war in the south and the novel, and in both cases there is a sense of loss for what was beautiful and valuable in 'the lost land'.

There is clearly something in the parallel, yet it is important to note how little is actually valued from the south and the past. Almost all that Twain cherishes in Huck Finn's Hannibal and Arthur's Britain is the weather, the flora and fauna and the naïve nobility of a few people – only Jim in *Huckleberry Finn*, but in *A Connecticut Yankee* both Arthur and Launcelot can be tender and brave and Hank finds deep fidelity and emotional contact in Sandy.

As if to justify that residual nostalgia a tremendous weight of criticism is directed at the negative features of the lost lands. Chivalry is ridiculed throughout *A Connecticut Yankee* and shown to be a super-structural mask for vicious oppression, just as the Scott-like 'nobility' of the feuding families in *Huckleberry Finn* was really a narcissistic and murderous stupidity. Twain is especially powerful and dedicated in his exposé of the evils of slavery. Jim in *Huckleberry Finn* is a timid, human and generous man who is both the result and a total critique of the slave-system. In *A Connecticut Yankee* Twain puts great effort into realising just what it might be like to be a slave, and insists that the difficult process itself is of crucial importance: 'Words realise nothing, vivify nothing to you, unless you have suffered in your own person the thing which the words try to describe' (28.264).

But he presses hard to make words do. Arthur himself is made a slave, hawked about at fairs, then finally thrown in with the Yankee as a job lot. Being treated like a commodity makes the king himself think in commodity terms (as Marx predicted in *Capital*) – he is offended by his own low price (35.325–6). Through the sequence, chilling details of slave life are enacted. They are in

a chain-gang, of course, and the pain of that is brought out fully
(35.327–9, realising emotively a topic dealt with before more
distantly, 21.188–91). The problems of an escaped slave are
developed after Hank and the King break out (ch. 37), and so is
the ease with which people can be enslaved, the burden of proof
being on them to show they are not slaves (34.320–1).

Twain wants each of his readers to become, like Arthur, 'the
bitterest hater of the institution I ever heard talk' (35.327). But he
is not merely exorcising for himself dramas of the south that partly
formed him. He was well aware of the need to keep before the
public the unacceptable face of slavery, because he knew well
how little the attitudes in the south had changed, and recognised
'the postbellum slavery apologists and newly militant racists who
were, just then, about to reimpose the yoke of white supremacy
upon the "reconstructed South" ' (Geismar, 1970, p. 120). Here
too, as in his critique of contemporary England, Twain is
speaking politically rather than personally, both in terms of the
general need for human freedom and in terms of the constant
specific vigilance needed to defend those freedoms which, in very
recent times, had been bitterly won in civil war.

The north had been a positive force in dispelling the evil of
slavery, but there is much in the novel that comes home to criticise
the industrial society of north-eastern America. Twain finally
scrutinised his own culture with a gaze more searching than most
Arthurian writers have cared to turn on the authorities basic to
their own context. Some of the material is related to specific
contemporary affairs. The Yankee speaks at length on behalf of
free trade against the protectionist argument (33.299–302,
developing 31.284). Here Twain sets out the position he took with
other 'Mugwump' Republicans who deserted their party to
support Cleveland, the Democratic free-trader elected president
in 1884.

Just as the anti-slavery material was partly directed against
contemporary reactionary pressures, so the anti-Catholic satire
was also relevant to the active and growing Catholic church in
North America, especially in its opposition to the emergent trade
unions (Budd, 1962, pp. 116–18). A similar specific anxiety seems
to be embodied in the lynching sequence in 'The Tragedy of the
Manor-House' (ch. 20), where an 'oppressed community had
turned their hands against their own class in the interest of the
common oppressor' (30.277). This appears to refer to the

execution of anarchists after the 1886 Chicago Riots. W. D. Howells, Twain's friend and literary confidante, was very unhappy about their trial and the editors of the Twain-Howells letters feel sure the episodes are linked (1967, pp. 275–6).

An equally radical pressure is felt in the latter part of Chapter 33, where after extolling free trade, Hank goes on to predict the excellent future of the working man under effective unions. This meshes with Twain's enthusiasm for the newly formed 'Knights of Labor', and the passage relates closely to a speech he gave in March 1886 called 'The New Dynasty' (Carter, 1957): both Twain and the unionists use metaphors to demonstrate the working man's claim on the power and the cultural legitimations once dominated by an aristocratic and chivalric class.

Just as unionists and workers could be presented as a new chivalry, so contemporary radicals saw their opponents in business as being tarred with the brush of chivalric evil from the past. Henry George, the tax reformer, talked of the developing monopolist organisation of capital as 'the new feudalism' (Smith, 1964, p. 9) and called the monopolists themselves 'Robber Barons'. The chief of these, and the one Twain hated most, was Jay Gould – whom Beard characterises as 'The Slave Driver' (Plate 26). Twain praised the illustrations, and must have accepted the idea.

But Twain's critique of business methods and morality goes much further than this. The fact is that while Hank Morgan has been the critical observer of all the 'ungentle laws and customs' discussed so far, he is also an active agent in the novel, and as such he seems himself to become a victim of its criticism. He is the focus of the feeling the book generates against industry and business practices typical in the American north east. He becomes a monopolist himself. His final slaughter of the knights of Arthur's England and his own defeat and lapse into inarticulate nostalgia must be associated with the industrial and business values that he represents. It is important to note that his democratic values only operate to any extent when he is a passive observer: when he is active he is quite dictatorial. Twain is by no means suggesting that democracy itself is the cause of chaos: rather he shows how the forces of capitalist industry frustrate the development of democracy and plunge the country into a deadly chaos in some ways worse than feudal oppression.

At first there is, it is true, a hopeful relation between democracy and industry. When the Yankee meets particularly stubborn or lively members of the oppressed classes, he sends them off to his factory (13.129–30). This he calls a 'man-factory', a place where through technological training men are taught to be true men, independent and self-respecting. This is not at first a 'de-humanising pun' as Kaplan thinks (1971, p. 22). It is part of the Yankee's programme to educate and reform the oppressed and produce 'a new deal' which was not a revolution (13.129). Roosevelt is supposed to have derived his famous phrase from this passage, and it certainly seems to fit his intentions – but the result of the Yankee's efforts seems to predict the development of capitalist industry in and beyond Roosevelt's day.

For all the Yankee's good intentions to restructure business in favour of the working majority, specifically promised in this scene, as the novel progresses he becomes more and more tyrannical, he does seem to be manufacturing men as a product, and so develops not them but his own profit and power. His actions become more and more exploitative and publicity-conscious, his contempt for the common people more obvious and so the disastrous ending of his industrialisation more inescapable. The factories finally become places where weapons are made to destroy men, and which are themselves destroyed. The idea was there from the start, for the Yankee came from Colt's factory at Hartford, where the famous '45 and the Gatling gun were produced, and making guns was his first mentioned skill (Preface, p. 36). However much Twain as an observer praised a new political deal, when he considered the industrial creation of a new world he only discovered, as he instinctively implied in his early notes, that the future of that world was violent, conflicted and ultimately disastrous.

The Yankee's name itself suggests that after his early dallying with 'Bob Smith', an everyman's name, Twain saw the malign side of his hero quite clearly. Hank is a name both colloquial and euphoniously Yankee, but the surname is ominous. First it suggests, in non-abbreviated, non-Yankee terms, Henry Morgan the notorious pirate. Secondly it makes him kin with Morgan le Fay, the cruel aristocrat. At first he watches her with an observer's horror, but then as an active participant he agrees with her when he sends the composer and the musicians to the gallows – she had only condemned the composer. It is a joke, but a disturbing, unsettling joke, typical of Twain's method of making his audience think again, and so recognise the link between Hank and this other Morgan, which she expresses herself (16.150). And lastly, his surname comes up-to-date: J. P. Morgan was one of the great monopolists of the period who, like Gould, Rockefeller and Carnegie were all born within a few years of Twain.

The Yankee's other name is 'Sir Boss'. That name too has connotations, equally bad from south and north. It implies the slave-master, as in the endlessly repeated phrase 'Yassuh boss'; and it suggests the big-city equivalents, especially 'Boss' Tweed, the lord of corruption in contemporary New York. In industrial terms, 'boss' implies a businessman rather than a technocrat and although the Yankee presents himself as a hero of technology, someone who has 'learned to make everything' (Preface, p. 36) and states his respect of the 'creators of this world' from Gutenberg to Bell (33.298), the emphasis of the novel and particularly of the Yankee's activities falls heavily on the entrepreneurial and the publicity side of industry. So much so that Twain had to backtrack to write Chapter 10 in order to lay the narrative basis for the technological tricks he was later to turn; he had to make the hats that had already delivered their rabbits.

When the Yankee does do something technical, it is either a rural complexity like re-stoning a well, using a lariat, or something everyday like using the telephone, smoking a pipe. No doubt Twain's own technical innocence is part of the cause, but the novel exploits this technological shortfall to make the Yankee not an Edison or a Bell, but essentially a business booster. That indeed was the context of the phrase 'a Connecticut Yankee' in Twain's earlier book *Roughing It*, and the circus boss P. T. Barnum was cited as a typical example (Sloane, 1979, p. 146). The Yankee acts like a public relations ringmaster. When he re-stones the well, the whole impact lies in the 'effect' he gets with mumbo-jumbo and explosives. The emphasis throughout is not on the productive factories and any improvement in the common lot through things like soap and matches: it is on the Yankee's conscious humiliation of knights as travelling salesmen and his own centralised power as the true boss – or the dictator. One critic has gone so far as to see the figure of modern totalitarianism emerging through the Yankee (Hansen, 1973), but however much dictators do depend on a mixture of technology, theatricality and centralised control, it seems that Twain has contemporary business most firmly in his sights. That extends to his rewriting of the traditional Arthurian plot. Launcelot does cause the final civil war, but his major sin is outwitting Mordred in a tricky stock deal (42.380).

Twain does not ignore the political side of the Yankee's meaning. He sees, instinctively perhaps, that control of the means of production and distribution is also a means of social control and that power and its corruption are the final products. The Yankee grows increasingly arrogant. He splashes money about embarrassingly in Chapter 32 to impress ordinary people, including Dowley – a blacksmith rejected and humiliated by the former blacksmith. He comes to dislike the newspaper he founded because it is too 'irreverent' and approves the 'dignified respectfulness' of the court circular which is identical each day, having no news, no vitality, no irreverence (26.247).

Early on the Yankee comes to like the name of boss, 'a good word to conjure with', especially because it overawes people so much (14.135). For long he is the second power in the kingdom, but towards the end he is more important than the king (37.347) and has plans for a democratic régime in which he, however, will be president (40.365–6). This brings to a head his long-developing contempt for the common people. As an observer he could see they were timid because of their oppressive circumstances and inherited ideas (8.87–8 and 13.126–8) but as an active exploiter he can only see them as 'these animals' (5.66). Finally, when the common people remain true to their old allegiance rather than accept his new industrial faith, they are 'human muck' (43.392).

The Yankee's use of physical power is as disturbing as his attitudes. In one bizarre episode, another disturbing joke, he harnesses a constantly bowing saint as the drive for a sewing machine, then sells him when he is wearing out (22.205–6). The jokes and actions grow grimmer: after he blows up ten knights with a mine there was 'a steady drizzle of microscopic fragments of knights and horse-flesh' (27.259). Then after beating eight knights humorously with a lariat he shoots down nine more with his revolvers and says 'The march of civilization has begun' (39.363).

Technology, business, autocracy – they all converge in uncontrollable violence to human beings, and finally in the destruction of those who practise them themselves. The ending to Twain's novel is famous – always a surprise to a new reader, always a central topic of discussion of the book. Into remarkably few pages

Twain packs the central issues of his powerful, creative and disturbing novel, one that the passing of time and the development of what Hank calls 'civilization' have only made to seem more compelling and more truthful.

The Yankee and his technicians are penned in their own redoubt; they kill the whole chivalry of England by an electrified fence, by flooding a ditch and then by Gatling fire. All the forces they have harnessed are used destructively. Then Hank blows up his own chain of factories throughout the country, all mined for the purpose. Earlier the whole network was described as a 'serene volcano', as 'the civilization of the nineteenth century booming under the nose of the sixth' (10.103). Now the volcano has gone up. And the technicians die as well, infected with plague by the dead thousands around them. Hank himself is carried into the cave at the centre of their redoubt. It is Merlin's cave: the Yankee's powers have become, like the old magician's, those of manipulative malpractice. Their competitive similarity is both emphasised and resolved as Merlin himself creeps in disguised as a poor old woman, to finish off his great enemy.

Nothing is left of the civilisation programme; the scene returns to the nineteenth century where the time-traveller is in the extremity of 'the torture of those hideous dreams' (Postscript, 410). His last feelings are nostalgia for the wife and child whom he has come to love (Plate 27). They are still in 'the lost land'; the human family and society, whose value has outlasted the industrial and capitalist edifice, is now unavailable to the man burdened with the experience of history and capitalist industrialisation.

Through Hank Morgan Twain has realised the course of the industrial revolution. He saw himself briefly as 'another Robinson Crusoe' (7.81) and the novel is a nightmarish replay of Defoe's bourgeois dream. Hank has the whole range of relevant skills, technical and entrepreneurial (Smith, 1964, p. 154); it is the latter which release his power and his dominance – and his appalling impact. His first institution is a patent office and widespread education; he creates a newspaper to publicise and a sale system to distribute his factory goods; he organises an army and a navy to protect his business system. The Yankee is the genius of the development of Western industrial capitalism. No doubt an economic historian might find that Twain has things out of order and has his emphases wrong, but he was directly involved in the whole process he was imaginatively recreating, not analytically alienated from it like Marx: he created an affective version of what rapid socio-economic change felt like, as it had happened in America in his lifetime.

Twain had experienced the whole process in a life that went from the rural south to the industrialised north-east. His own professions had been the skills that disseminated the power of the capitalist industrial monolith: first a journeyman printer, then a riverboat pilot – and they were the distributive predecessors of the railways in 'civilising' American (Schivelbusch, 1980) – then a newspaper editor and coal-baron's son-in-law, a Washington lobbyist and place-seeker. Finally, as a highly-paid entertainer and bad conscience of the eastern establishment, settled in Nook Farm with the others from the upper-middle class élite, he moved into his own entrepreneurial activities, opening a publishing house, sinking his money in the ill-fated Paige typesetter and – after his personal bankruptcy – becoming friendly with the monopolist millionaire Carnegie.

But his work and his attitudes did not automatically follow his social ascent. His earlier books were sold not in bookshops like those of the élite New England writers, but by door-to-door subscription salesmen, remarkably like Hank's travelling knights. His audience was not 'the better class of readers' as the editor of *Literary World* pointed out (Foner, 1958, p. 56). Bliss, the subscription publisher, called Twain 'The People's Author' (Kaplan, 1967, p. 106) and Twain accepted that role happily; he later wrote to Andrew Lang that his essential audience was 'dumb' – he did not mean they were stupid, but that he was 'the mighty voice of the uncultivated' (Kaplan, 1967, pp. 43 and 169).

A marginal man, like so many powerful creative artists, Twain knew the forces of his period from the inside, as Tennyson only knew them from an alarmed distance. Into the Arthurian legend he injected a new value, a new type of authority. In one sense his new figure, Hank Morgan is like Galahad, consumed by his own fires. Yet more fully he is like Malory's Launcelot, a figure destroyed by his double values, here those of a democratic observer and those of a capitalist technological intervener. Twain too was torn between revelling in the riches and power of a literary entertainer in 'the Gilded Age', and the role of an outsider, criticising that world with other values, seeing the true gold that devalued the gilt. He coined the stinging phrase himself as the title of an earlier novel, *The Gilded Age*, which pilloried the corrupt boosting world of American politics and business.

The result of Twain's own position and of his power to realise his imaginative response to his world is a remarkably modern Arthuriad, a frontal challenge to Tennyson's conservative Victorian version. In its daring, its vitality and its remorseless refusal to settle for any ideological consolation other than regret and something close to despair, *A Connecticut Yankee at King Arthur's Court* presents a model of vigour and veracity which the writers of more modern Arthurian stories and poems have found it very difficult to match.

IV

The best-known Arthurian writer of the twentieth century and the one who approaches most closely to Twain's power and feeling is T. H. White. The first book of his Arthuriad, *The Sword in the Stone* was very successful in 1938 and became the basis for a Disney cartoon. The four-book collection, *The Once and Future King* (1958), was a best-seller and gained wider fame as the source of the New York hit musical *Camelot*, which then became a widely popular film. But the development of the Arthuriad, like the progress of White's life, was by no means smooth or happy. His biographer gives many details (Warner, 1967) and some literary points are filled out in the only critical book on his work (Crane, 1974).

White had to rewrite the second book, *The Witch in the Wood* (1941, called *The Queen of Air and Darkness* in the 1958 omnibus volume) and his publishers would not publish separately the fourth volume, *The Candle in the Wind*, holding it over from 1942 till the 1980 collection. But they completely refused to print the projected fifth part, *The Book of Merlyn* (1977). Originally they blamed paper shortages during the early forties, but the fiercely anti-war tone of the last books, especially the rejected fifth, could not have appealed to a patriotic, paper-hungry publisher.

If White's hatred of war is the most powerful issue in his Arthuriad, the most inventive contribution he makes to the Arthurian legend is *The Sword in the Stone*. He presents, for the very first time, Arthur as a child. Formerly in the legend his growing-up had been invisible: his off-stage foster-father Ector played in the story the role of servants, governesses and tutors among the wealthy and powerful. White's new segment brings into the Arthurian legend a recognition of new practices and new ideas of child-rearing. The romantic interest in the child as a natural source of unfettered imagination, the rise of interest in education as a means of developing and improving the world, the increasing affective confrontation between parents and children – these socio-cultural forces are all implicit in White's imaginative innovation.

Throughout *The Sword in the Stone* Arthur is tutored in wisdom. His master is Merlyn. Twain had made him remain through the whole story for the first time, but as the enemy of modernity. White uses him in a way like Hank Morgan, as a time-traveller bringing knowledge of the present into the past, but Merlyn's force is entirely positive and he is empowered by scholarly whimsy and natural values, not science, technology and business. He understands formal learning but he also has access to the deep springs of true wisdom among birds and animals. It is there, in a series of vigorously imagined animal transformations, that Arthur learns true wisdom: the evil of sheer might among the fish, raw courage from the hawks, evolutionary history from the snake, time and relativity from the owl, mercy from the hedgehog, man's complex role in creation from the badger.

In his experiences among the ants and the geese he sees two model communities, the military fascism of the ant-hill and the primitive communism of the goose flock. These two sequences written for Book 5, fit rather well into Book 1 where they were placed for the four-book 1958 volume. They displace the rather dry sequences with the owl and the snake and both dramatise and sophisticate what was originally a rather limited discussion by developing naïve values into political forces, and so giving a sound, if postdated, basis for Arthur's attempt in the later books to use 'Might' in the service of 'Right'. That lesson, learnt by Arthur as Wart the child of nature, is retained and made urgent when he becomes king at the end of the first book, where White picks up Malory's story at its beginning.

But added to the thoughtful and naturally wise aspect of *The Sword in the Stone* there is a welter of whimsical comedy. Quaint medieval lore, the pantomime-like Questing Beast, minor knights as elderly London clubmen, Merlyn as an absent-minded professor – these elements should not be dismissed as a sugary top-dressing. They are typical of that deliberate and defensive unseriousness that is a feature of the self-conscious English upper-middle class, from whom White came and among whom he found his friends. Where Twain's irreverence had a political bite, White's is no more than a nervous self-protection in case he is caught being too earnest. He opened the way himself for a Disney trivialisation.

The three other books published in *The Once and Future King* are all much closer to Malory, using his narrative structure and modernising it in various ways. One is a development of the twentieth-century faith in individualist psychology. The touchy hostility of the Gawain brothers is traced to their mother – White's own problem is glanced at: he was a homosexual sado-masochist discontented with his lot, and he blamed it on his own mother.

In a similar personal and reductive way White explains Lancelot's passion for Guinevere as a repressed diversion of his violent potential and her own role of *femme fatale* as being quite against her own will (pp. 331 and 468). But throughout the story Arthur is central, a figure owing more to Tennyson than Twain or Malory: a king constantly fretting over disorder and how he can make a non-violent law prevail. He and White finally decide that the trouble is competition, that people just will not pull together as the geese do, or as the ants are made to do. It is a sharp recognition of the force of competitive individualism, but White's curious mixture of depth and shallowness is clear when Arthur can only talk about the 'games ethic' (p. 362) – White's power of analysis, like his sexual persona, cannot escape the confines of the public school.

Arthur, faced with the destruction of his Round Table, like White contemplating the Second World War, felt the world had gone mad (pp. 588–9). Politics is no longer Twain's world of democracy and oppression within a nation: it has become the desperate conflict of nations and mass slaughter. White vividly recreates the common sense of impotent despair as the world slid into war again, only twenty years after the holocaust of 1914–18. As his fourth book ends, and as the published quartet concludes, Arthur is waiting for the last terrible battle, feeling that somehow he may return, and at least hoping that someone will record his attempt to civilise might into the service of right. With an imaginative touch that returns to the world of youthful positives and the value of the literary past, White makes Arthur's squire at the end the young Thomas Malory.

For years that conclusion seemed satisfactory – tense, despair-ing yet not desperate. Crafted in 1942, it seemed valid for the whole period of the Cold War. Yet White had not ended there; he had felt that another book was needed. He saw his fifth book as a return to the animal wisdom and company of *The Sword in the Stone*, a withdrawal from the world of *homo ferox*, man the ferocious. White's urge to escape is in many ways simplistic, avoiding the historical and political reasons why cities and nations have become as they are. But those feelings have become increasingly common: in recent years many people have felt a need to leave the ferocious and unclean cities, and if they cannot leave, to find company with domestic animals. White's insights, like Twain's, have the power of prediction.

The fifth and final book also contains a flight from fiction itself. Arthur and Merlyn and many animals meet in the badger's sett and discuss the world and men. It is a debate, not a story. The fictional mould is broken – an interesting prediction of the general modern loss of faith in the conventional forms of fiction, but unfortunate for a novel that has till now accepted those conven-tions. Apart from that disconcerting rupture, there is much about the debate that is unsatisfactory. The views put forward are narrow and extreme: White's hatred and contempt for politicians has become a general misanthropy. His love of animals is itself compromised, made cramped and inauthentic because it is only a substitute human world. The badger's sett is in effect a Cambridge senior common-room. Nevertheless, there are moments of positive force as Arthur comes out with the hedgehog at night to enjoy the physical world (pp. 108–9) and when White savours the popular faith in Arthur because 'the legends of the common people are beautiful, strange and positive' (p. 136).

Like Twain's final traces of positive feeling, this is no more than nostalgia, and it even extends to a dream family life. In the goose episode White wrote for this book, Arthur longs to remain with the flock and marry Lyo-Lyok, the calm and generous companion of his adventure. Like the Yankee, Arthur ends in despair, but unlike Twain White turns to literature and the Arthurian legend for consolation. The sonorous finale of the book returns to the last battle and the hint of Arthur's return; in culture White, like King Arthur, can escape from history and live in the past, present and future without pain.

Both Twain and White bring to the Arthurian legend the

vitality and the danger of experimental creative thinking, a dynamic response to the world about them. In their different ways both interpret their own worlds by a questioning of the authorities that appear to dominate them. Twain's greater impact comes from his fuller, more experiential understanding of the industrial and democratic forces he saw in conflict. White, responding to destructive international politics, could only do so from a position of limited comprehension that led easily to baffled rage.

The value of the two Arthurian novels is indicated by the great success their works have had with the public. Being instinctively aware of the threats posed both by industrial capitalism and the politicians' exploitations at home and abroad, readers have assented strongly to artists capable of re-using the Arthurian legend in order to question and expose the authorities by whom the contemporary world is controlled.

V

The other major areas of the contemporary Arthurian legend are not radical or searching like the work of Twain and White. Rather, they use the legend as a means of constructing ideological edifices that support existing authorities and responses to the world.

In some cases, that response is no more than a statement of the value of Malory's Arthuriad and the validity of reshaping it for a modern period. Such work ranges from the many simple modernisations of Malory, through the assembling by Roger Lancelyn Green of a very popular modern Vulgate based on Malory (1953) to the subtle but basically Malory-rewriting poems by Edwin Arlington Robinson, *Merlin* (1917), *Lancelot* (1920) and *Tristram* (1927); a helpful account of Robinson's Arthurian work is given by Fisher (1966).

In recent years there has been a good market in America for similar work, novels which are the medieval legends brought up-to-date with some modern characterisation and sexual activity. Thomas Berger's *Arthur Rex* (1978) is based on Malory and Richard Monaco's *Parsival, or A Knight's Tale* (1977) uses the German grail legend, taken more from Wagner than the complex thirteenth-century *Parzival* by Wolfram von Eschenbach. A more intriguing effort was by John Steinbeck: as his letters and unfinished draft show, he respected Malory's Tale I too much for success, and only when he started afresh on Tale III did a Steinbeckian problem romance begin to emerge (1976).

These twentieth-century Arthurians have faced backwards, though they all contain aspects of modernity. In looking at genuinely new versions of the Arthurian legend, there are two main areas to consider – first, the religious modernisation of the legend and second, the historical Arthur industry, with its associated fictional re-creation of the notional Arthurian reality.

At the centre of the modern British revival and development of religious Arthuriana has been, naturally enough, the holy grail. The full medieval treatment, before the redirection and reduction by Malory and Tennyson, was disseminated by a number of writers – particularly influential were Sebastian Evans at a popular level (1898), Jessie L. Weston in first a scholarly (1913) and then a mythical context (1920) and A. E. Waite in the distinct aura of mysticism (1909 and 1933). The idea that the grail itself visited Britain with Joseph of Arimathea was very attractive; Geoffrey Ashe describes the modern promotion of Glastonbury as a spiritual centre in *King Arthur's Avalon* (1957), a book which is itself an influential part of this modern development.

Through Joseph, Glastonbury and the grail, British spiritual Christianity is given an ancient legitimisation, a contact with the early church before the development of Roman Catholicism – even a link with Christ himself. The patriotic Christianity of the Glastonbury legend has linked up with the much wider and non-specific modern mysticism which has embraced Glastonbury as a central focus of supernatural forces. One sign of this is the weight given to Glastonbury and the grail in one of the bibles of this movement, *Mysterious Britain* (J. and C. Bord, 1972, chs 11 and 12): others have been modern manifestations at Glastonbury like the 'hippie' Glastonbury Fayre in 1971 and the more recent parties of 'druids' walking the earthwork 'maze' around Glastonbury Tor which is believed to be a symbolic grail quest. These have been English versions of the international movement that in recent decades reacted to materialism and consumer society with an interest in all things that appeared non-material and spiritually consoling.

That movement provided a rich field for writers and publishers of the supernatural a decade or so ago, and John Cowper Powys's huge novel *A Glastonbury Romance* (1933) was republished by Picador, a leading imprint in that field. The cover itself sought out the desired audience, showing the mysterious ruins of Glastonbury Abbey framing the even stranger Tor reaching to the sky; the colours selected were among those sacred to the drug culture, purple, orange, lime green. In fact, Powys's novel uses only parts of the Arthurian legend to extend through myth the forces of the modern world. Many looking for a mystical experience would be surprised, partly by the remorseless naturalism of the novel which coexists with its moments of heady mysticism, and even more by its juxtaposition of material and spiritual things: Glastonbury has become a modern and distinctly Marxist commune and the holy grail appears to sanctify a man hurrying to give a much-needed enema to a bad-tempered pensioner who suffers from piles.

A literary use of the grail myth more in keeping with conventional religious thought is in two poems by Charles Williams. *Taliessin through Logres* (1938) and *The Region of the Summer Stars* (1944) tell how God sent the grail to Logres. This Arthurian country symbolises the possibilities of human contact with God, but because of a series of sinful miscomprehensions and vicious deeds, Logres has been reduced to modern Britain where the few pure spirits hope the grail will once more be offered. This pattern was made clear in *Arthurian Torso* (1948) in which C. S. Lewis published both his own exposition of the poems and Williams' unfinished essay on 'The Figure of Arthur' from which came the whimsical, somewhat self-protective title.

Williams' curious career as a religious bachelor promoting grail thoughts is strangely like a modern version of those monks who first projected the grail legends into the mainstream of the Arthurian legend. He too had a social base; as well as his church activities, he was one of 'The Inklings', a private Oxford society of the thirties and forties (Carpenter, 1978). Meeting in Oxford college rooms, with clever talk, group jokes, moderate drinking and heavy pipe smoking, they spent long evenings in a life-style partly boyish, partly hostile to the real modern world. Both evasions show in the literature they produced, Williams' poems, C. S. Lewis's children's stories (the 'Narnia' series) and, the best-known of them all, J. R. R. Tolkien's *The Lord of the Rings*.

Two more prestigious poets, T. S. Eliot and David Jones have worked primarily on the modern experience – cities in *The*

Waste Land (1922), war in *In Parenthesis* (1937) – but they employ spiritual aspects of the Arthurian legend for mythic extensions of their modern sensitivities. They ultimately find in Arthur's world some elements of authority to support their belief in a religious calm outside the material and political world.

The continued, even growing, value of such a spiritual Arthurian authority is shown by the recent publication of two wholly speculative, even fantastic, books in this area. *The Real Camelot* (Darrah, 1981) mythicises Arthur and traces the whole structure back to pre-Celtic British paganism, a project which quite dwarfs Rhys's earlier efforts, made in the high tide of myth criticism (1891). Much more dramatic though, has been the response to *The Holy Blood and the Holy Grail* (Baigent, Leigh and Lincoln, 1981), which finds that the Merovingian kings of France are direct descendants of Christ through his secret marriage to Martha – the grail is a family heirloom. This book, an Arthurian equivalent of the flying saucer publishing phenomenon, was outstripping all other book sales in London in early 1982. It is clear that the mythical and mystical world is a place of comfort to many.

VI

A different response to the legend has been made by those in quest of the 'historical' Arthur, who overtly study the notional man and his period, and covertly re-create through him several modern ideologies. It is plain that this Arthur provides a sharply focused version of the 'great man' approach to history, which supports both individualism and autocracy. This was clear in the work of the historian who really started the modern historical Arthur industry. At the very end of his discussion of 'Roman Britain' (1936, pp. 320–4) R. G. Collingwood let himself go on Arthur, suggesting he did exist as a Romanised Celt with a name coming from the Roman Artorian family, that he was the commander of a 'mobile field army' who fought the Germanic invaders all over Britain, that he used as his secret weapon the heavy cavalry the Romans had faced at Adrianople in 378.

The evidence itself is sketchy, but it enabled Collingwood to find a man central to the period, to attach the undoubted British defence to one superior spirit. He could see 'a country sinking into barbarism, whence Roman ideas had almost vanished; and the emergence of a single man intelligent enough to understand them, and vigorous enough to put them into practice' (1936, p. 324).

This hero not only validated at one blow the intelligence and will-power which are central totems of bourgeois individualism; he was also 'the last of the Romans' and so 'the heritage of Rome lived on in many shapes' (1936, p. 324). Two of the shapes, undoubtedly, were the classical curriculum of the English public schools and the intimately related ideology of empire whereby the English, like the Romans before them, justified their exploitative world-wide practices by the imposition of 'civilisation' and a 'peace' suitable to their interests.

Collingwood's imperialism has survived in a number of the more recent labourers in the industry of Arthurian historicism, this most modern recreation of the Arthurian legend. Beram Saklatvala called his book *Arthur, Roman Britain's Last Champion* (1967); Geoffrey Ashe pressed the imperial connection in *From Caesar to Arthur*, even identifying the hero as the last emperor, Artorius Augustus (1960, p. 205). John Morris, like Collingwood a professional historian, gave the same opinion and even saw the mirage of a continuity from this last Roman to the British present: 'Many permanent institutions, customs and conventions that still influence modern political behaviour begin their history in the Arthurian age' (1973, p. 506). The absolute invalidity of all this can be judged by reading the twenty-thousand word review of Morris's book which lists the major errors of fact and emphasis in this 'tangled tissue of fact and fantasy' (Kirby and Williams, 1975–6). The 'objective' historians are dealing in a consoling English fantasy, as real power passes from that second world empire.

Another piece of patriotism – in this case closer to racism – is sometimes to be found as the sting in the tail of this allegedly historical writing. Ashe not only argues for a transfer of imperial right from Rome to Britain, but also insists that because of Arthur's defence the Celts intermingled culturally and racially with the Germanic invaders much more than would have happened after an Arthur-less rapid conquest. So Arthur's 'dim, tremendous reversal' was able to dilute 'the German tide' (1960, p. 10). The notion seems to relate to Hitler's embarrassing habit of claiming the English as Aryan cousins. The English find it advantageous to become British – but still remain distinct from both despised relatives. Saklatvala sums the ideological exercise up crisply: thanks to Arthur, 'they are as unlike their cousins in Germany as they are unlike their purely Celtic neighbours' (1967, p. 192). There is, of course, no truth in this Celtic-Germanic racial theory. K. H. Jackson's important yet apparently little-consulted map of English river-names shows, as one might expect, that Celtic influence was only strong near the surviving Celtic areas (1953, ch. 6) and Leslie Alcock, the most thorough of the recent historians says flatly 'There is no reason to believe that the character of the English settlement was changed in any way by Arthur's victory' (1971, p. 364).

Apart from these specific ideologies, historicism is in itself a dynamic force in this modern redaction of the Arthurian legend. Instead of the knightly adventures and hermit dreams of medieval romance or the fictional devices of a more recent literature, the techniques of a modern and quasi-objective science process the material for a modern consciousness. The photographs, maps, appendices themselves mean so much: Morris, the most fantastic of the historians, is also the busiest with technical data (Plate 28). Arthur is incorporated into and supports the world of academic, expert authority where the highest excitement comes from a possibly unquestionable fact. In 1966 when Alcock investigated Cadbury Camp, a notional site of Camelot, almost the first thing excavated was, incredibly enough, a gilt bronze letter A. The excitement was intense; it caused, Alcock says drily, 'an unnecessary flutter among the Arthurian romantics' (1972, p. 51). The BBC and the 'serious' Sunday papers sent station-wagon-loads of journalists and cameramen down to Somerset to nail the story. Unfortunately, the letter was centuries too old: it was not Arthur's personalised belt-buckle or some other individualist fantasy-object. How irreverently Mark Twain would have enjoyed this little modern passion-play, revealing as it does both the urgency and the fragility of the need – not merely the quest – for the historical Arthur.

There has also been a more broad-based fictional deployment of the historicist approach. A whole series of novels have depended on the idea Collingwood put forward and others amplified. John Masefield's *Badon Parchments* (1947) was one of the earliest, an austere imitation of the Arthurian 'reality'. Other writers have laid the patterns of romance, both sexual and mystical, over the historical basis. Henry Treece made Arthur one of his many exercises in ancient sensual excitements (*The Great Captain*, 1956). Rosemary Sutcliff's work has been the most widely-known and among historians the most respected. *Sword at Sunset* (1963), offers itself as an account of Arthurian Britain. It contains a lot of thoughtful historical re-creation as well as a distinctly 'poetic' element, a more sophisticated version of the rugged heroes and storm-tossed heroines of that very successful genre known as 'women's fiction' (Sutherland, 1981, ch. 6).

An ingenious, well-crafted and highly successful variant of this pattern is Mary Stewart's trilogy which uses Merlin as hero and Geoffrey of Monmouth as base, *The Crystal Cave* (1970), *The Hollow Hills* (1973) and *The Last Enchantment* (1979). She weaves an appealing modern pragmatism into the traditional story by making Merlin a trained engineer whose contact with the Roman technicians of his father Ambrosius' legion empowers him to move Stonehenge to Salisbury plain; he diagnoses the trouble with Vortigern's castle not as subterranean dragons but poor foundation work. In the second and third books, Malory's story and romantic mystery gain strength as influences, but the element of modernity remains.

These fictional patterns all have some relation, however distant, to the idea of a historical Arthur, the underpinning of most recent reactions to and re-creations of the legend. But the historicity of Arthur does not have to be ideologised in those partial and manipulative ways, whether academic or fictional. It can be studied with rigorous positivism and the attempt reveals the limits of the method. Alcock worked very hard to tell the truth and no more about the Arthurian reality. He believes in the existence of the man, and would assent cautiously to some elements in the Collingwood thesis – the Roman connection, the mobility at least. But he is aware that these are mere facts, reductively lifeless, and he finally comments about Arthur 'As a person, his significance comes later, in the realms of literature and romance' (1971, p. 364). His publishers humanised his text more insidiously, by giving both the hard and softback first editions a lusciously romantic photograph of Cadbury Camp at sunset.

Another scholar was equally rigorous in excluding the romantic and the erroneous from his work; oddly enough, he was the earliest serious Arthurian historian, as Alcock is the most recent. Joseph Ritson's last work of ground-clearing scholarship was his posthumously published *The Life of King Arthur* (1825) and in it he worked carefully over the Arthurian documents, giving each its précis, analysis and assessment of value. The work stands up extraordinarily well against that of later scholars (Hopkins, 1928) yet it is clear from his life that for Ritson his work was itself not value-free but was an assault on murky ignorance, and not only that found in books. His scholarship was a part of his political radicalism, two forms of enlightenment working together – 'The Life of Robin Hood' in his collection of Robin Hood ballads (1823) is a classic of this socially and politically active intelligence.

A modern scholar with Alcock's clarity and Ritson's humane engagement is Jack Lindsay; it may be no accident that he has always worked outside the academic establishment. *Arthur and his Times* (1958) is an admirable history of Arthur for the reason that it says relatively little about Arthur, and even not a great deal about Britain in his notional times. Lindsay accepts broadly the Collingwood theory, but writes an account of the socio-economic and human forces of the period, drawing heavily on the little-known letters of late Roman Gaul and on the evidence of archeology to build up what he would call a 'totality' of the period. Arthur and his times are seen partly as the force-field where mighty powers operate, but Lindsay's Marxism, like Marx's, is not simple determinism: he also sees Arthur as being in war what Pelagius, the early British heretic, was in religion, symbols of the fact that human beings can stand dialectically against their economic, social and cultural conditioning and struggle to make a world fit for themselves and their aspirations. Lindsay's book interprets the totality of the Arthurian world so fully as to draw from it meaning for another period in crisis; and he develops neither the despair nor the self-satisfaction of other modern Arthurians, but a sense that through comprehending the material and political pressures in the world it is possible to exert against them a collective will, and so remake an authoritarian world in the mould of a more humane and more egalitarian authority.

That position implies a role for knowledge which rejects the consoling academic ideology that knowledge is value-free, opinionless, comfortably impotent. As should by now have become clear, that is also the position from which this particular survey of Arthurian literature and its social context has been written. It is not sufficient merely to trace the development of the legend for some fifteen hundred years, to suggest as some writers do that the Arthurian legend is a world of its own floating above historical and material reality. Such books (Maynadier, 1907; Reid, 1938) only create the position of the separate academic, without responsibility, without guilt for what goes on in the real – disturbingly real – world.

To see the social and political functions that the versions of Arthurian literature have served in the past and are still serving in the present is to recognise the intimate relationship between culture and material reality, between a world of words and a world of actions, reactions, penalties and rewards. To insist on treating the legend of King Arthur in that way, to press it towards social relevance as firmly as most modern commentators have severed it from such a connection is, of course, a political treatment. That has been the conscious purpose of this book. It is a practice that is itself connected to its time, as more and more people become aware of the link between culture and authority, and more and more people recognise the social and political functions of cultural production.

REFERENCES

Primary Sources
Berger, T. (1978) *Arthur Rex* (New York: Delacoste).
Eliot, T. S. (1922) *The Waste Land* in *The Waste Land and Other Poems* (London: Faber).
Green, R. L. (1953) *King Arthur and his Knights of the Round Table* (London: Puffin).
Jones, D. (1937) *In Parenthesis* (London: Faber).
Masefield, J. (1947) *Badon Parchments* (London: Heinemann).
Monaco, R. (1977) *Parsival, or a Knight's Tale* (New York: Macmillan).
Powys, J. C. (1933) *A Glastonbury Romance* (London: Macdonald; Picador edition, London, 1975).
Robinson, E. A., *Merlin* (1917), *Lancelot* (1920), *Tristram* (1927) in *Collected Poems* (New York, Macmillan, 1937).
Steinbeck, J. (1976) *The Acts of King Arthur and His Noble Knights* (London: Heinemann).
Stewart, M. (1970) *The Crystal Cave* (London: Hodder and Stoughton).
—— (1973) *The Hollow Hills* (London: Hodder and Stoughton).
—— (1979) *The Last Enchantment* (London: Hodder and Stoughton).
Sutcliff, R. (1963) *Sword at Sunset* (London: Hodder and Stoughton).
Twain, M. (1971) *A Connecticut Yankee at King Arthur's Court*, ed. J. Kaplan (London: Penguin).
—— (1975) *Notebooks and Journals*, vol. II, ed. F. Anderson, L. Salamo and B. L. Stein (Los Angeles: University of California Press).

—— (1980) *Notebooks and Journals*, vol. III, ed. R. P. Browning, M. B. Frank and L. Salamo (Los Angeles: University of California Press).
—— and Howells, W. D. (1967) *Selected Mark Twain – Howells Letters, 1872–1910* ed. F. Anderson, W. M. Gibson, H. N. Smith (Cambridge, Mass.: Harvard University Press).
Treece, H. (1956) *The Great Captain* (London: Bodley Head).
White, T. H. (1938) *The Sword in the Stone* (London: Collins).
—— (1941) *The Witch in the Wood* (London: Collins).
—— (1942) *The Ill-Framed Knight* (London: Collins).
—— (1958) *The Once and Future King* (London: Collins).
—— (1977) *The Book of Merlyn* (Austin: University of Texas Press).
Williams, C. (1938) *Taliessin through Logres* (London: Oxford University Press).
—— (1944) *The Region of the Summer Stars* (London: Editions Poetry).
—— and Lewis, C. S. (1948) *Arthurian Torso* (London: Oxford University Press).

Secondary Sources
Alcock, L. (1971) *Arthur's Britain* (London: Lane).
—— (1972) *Was This Camelot? Excavations at Cadbury Castle 1966–70* (London: Thames and Hudson).
Anderson, F. and Sanderson, K. M. (1971) *Mark Twain: The Critical Heritage* (London: Routledge).
Ashe, G. (1957) *King Arthur's Avalon* (London: Collins).
—— (1960) *From Caesar to Arthur* (London: Collins).
—— (1971) *Camelot and the Vision of Albion* (London: Heinemann).
Baetzhold, H. G. (1961) 'The Course of Composition of *A Connecticut Yankee*: A Reinterpretation', *American Literature* 33, 195–214.
Baigent, M., Leigh, R. and Lincoln, H. (1981) *The Holy Blood and the Holy Grail* (London: Cape).
Bord, J. and C. (1972) *Mysterious Britain* (London: Garnstone).
Budd, L. J. (1962) *Mark Twain: Social Philosopher* (Bloomington: Indiana University Press).
Carpenter, H. (1978) *The Inklings: C. S. Lewis, J. R. R. Tolkien, Charles Williams and their Friends* (London: Allen and Unwin).
Carter, P. J. (1957) 'Mark Twain and the American Labor Movement', *New England Quarterly*, 30, 383–88.
Collingwood, R. G. (1936) 'Roman Britain' in R. G. Collingwood and J. N. L. Myres, *Roman Britain and the English Settlements* (Oxford: Clarendon).
Crane, J. K. (1974) *T. H. White* (New York: Twayne).
Darrah, J. (1981) *The Real Camelot* (London: Thames and Hudson).
Evans, S. (1898) *In Quest of the Holy Grail* (London: Dent).
Fisher, J. H. (1966) 'E. A. Robinson and Arthurian Tradition' in *Studies in Language and Literature in Honour of Margaret Schlauch*, ed. M. Brahmer *et al.* (Warsaw: Polish Scientific Publishers).
Foner, P. S. (1958) *Mark Twain: Social Critic* (New York: International).
Geismar, M. (1970) *Mark Twain: An American Prophet* (Boston: Houghton Mifflin).
Hansen, C. (1973) 'The Once and Future Boss: Mark Twain's Yankee', *Nineteenth Century Fiction*, 28, 62–73.

Hopkins, A. B. (1928) 'Ritson's Life of King Arthur', *Publications of the Modern Language Association of America*, 43, 251–87.
Jackson, K. H. (1953) *Language and History in Early Britain* (Edinburgh University Press).
Kaplan, J. (1967) *Mr Clemens and Mark Twain* (London: Cape).
—— (1971) Introduction to *A Connecticut Yankee* (London: Penguin).
Kirby, D. and Williams, J. C. (1975–6) review of Morris, J. (1973) *Studia Celtica*, 10/11, 454–86.
Lindsay, J. (1958) *Arthur and His Times: Britain in the Dark Ages* (London: Muller).
Maynadier, H. (1907) *The Arthur of the English Poets* (Boston: Houghton Mifflin).
Morris, J. (1973) *The Age of Arthur* (London: Weidenfeld and Nicholson).
Reid, M. J. C. (1938) *The Arthurian Legend* (Edinburgh: Oliver and Boyd).
Rhys, Sir J. (1891) *Studies in the Arthurian Legend* (Oxford: Clarendon).
Ritson, J. (1823) 'The Life of Robin Hood' in *Robin Hood: A Collection of all the Ancient Poems, Songs and Ballads* 1 vol. edn (London: Stocking).
—— (1825) *The Life of King Arthur from Ancient Historians and Authentic Documents* (London: Payne and Foss).
Saklatvala, B. (1967) *Arthur, Roman Britain's Last Champion* (Newton Abbot: David and Charles).
Salomon, R. B. (1961) *Twain and the Image of History* (New Haven: Yale University Press).
Schivelbusch, W. (1980) *The Railway Journey: Trains and Travel in the Nineteenth Century* (Oxford: Blackwell).
Sloane, D. E. E. (1979) *Mark Twain as a Literary Comedian* (Baton Rouge: Louisiana State University Press).
Smith, H. N. (1964) *Mark Twain's Fable of Progress* (New Brunswick: Rutgers University Press).
Sutherland, J. (1981) *Best Sellers* (London: Routledge).
Waite, A. E. (1909) *The Hidden Church of the Holy Grail* (London: Rebman).
—— (1933) *The Holy Grail, its Legends and Symbolism* (London: Rider).
Warner, S. T. (1967) *T. H. White* (London: Cape).
Weston, J. L. (1913) *The Quest for the Holy Grail* (London: Bell).
—— (1920) *From Ritual to Romance* (London: Macmillan).
Wilding, R. M. (1980) *Political Fictions* (London: Routledge).

Index

(Characters are entered under the versions of their names found in Malory; other versions are given as cross-references)

217